Richard Cross is John A. O'Brien Professor of Philosophy at the University of Notre Dame. He has published widely on the history of philosophical theology, and his books include *Duns Scotus* (1999), *The Metaphysics of the Incarnation* (2002) and *Duns Scotus on God* (2005).

D1596593

Richard Cross has written a clear and engaging guide to the emergence of medieval philosophy in the Latin Christian West. Beginning with the consolidation of the inheritance of antiquity (roughly 1050–1200), Cross traces the development of philosophical thought in its successive phases: the assimilation of new translations of Aristotle and his commentators (1200–77); the refinement of the neo-Aristotelian synthesis (1277–1300); and its re-evaluation (1300–50). Anselm, Abelard, Aquinas, Scotus, and Ockham are key players, of course, but they are contextualized in their social and intellectual milieu, so that the contributions of Grosseteste, Bacon, Albert, Henry of Ghent, Godfrey of Fontaines, Peter Auriol, and many others are recognized as well. With insight and grace, Cross discusses the philosophical topics that motivated these thinkers: the problem of universals, the nature of scientific knowledge, the relation of the soul to the body, the mechanisms of human cognition, divine power and foreknowledge, and much else besides. This masterly presentation is lucid and accessible, providing beginners and specialists alike with a thorough account of the period, enlivened by Cross's erudition and wit.

Peter King, Professor of Philosophy and of
Medieval Studies, University of Toronto

Richard Cross's book provides a lucid introduction to the accepted great figures of medieval philosophy – Aquinas, Henry of Ghent, Scotus and Ockham – beautifully nuanced treatments of a number of more minor figures and, despite the deliberately old-fashioned choice of material, an important new perspective on it. Cross's presentation is outstanding because, although most of the men he considers were theologians, he treats them, rightly, as doing philosophy of the highest order. Without technical jargon and always in a way fully comprehensible to a beginner, Cross engages philosophically with these thinkers' positions and arguments, so that the reader comes to understand not just what they thought, but the reasons for which they thought it. His big innovation – foreshadowed in much recent specialized work, but never stated so clearly as here – is to see the half-century or so immediately *after* the lifetime of Aquinas as the great period of discovery and achievement in medieval philosophy, with Duns Scotus the pre-eminent philosopher, and Ockham as providing a radical simplification, which however left him and his followers unable to answer fundamental metaphysical questions. I would strongly recommend this book to any student looking for a sober, clear, elegant and stimulating introduction to the recognized great medieval philosopher-theologians.

John Marenbon, senior research fellow,
Trinity College, Cambridge

Richard Cross's highly intelligent treatment slides easily between historical context and doctrinal exposition, both to orient students to a challenging period and to acquaint contemporary Christian philosophers with the formidable range and creativity of their medieval predecessors. Besides individual chapters on his 'top four' – Anselm, Aquinas, Scotus, Ockham – Cross includes substantial discussions of authors rather less studied: Gilbert of Poitiers, Peter John Olivi, Giles of Rome, Hervaeus Natalis and Peter Auriol, among others, the better to provoke more work on such important medieval thinkers.

Marilyn McCord Adams, Distinguished Visiting Professor
of Philosophy, Rutgers, The State University of New Jersey,
and formerly Regius Professor of Divinity, University of Oxford

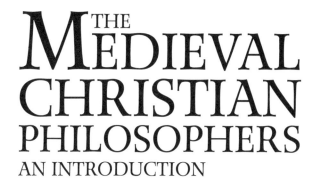

THE MEDIEVAL CHRISTIAN PHILOSOPHERS
AN INTRODUCTION

RICHARD CROSS

I.B. TAURIS

LONDON · NEW YORK

Published in 2014 by I.B.Tauris & Co Ltd
6 Salem Road, London W2 4BU
175 Fifth Avenue, New York NY 10010
www.ibtauris.com

Distributed in the United States and Canada Exclusively by Palgrave Macmillan
175 Fifth Avenue, New York NY 10010

Library of Medieval Studies, vol. 1

Cover illustration – St Thomas Aquinas (1225–74) by Fra Bartolommeo or Baccio
della Porta (1472–1517), Museo di San Marco dell'Angelico, Florence/Bridgeman
Art Library

ISBN: 978 1 84885 542 7 (HB)
       978 1 84885 543 4 (PB)

A full CIP record for this book is available from the British Library
A full CIP record is available from the Library of Congress

Library of Congress Catalog Card Number: available

Typeset in Caslon by Free Range Book Design & Production Limited

Printed and bound in Great Britain by T.J. International, Padstow, Cornwall

For Freddie

Contents

Part III: INNOVATION

Part IV: SIMPLIFICATION

Preface

This book aims to cover a huge amount of material, and it attempts to do so in a manageable kind of way. So I have had to make some hard choices. I start at 1050 – reasonably thought of as the beginning of the scholastic period, as I outline in the Introduction. But for reasons that I explain in my final chapter, I have basically taken 1350 as my cut-off date. There is a great deal that could be said about the later period; but, apart from a brief discussion of Wyclif, it will not be said here. Equally, I have treated merely of Western Christian philosophy, against the prevailing trend of seeing medieval philosophy not merely as an international affair but as an intercontinental one. To this, I say merely that I do not want to write on things that I do not know enough about. I know well enough how the Latin translations of Arabic writers were received by the Latin speakers of the West, for example; but I do not know Arabic, beyond the little it has in common with Syriac, and cannot comment on the relation between the translations and the original texts; or, indeed, on the philosophy of the thinkers themselves. The translations are another matter: philosophical texts in their own right, authored partly by their Arabic originators, but hijacked and transformed, consciously or not, skilfully or recklessly, by their translators. And it is these texts that were of relevance in the West, the topic of my study here.

In some ways, then, I have ended up writing a rather more old-fashioned book than I had anticipated – and not just in terms of my timescale. It is not without reason, for example, that Anselm, Aquinas, Scotus, and Ockham are often highlighted as the greatest of the medieval philosophers; and I think it makes for more philosophically interesting reading (and writing) to structure the text around these thinkers. But, of course, focusing on 'big' thinkers – those thinkers judged great with the benefit of hindsight, judged by the light of history – is anachronistic, for all its philosophical wealth; and it is in this way that my text has come out rather traditional, somehow falling into the inheritance of twentieth-century historiographies that I have until now rather attempted to avoid. But I have tried to impose or discern some kind of overarching narrative that is rather different, I think, from any that has been suggested before.

And the choice of second-league figures, so to speak, has not been easy. In the end, I thought it most helpful to go with those who have, I think, been central to many twentieth-century histories, rather than introduce large collections of lesser-known figures. There are too many very good thinkers who fundamentally found themselves agreeing with some kind of party line; I have tried to focus on thinkers who had sparks of innovative originality. So, for example, among the Franciscans of the late thirteenth century, Roger Marston, Richard of Middleton, Gonsalvus of Spain, and the urbane and civilized Matthew of Aquasparta, do not appear. And of the Dominicans, I do not discuss solid and reliable figures such as John of Naples. I have not discussed Meister Eckhart (perhaps I should have done), since he ultimately seems something of an outlier for academic philosophy. At any rate, perhaps secular theologians – those that do not belong to religious orders – suffer most of all from this approach. But the best of them are included here (e.g. Henry of Ghent, Godfrey of Fontaines); some of the second-league figures are really rather dull, though I discuss William of Auvergne in some detail since he was notable for his assimilation of some of the novel philosophical texts of the early thirteenth century.

In terms of the structure of the work, it will become immediately apparent that, while the main treatments of particular philosophers are in the sections devoted to them, I have not used this structure like a straitjacket. While I have tried to give individual philosophers sustained attention in this way, I have also tried to give some sense of the *dialectic*: and this means allowing discussion of one thinker to bleed into discussion of another. So for a full sense of what I have to say about an individual thinker, it is necessary to use the index.

Discussions with friends and colleagues have helped me sort out particular points: thanks to Marilyn Adams, Eileen Botting, Eric Hagedorn, Isabelle Moulin, John O'Callaghan, Stephen Dumont, and Cecilia Trifogli, all of whom helped me, even if sometimes they did so without realizing it. Faults, of course, are mine and mine alone. Except where noted, translations are my own too. When I cite existing translations, I include page references to the translations but not to the Latin texts; when I provide my own translations, I include page references to the Latin texts.

Introduction
Institutions and Sources

Western Europe in 1050 was something of an intellectual back-water. Compared to the phenomenal achievements of philosophers in India, China, and (more relevantly) the Islamic world, thinkers in Western Europe had accomplished very little for perhaps five or six hundred years. Even moribund Byzantium was intellectually livelier. For reasons that are not altogether straightforward, or even particularly evident, things started changing radically, particularly from around 1100, and the Latin West was able not merely to catch up with the intellectual attainments of these other civilizations, but to surpass them. No one really knows what brought this renaissance about. But we know quite a lot about *how* it was brought about, and this is the topic of my first chapter. The answer is, in some ways, rather dull and predictable: philosophers massively increased the range of sources available to them, and they managed to create institutions that gave them the opportunity to study these sources in a structured way.

The sources: twelfth-century (re)discovery, thirteenth-century effects

Someone living in 1100, interested in developing philosophical ideas, had a number of useful sources to turn to. Foremost in importance from a philosophical point of view are a couple of Aristotelian works, and texts of Aristotelian inspiration: Aristotle's *Categories* and *On Interpretation*; and Porphyry's *Isagoge* or introduction to the categories, all in the translation prepared by Boethius (*c.* 475/7–525/6). Along with an anonymous early twelfth-century treatise once thought to be by Gilbert of Poitiers (1085/90–1154), the *De sex principiis*, this gives us the so-called '*logica vetus*' ('old logic').

Boethius authored a couple of important logical works of his own (on categorical and hypothetical syllogisms, and on topics) which were likewise available, along with his commentaries on the *Categories*, *On Interpretation*, and the *Isagoge*. In fact, Aristotle, albeit in this highly restricted *corpus*, was the most important philosophical influence throughout this early period. John Marenbon has shown that the earliest significant medieval thought was fundamentally Aristotelian in orientation, with a strong emphasis on logic and language (see Marenbon, 1981). And it is likely that a standard education from antiquity onwards would have equipped students with the rudiments of the *Categories*, along with Porphyry's *Isagoge*, thus giving notions of primary and secondary substance (particular and universal), and the accidental (non-essential) categories or predicates (quantity, quality, relation, place, time, position, state, action, affection) from the *Categories*; and genus, specific difference, definition/species (constituted of genus and specific difference), *proprium* (necessary but non-defining feature), and accident – the so-called 'predicables', varieties of universals – from Porphyry's *Isagoge*.

So it is unsurprising that, once the cultural and political situation facilitated it, it would be Aristotle whose complete *oeuvre* would hold sway in the twelfth and thirteenth centuries. And this is precisely what happened. Boethius had translated too the rest of the logical works of Aristotle (the *Organon*) with the exception of the *Posterior Analytics*, and these texts (*Prior Analytics*, *Topics*, and *Sophistical Refutations*) became widely available from the 1120s. This gives us the *'logica nova'* ('new logic'): *Prior Analytics*, *Topics*, and *Sophistical Refutations*. It is fair to say that the overwhelming philosophical achievements of the twelfth century lie in the area of logic: pre-eminently Peter Abelard (1079–1142) in terms of quality; but more influential was a range of works collectively containing what is known as the *logica modernorum*, themselves largely inspired by the contribution of Abelard (for these treatises, many of which are anonymous, see L. M. de Rijk, 1962–7). Thirteenth-century logic did little to expand the insights contained in these texts, and the works themselves were known to later thirteenth-century writers largely through high-quality summaries produced by certain key thirteenth-century logicians – most notably Peter of Spain (*fl.* 1230s–40s), and also William of Sherwood (1200/5–66/72) and Lambert of Auxerre (*fl.* 1250s). It is not until the fourteenth century that we find further significant developments in logic: in particular, a grasp of the general principles of propositional logic, spelled out most notably in Walter Burley (1274/5–1344/5), and the development of the so-called *Obligations* literature, focusing on different disputational puzzles or *sophismata*.

Boethius's stated plan was to translate all of the works of Plato and Aristotle, and, through commentaries, to demonstrate that these two thinkers were not in disagreement with each other. (This is not as absurd a project as it perhaps sounds: the standard Neoplatonic approach to the issue was to insist that Plato's work dealt with the world of intelligence and the Forms, and Aristotle's with the material, sub-lunar, world.) In setting out his programme, Boethius hinted at a great body of learning that was not known in the West in 1100: namely, the remaining works of both Plato and Aristotle. The medievals never got any further in the task of locating and translating Plato – this was something that would have to wait until the fifteenth century. There is one exception to this: Calcidius's fourth-century translation of the first half of Plato's cosmological dialogue, the *Timaeus*, a work of vital importance for twelfth-century thought. Interest in this work was almost entirely eclipsed by the focus on Aristotle in the thirteenth century – presumably because of its inconsistency with central features of Aristotelian metaphysics (for example, its commitment to atomism, vigorously rejected by Aristotle as a response to Zeno's paradoxes). But the remaining works of Aristotle revolutionized the medievals' world view from the beginning of the thirteenth century onwards, in ways that I will try to describe here and in later chapters. I have already mentioned most of the works of the *Organon*. The remaining work, the *Posterior Analytics*, was translated by James of Venice in the first half of the twelfth century (though, as arguably the densest and least accessible of Aristotle's logical works, it attracted no sustained attention until Robert Grosseteste's commentary in the 1220s). James translated the *Physics*, *De anima*, and *Metaphysics* A–Γ (1120–50). The more-or-less complete *Metaphysics* was translated anonymously sometime later in the twelfth century too; and again, not from Greek but from Arabic, by Michael Scot around 1220–35. Michael's version – the so-called '*nova*' ('new') – proved the most popular by far (contrasting with James's '*vetutissima*' ('very old'), its early thirteenth-century revision (the '*vetus*') and the anonymous twelfth-century '*media*' ('middle')). The *Nicomachean Ethics* was not translated completely until 1246–7, by Robert Grosseteste (*c.* 1170–1253); a good translation, from

Greek, of the complete *Metaphysics*, and a translation of the *Politics*, were not produced until Aquinas's translator, William of Moerbeke, did so in the 1260s and 1270s.

The rediscovery of the rest of the Aristotelian *corpus* affected all aspects of thirteenth and fourteenth-century philosophy. It was impossible that it should not: doing philosophy and theology while ignoring Aristotle would be the thirteenth-century analogue of someone attempting to do philosophy or theology today while ignoring almost everything that twentieth and twenty-first-century science has discovered. Thinkers did not slavishly follow Aristotle on everything: quite the contrary, they engaged with his arguments and rejected them when they found them wanting. And, of course, being philosophers, they all did so in different ways. Aristotle was a catalyst for them to engage more deeply with each other too. But, as we shall see, they all adopted certain fundamental Aristotelian insights on the nature and structure of material beings.

Aristotle's logic was not the only philosophical source available in 1100. Augustine of Hippo (354–430) was not only the most significant of the early Christian theologians, but also a conduit for a great deal of philosophical thought from antiquity. Augustine was clearly acquainted with the rudiments of Aristotelian logic – that much is plain from the crucial central chapters of his *De trinitate*. But he was also perhaps the main route for the transmission of Platonism – to which he was remarkably sympathetic – to the later Middle Ages. For example, Augustine takes from the Platonists the crucial idea that there are universal forms. Plato posited such forms, at least for part of his life, in order to explain how it is that different things of the same kind seem to have features *in common*: two egg yolks are both yellow, and the yellowness of one might be exactly the same as the yellowness of another. So, Plato reasoned, the explanation for this must be that there are abstract properties – yellowness, whiteness, and so on – in which the eggs 'participate'. These Forms exist eternally, changelessly, and necessarily, apart from the temporal, changeable, contingent material world. They explain how it is that material things are the kinds of things that they are (for a typical discussion of the issue in Plato, see *Republic* VII (517–518B)). Obviously, it would be hard (though not impossible) for a Christian theologian to be happy with the thought that there are eternal and necessary items apart from God. But Augustine (following the example of Philo of Alexandria and Plotinus) suggested that divine thoughts – divine *ideas* – might be able to perform the same function as the Platonic forms. In effect, Augustine simply places the forms in the mind of God:

> The ideas are certain original and principal forms of things, that is, reasons, fixed and unchangeable, which are not themselves formed, and, being thus eternal and existing always in the same state, are contained in the divine intelligence. And though they themselves neither come into being nor pass away, nevertheless, everything which can come into being and pass away, and everything which does come into being and pass away, is said to be formed in accord with these ideas. (*De diversis quaestionibus*, q. 46, n. 2 (trans. Mosher, p. 80))

Augustine's divine ideas are ideas of universal kinds, not of particulars, and discussion of the existence and nature of universals constitutes one of the central areas of medieval philosophical debate. A considerable part of what follows will trace some of these debates through the High Middle Ages. As we shall see, most thinkers rejected Platonic forms; and, perhaps surprisingly, few thinkers appeal to the divine ideas to explain kind-membership. The reason for this is that a powerful alternative tradition on the question of universals existed in antiquity: one coming from Aristotle, and initially mediated to the Middle Ages through Boethius. I will come back to all of this in a moment.

Augustine provided many other things of philosophical interest for the intelligent reader. For example, he adopts Plato's fundamentally visual model of thinking: thinking of a universal is something like 'looking' at the form. Since according to Augustine the forms are items in the divine mind, human knowledge is fundamentally a matter of divine illumination. As Augustine understands it, intellectual cognition involves 'judging corporeal things in accordance with incorporeal and eternal reasons (*rationes*)' (*De trinitate* XII, c. 2, 2), something achieved when the 'mind's eye' (*acies mentis*) 'grasps' the forms in the divine mind (*De trinitate* IX, c. 6, 11). Some medievals adopt this wholesale, and attempt to integrate it into Aristotle's philosophy of mind – with the 'agent intellect' from book 3 of *De anima*: a text not known to Augustine.

Talking of the ideas as *reasons* (*rationes*) suggests that Augustine is perhaps integrating his theology into another bit of ancient philosophy as well, not Platonic but Stoic: the notion of 'seminal reasons' (*logoi spermatikoi* in Greek, or *rationes seminales* in Augustine's Latin) – the organizing principles of the Stoics' material world. Augustine's philosophy of mind mediated a further component of Stoic philosophy to the medievals too: the notion that thought is somehow fundamentally *linguistic*. The Stoics talk of a concept as a kind of internal 'word' (a '*logos endiathetos*', contrasted with a spoken or uttered word – the *logos prophorikos*). Augustine takes up this way of thinking enthusiastically, perhaps because of the identification of the second person of the Trinity as a kind of word, made at the beginning of John's Gospel (see John 1.1). As we shall see, later medieval speculations in the philosophy of mind take their lead from these ideas, and attempt to integrate them – and sometimes reject them – in the light of insights from Aristotle's *De anima*. Basically, Aristotle rejects both Platonic forms and (in some sense) the notion that knowledge is by some kind of illumination or direct vision of the forms. He holds, rather, that knowledge is a matter of abstracting universal concepts from particulars. How this happens, of course, became a matter of considerable debate, and I will look at it in later chapters.

Augustine was not the only conduit for Stoic ideas from antiquity. More important are the works of Cicero and (particularly) Seneca, critically translating and transmitting Stoic ideas in Latin. For example, one of the key features of Middle Stoicism, from Posidonius in the first century BCE, is the view that morality can be codified in some kind of natural *law* – not just legal norms, but universal *moral* norms binding all peoples. Perhaps the most significant statement of this for medieval philosophers is Cicero's *De officiis* (*On Duties*). Cicero structures *De officiis* around a possible conflict between the beneficial (*utile*) or advantageous (*commodi*), and the virtuous (*honestum*), of which latter the key component is justice (*iustitia*) (see *De officiis* II, c. 9 for a useful summary of the work's overall argument). Cicero's view is that there can never be any such conflict, since acting unjustly can never be truly advantageous (see *De officiis* III, cc. 21–4; c. 81); and given this he strives to show that justice is natural and thus that calculations of advantage are always subordinated to considerations of justice (see *De officiis* III, c. 11). He argues for this by claiming that just acts are regulated by 'the law of nations': a law that obtains independently of any established political power, and that states that 'one is not allowed to harm another for the sake of one's own advantage' (*De officiis* III, n. 23 (trans. Griffin and Atkins, p. 108)). This 'rule of procedure' is supposed to provide a way for utility to coincide with virtue – since acting against the rule would tend to 'shatter […] the fellowship of the whole human race' (*De officiis* III, n. 21 (trans. Griffin and Atkins, p. 108)): something that cannot be advantageous to the individual. (As he himself tells us, Cicero's Stoic source, incidentally, is Panaetius, not Posidonius.)

Stoic ethics are significant for much twelfth-century ethical thinking. Peter Abelard, for example, accepts the kind of natural law tradition that we can find in Cicero, but adds to it a very distinctive twist, adapting other aspects of Stoic action theory. The Stoics hold that a necessary condition for human happiness is *apatheia*: the ability not to be overcome by negative emotion or passion. The idea is not that the philosopher lacks emotions, but that he holds these emotions at some kind of distance, as it were: he refuses his *consent* to the emotion. Abelard adopts this notion of consent to give an account of the moral value of human action: moral evaluation depends on 'consent' to an action – not actually to performing the action, but simply being such that, if one could perform it, one would, where the rightness or wrongness of the consent depends on the action's status relative to the norms of natural law. (For the whole discussion, see Abelard, *Ethics* (also known as *Scito teipsum*).) Abelard's ethic of intention was unique in the Middle Ages, as far as I know. But his emphasis on law was not. For example, as we shall see, Thomas Aquinas (*c.* 1225–74) proposes a full-scale adaptation of this way of thinking about ethics into an Aristotelian, teleological, context, using the legal approach as a way of radically recasting traditional Aristotelian virtue-ethics.

Augustine's thought was very influential on Boethius. I have already mentioned Boethius's role in transmitting the logical works of Aristotle and Porphyry, and I examine some of Boethius's own insights in Chapter 2, because they relate very particularly to twelfth-century thought, and I want to think about them in detail in that context. But Boethius too was also a significant transmitter of Platonic thought. For example, his very influential *Consolation of Philosophy* constitutes, among other things, a summary of Plato's *Timaeus*. It also contains perhaps the single most important discussion of God's knowledge of future contingents: God is timeless, and can thus 'see' the whole of time, including the future, laid out before him. But, generally, seeing something does not prevent it from being contingent; neither is God's knowledge past or future, so it is not subject to the necessity of the past (if God knew *yesterday* what I would do today, then, since the past is fixed, what I do today is likewise fixed or pre-determined). (For the whole discussion, see Boethius, *Consolation of Philosophy* V, pr. 6.) Boethius also wrote theological treatises on the doctrines of the Trinity and Incarnation, and on divine goodness, and these treatises themselves mediate vast amounts of basically Aristotelian metaphysics read through the lens of developments in Platonism and Augustine's theological version of Neoplatonism.

I have spoken of the significance of Augustine and Boethius in the transmission of broadly Platonic themes to the later Middle Ages. One further source for such material should not be overlooked: Pseudo-Dionysius, translated by John Scottus Eriugena in the ninth century, and of considerable importance for a theologically-inflected Platonism. We now know that this theologian was writing in the early sixth century. But he wrote under a pseudonym, and was throughout the Middle Ages believed to be St Paul's Athenian convert (see Acts 17.34). He was thus thought to be the first of the Church Fathers, and his writings were correspondingly given significant weight. Particularly important was Pseudo-Dionysius's analysis of religious language in *The Divine Names*. Each of the many discussions he includes of Biblical and Platonic names for God is structured according to the same dynamic: affirm the name of God – since God truly is such-and-such; deny the name of God – since God is not such-and-such in the same way as his creatures; and affirm that God transcends the name – since God is such-and-such in a 'supereminent' way. Dionysius presented a form of Christianity heavily influenced by the rather baroque Platonism of Proclus (*c.* 412–85). And Proclus himself later found his way into the West through another rather dense source: the so-called *Liber de causis* (a kind of summary of Proclus's *Elements of Theology*), translated by Gerard of Cremona from an Arabic text towards the end of the twelfth century. In all of these sources, the medievals found a potently hierarchical universe, full of participation relationships – quite un-Aristotelian. Eriugena himself was a rather suspect figure, and I think his influence on my period was more indirect – particularly through the translation work – than direct. And one Greek writer, translated into Latin in 1154/5 by Burgundio of Pisa, surpassed all Patristic theologians other than Augustine in influence: John of Damascus († *c.* 750), a magnificent and highly intelligent encyclopedist of the entire earlier Greek theological tradition, and philosophically as much inclined towards Aristotelianism as towards any other kind of thinking.

An apophatic approach similar to Dionysius's can be found in another thinker too, likewise influential on the medieval Christian philosophers: the Jewish philosopher Moses Maimonides (1138–1204). Maimonides argues that God is completely non-composite: he cannot have attributes, and the only true positive predications that can be made of both God and creatures in the same sense relate to activities (*Guide of the Perplexed* I, c. 52). God has nothing in common with any creature, and predications other than those of activity share nothing more than a name ('these attributions have in common only the name and nothing else') (*Guide of the Perplexed* I, c. 56 (trans. Pines, I, p. 131)). According to Maimonides, this does not result in the meaninglessness of these kinds of predications: he asserts that affirmative predications remove certain negations ('living' = 'not dead'; 'powerful' = 'not powerless'). Maimonides summarizes:

> Every attribute that we predicate of him is an attribute of action or, if the attribute is intended for the apprehension of his essence and not of his action, it signifies the negation of the privation of the attribute in question. (*Guide of the Perplexed* I, c. 58 (trans. Pines, I, p. 136))

Furthermore, God is a necessary existent; hence, given non-compositionality, his essence is just his existence (*Guide of the Perplexed* I, c. 57) – an insight that is important for Aquinas later on.

I said a moment ago that Aristotle revolutionized the medieval world view, and in later chapters I will suggest some of the ways in which this is the case. But as we have seen Aristotle in part initially came from the Islamic world, and in mining this sphere for philosophical texts the Christians found many additional resources: in particular, significant pieces of Muslim philosophy and theology. Relatively unproblematic was the reception of the greatest of all Muslim philosophers, Avicenna (ibn Sīnā) (980–1037), whose most important works were translated by Dominicus Gundisalvi sometime between 1160 and 1190. Avicenna seems to me to have been, along with Aristotle, by far the most important single philosophical influence on the Christian philosophers of the High Middle Ages – and something of the extent of this influence will, I hope, become clear in later chapters. For example, medieval discussions of universals after the beginning of the thirteenth century typically take as their starting point neither Aristotle nor Augustine, but rather Avicenna. According to Avicenna, a universal is 'what can be predicated of many'; as such, it includes neither its existence in a singular, nor its existence as a concept. Avicenna illustrates this with an example that was famous in the later Middle Ages: horseness, the nature of horse:

> In itself, [horseness] is nothing at all except horseness; for, in itself, it is neither one nor many, and exists neither in concrete things nor in the soul, existing in none of these things either in potency or in act, such that [these] are included in horseness. Rather, in terms of itself, it is only horseness. Rather, oneness is an attribute that conjoins with horseness, whereby horseness with this attribute becomes one. Similarly, in addition to this attribute, horseness has many other attributes that enter it. Thus, horseness – on the condition that, in its definition, it corresponds to many things – becomes general. (Avicenna, *Metaphysics* V, c. 1 (trans. Marmura, p. 149))

The idea is that horseness, as such, is simply the essential properties of horses; it exists in horses provided that there are horses, and it exists in the soul, as a concept, provided that someone is thinking of it. Neither does horseness, as such, include any kind of unity or multiplicity. Provided that there is one horse it is one, and provided that there is more than one horse it is many – as many as there are horses.

These insights of Avicenna's were of crucial significance for the understanding of universals in the thirteenth century. The background to Avicenna's account is Alexander of Aphrodisias, and the kind of view that Avicenna defends was explicitly associated with Alexander in Boethius's *Second commentary on Porphyry's Isagoge*. (For discussion of all this, see Tweedale, 1984, pp. 279–303.) According to Alexander,

> The common and universal [...] have their actual existence in material particulars; it is only when they are being known by an intellect that they become common and universal. (*De anima* III, § 28 (trans. Fotinis, pp. 118–19))

And Boethius claims that the solution to the problem of universals 'agreeing with Alexander [of Aphrodisias]' (*Second commentary on Porphyry's Isagoge*, n. 23 (trans. Spade, p. 23)) involves claiming that

> there is one subject for singularity and universality. But it is universal in one way, when it is thought, and singular in another, when it is sense in the things in which it has being. (*Second commentary on Porphyry's Isagoge*, n. 32 (trans. Spade, p. 25))

Since Avicenna doubtless knew Alexander's teaching too, we have in effect two routes through which it arrived in the Latin High Middle Ages: for the twelfth century, through Boethius; and for the thirteenth, through Avicenna as well.

Avicenna's thought was not wholly unproblematic for Christians; but many of his insights were at least friendly to theologians. This is in stark contrast to another great Islamic philosopher, the Aristotelian commentator Averroes (ibn Rushd) (1126–98) – known from the thirteenth century in the West simply as the 'Commentator', such was his global importance in the interpretation of Aristotle (the 'Philosopher'). The most significant commentaries of Averroes were translated by Michael Scot sometime between 1220 and 1235. Averroes's close textual readings of Aristotle did nothing to attempt to mitigate theologically troublesome issues in Aristotle's thought. For example, Aristotle believed that the world must lack a beginning. The world is in motion, and a thing cannot just start to move, with no explanation. So there must always have been motion (*Physics* VIII, c. 1 (251a8–b10)). Averroes, similarly, objected to creation, but for a different (though still Aristotelian) reason. According to Aristotle, production requires some kind of substrate – something to be *altered* in the production. Averroes agreed, and rightly saw that creation does not satisfy this condition. Creation is thus unintelligible (see Averroes, *The Incoherence of the Incoherence* (trans. van den Bergh, I, p. 273)).

All of this is evidently problematic for monotheistic religions that believe in a created universe. What interpretative strategies were available for a Christian theologian? One could attempt to read Aristotle charitably – in such a way that he is not read as definitively positing a beginningless universe, but merely as making a suggestion for dialectical purposes. In all of his works up to and including the *prima pars* of the *Summa theologiae*, completed by the middle of 1268, Aquinas takes this line. He basically makes three exegetical proposals, all of which claim that the arguments are not 'strictly speaking demonstrative'. The first is that the Aristotelian arguments are merely *ad hominem*, designed to challenge the views of his opponents. Secondly, Aristotle's use of authorities means that he aims to persuade in a case that he knows no genuine arguments. And, thirdly, in any case, it seems that Aristotle explicitly states elsewhere that there are no good arguments on either side of the issue. (For all three strategies, see *Summa theologiae* I, q. 46, a. 1 c.)

In his *Physics* commentary, written in late 1268 and 1269, Aquinas argues against his own sympathetic take on Aristotle:

> Others, trying in vain to show that Aristotle did not speak against the faith, said that Aristotle did not intend to show, as something true, that that motion is perpetual, but to introduce arguments for both sides, as for something doubtful. But this seems foolish, given [Aristotle's] way of proceeding. And furthermore, he used the perpetuity of time and motion as a premise to show that the first principle exists, both here in [*Physics*] VIII, and in *Metaphysics* XII. So it is evident that he took this to be something proven. (*In octo libros Physicorum expositio* VIII, l. 2, n. 986)

By 'others', of course, Aquinas means himself – and he here takes a rather dim view of his earlier efforts.

Another interpretative strategy, by way of mitigation of Aristotle's apparent view, would be to claim that God's perfect nature, as creator, requires that there are some things that he always causes. This was Avicenna's take on the issue: Avicenna held that God necessarily and eternally causes the highest immaterial being, but that this eternal causation is compatible with that being's being created (see *Metaphysics* VI, c. 2). Or, alternatively, one could embrace the Aristotelian view about the factual eternity of the world, and argue from this that the world cannot be created. One could, in short, maintain a view incompatible with monotheism. Averroes and his thirteenth-century Latin enthusiasts (on whom, see the last section of Chapter 5 below) did not quite do this, though they certainly held that Aristotle was committed to the eternity of the world and that it was not possible to find intellectual grounds on which to rebut the view. This kind of position is known as *fideism*: believing something even when it appears that there are good reasons against the belief. It is not the healthiest of intellectual attitudes, though it has been embraced by some eminent theologians, motivated by the view that faith and reason have nothing to do with each other, or are properly hostile to each other.

One way of avoiding fideism on this question would be to agree that the view is indeed Aristotelian, but to hold too that it can be shown to be false. This was the line followed by Bonaventure (*c.* 1217–74) – partly using arguments about the infinite that originate in the Persian philosopher al-Ghazālī (*c.* 1058–1111; translated by Dominicus Gundisalvi and Magister Johannes sometime between 1160 and 1190). Bonaventure argues that, if the universe were infinitely old, then there would already have been infinitely many days. But this is impossible since (as Aristotle himself points out) it is impossible to reach the end of an infinite distance:

> It is impossible to traverse infinitely many things. But if the universe did not begin, then there will have been infinitely many revolutions [of the sun]; therefore it is impossible to traverse them; therefore it was impossible to reach up to this [current one]. If you say that they are not traversed, because none was first, or that they can certainly be traversed in infinite time, you do not in this way evade the conclusion. For I ask from you whether some revolution infinitely distant preceded today's one, or none did. If none, then they are all finitely distant from today's one; therefore they had a beginning. If one was infinitely distant, then I ask about the revolution that immediately followed it, whether that one was infinitely distant [from today's one]. If not, then neither was the first one infinitely distant, because a finite distance will be between both of them; if it was indeed infinitely distant, then I ask likewise about the third, and the fourth, and so on to infinity. Therefore one was no more distant from this one than from another; therefore one is not prior to another; therefore they are all simultaneous. (*Commentaria in libros sententiarum* II, d. 1, p. 1, a. 1, q. 2, arg. 3)

Clearly, there are defects in this argument, and I will return to them in a moment. The opponents of Bonaventure found a different argument about the infinite more challenging:

It is impossible for an infinite number of things to exist all at once. But if the world was eternal, without a beginning, since it does not exist without human beings (for it is in some way on account of human beings that all things are), and since a human being only exists for a finite time, it follows that infinitely many human beings have existed. But there have been as many rational souls as there have been human beings. Therefore there have been infinitely many souls. But there are as many souls as there have been, since souls are incorruptible. Therefore there are infinitely many souls. (*Commentaria in libros sententiarum* II, d. 1, p. 1, a. 1, q. 2, arg. 5)

And Bonaventure claims, too, that the proofs for the existence of God all show that the universe must have been created: and what is created is brought about *from nothing* (*ex nihilo*) – and thus, *after* nothing (*Commentaria in libros sententiarum* II, d. 1, p. 1, a. 1, q. 2, arg. 6).

These arguments are hard to refute. But Aquinas, who was generally notably sympathetic to Aristotle's views, and who as much as anyone else attempted to make them his own, had a try. Aquinas's position is that it is impossible to show that the world had a beginning, and impossible to show that it did not. Given the requirements of Christian orthodoxy, this view is, I think, a position maximally generous to Aristotle. For Aquinas, it is entirely a matter of faith that the world – even if created – had a beginning (*Summa theologiae* I, q. 46, a. 2 c). This might sound like an odd claim, but we can get a good sense of how Aquinas understood it if we look at Aquinas's reply to the last of Bonaventure's objections to Aristotle's view just mentioned. To make something from nothing does not mean that there is a very thin kind of something – call it 'nothing' – from which God crafted the universe. What it means is that it is not the case that God, in making the universe, made it from something:

Those who posit an eternal world would say that the world is made by God from nothing, not because it was made after nothing (which is how we understand the term 'creation'), but because it was not made from something. (*Summa theologiae* I, q. 46, a. 2 ad 2)

This has the startling consequence that the universe could be both created and yet lack a beginning. In exploring the implications of Aristotle's view of the universe, Aquinas has in effect produced a wholly new version of the Christian doctrine of creation: creation is the *total dependence* of the universe on God; and this total dependence is not itself a function of the universe's having a beginning.[1]

I say that Aquinas's view has this startling consequence. I should say that it *would* do, were it the case that Aquinas knew how to refute Bonaventure's arguments about the infinite. He makes an attempt. On the impossibility of traversing an infinite distance, he suggests that Bonaventure is thinking of the extension the wrong way round, as it were: it is not as though we have to reach a point infinitely far from us (impossible, since there is no such point); rather, we have already traversed the magnitude: it is bounded at the *present* end:

> Traversal is always understood to be from one end to another. But whatever past day is pinpointed, there are finitely many days from that one to this; and these can be traversed. The objection proceeds as though there are infinitely many intervening days, given the extremes. (*Summa theologiae* I, q. 46, a. 2 ad 6)

Aquinas thus puts his finger precisely on the mistake in Bonaventure's argument. It does not follow, contrary to Bonaventure's assertion, from the fact that 'all [days are] finitely distant from today's one' that 'therefore they had a beginning'.

But this, of course, still relies on the possibility of an actual infinite – there is, after all, the set of all past days, and this set is infinite; and making sense of this requires the transfinite mathematics first proposed by Georg Cantor in the 1870s and 1880s – though we shall see in subsequent chapters a couple of thinkers start to make a little progress on the mathematical issue. In fact, Aquinas persistently and rightly asserted, from his earliest writing on the subject (the *Sentence* commentary) to the latest (*De aeternitate mundi*), that the problem of an infinite set is raised most acutely by the second of Bonaventure's arguments quoted above. In the *Summa theologiae* he gives solutions proposed by others (but that he would reject – e.g. al-Ghazālī's assertion that an actual infinite is possible (see *Metaphysics* I, tr. 1, div. 7 (trans. Muckle, pp. 41–2)) – and then comments, rather indecisively, that the objection relates merely to human beings, not to creation in general (see *Summa theologiae* I, q. 46, a. 2 ad 8). Aquinas does nothing to address Bonaventure's supporting argument here, that 'it is in some way on account of human beings that all things are'. Behind Aristotle's eternity argument is a very different assumption: that the universe exists invariantly – it is always fully formed, and at any given time contains all the kinds that it ever does. This is quite unlike the Christian view, and I provide some contrasting accounts (in Augustine and Bonaventure) in Chapter 3. At any rate, making humanity the *telos* or goal of the material world does the same work in Bonaventure's criticism as invariancy does in Aristotle.

Elsewhere, Aquinas takes a different and more radical path – agreeing (against his view in the *Summa theologiae*) with al-Ghazālī's affirmation of the possibility of an actual infinite: 'Besides, it has not been proven that God could not create an actual infinite' (*De aeternitate mundi* (trans. McInerny, p. 717)). Of course, Aquinas himself had spent many years endeavouring, as a good Aristotelian, to prove just that; and in effect this puts Aristotle in conflict with Aristotle, since, in order to maintain the coherence of Aristotle's view on the possible eternity of the world, Aquinas has to reject what Aristotle has to say about the actual infinite.

The problems Aristotle's views on topics other than logic might raise for Christian theology led to his rather stormy reception in the thirteenth century. Philosophers and theologians were, on the one hand, strongly motivated to study Aristotle; on the other hand, at least some of them also perceived the dangers. Difficulties started almost immediately. One of the most interesting condemnations at the Fourth Lateran Council (1215), under Pope Innocent III, surrounds the rather Platonic thinker Amalric of Bène (d. 1206), tending to identify God and the world (a development of a strong Neoplatonic emphasis, mediated through John Scottus Eriugena, on divine immanence). Amalric (none of whose writings survive) was condemned at a synod, under Peter Corbeil (Archbishop of Sens) and Peter of Nemours (Bishop of Paris), at Paris, in 1210, and again at Lateran IV in 1215. From the point of view of the assimilation of Aristotle, this condemnation is significant for its connection with another thinker, David of Dinant (d. 1214). David is one of the key reporters of Amalric's view, surviving in David's now fragmentary *Quaternuli*. David develops some of Amalric's insights in a decidedly Aristotelian direction. He starts from

Aristotle's distinction between the possible intellect and the agent intellect. Aristotle's agent intellect somehow abstracts the forms of particulars, and thus has a role in our forming universal concepts; the possible intellect is somehow receptive of such concepts. David argues that the possible intellect understands matter, and can do so only if 'it has some similarity to it or is identical with it'. But, David reasons, it cannot be similar to matter, because that would involve both matter and intellect being 'passive and subject to the same received attribute, such as two white things or two black things'. Since mind and matter cannot satisfy this condition, they must be 'identical' with each other; from which David concludes

> It is clear, therefore, that there is only one substance, not only of all bodies but also of all souls, and this substance is nothing other than God himself. And the substance from which all bodies come is called 'matter' [...] while the substance from which all souls come is called 'reason' or 'mind'. [...] It is therefore manifest that God is the reason of all souls, and the matter of all bodies. (*Quaternuli*, p. 71, in Dronke, 1988, p. 440)

Despite apparently being an associate of Innocent III, David's writings (though not person) were condemned at the Synod of Paris in 1210 (for relying excessively on Aristotle's *libri naturales*), though neither David nor his work was mentioned at Lateran IV. Clearly, his is a very odd reading of Aristotle. It is perhaps, more than anything else, a testimony both to the difficulties that faced early interpreters of Aristotle, and to the problems that Aristotelian philosophy might in principle raise for the Christian faith.

Lateran IV was interesting from another Aristotelian perspective, too: it defined the doctrine of transubstantiation using, in effect, notions from Aristotle's *Categories* (a work which, as I have already noted, was dominant in twelfth-century philosophy): the substance of the Eucharistic bread is transubstantiated into Christ's body, but the species (i.e. the *accidents*) of the bread remain (Lateran IV, const. 1).

The Parisian synod was, at least temporarily, rather important in the reception of the rest of Aristotle, however, for, along with condemning both Amalric and the works of David, it banned 'lectures in Paris, either publicly or privately [...] on Aristotle's books about natural philosophy' (*Chartularium universitatis parisiensis*, n. 11 (I,

70)). This ban was repeated by Robert of Courçon, whom Innocent III put in charge of drawing up the Arts syllabus at Paris in 1215. In 1231, Pope Gregory IX, in the Bull *Parens scientiarum*, repeated the ban on teaching Aristotle, but with the following important restriction: that the ban obtained only until the books had been examined for errors. By this time, the earlier ban seems not to have been taken with much seriousness, for we know that Roger Bacon (*c.* 1214/20–*c.* 1292) was lecturing on Aristotle's natural philosophy at Paris during the 1240s. And at any rate, in 1255 the statutes of the Arts Faculty in Paris mandated the study of all Aristotelian works as part of the Arts syllabus.

The study of Aristotle was secure from this time onwards. But it is one thing to study a work; it is another to be free to assent to whatever it contains. And difficulties quickly arose at both Paris and Oxford. In 1270 the Bishop of Paris, Stephen Tempier, condemned 13 propositions taken largely from teachings of members of the Paris Arts faculty (*Chartularium universitatis parisiensis*, n. 432 (I, 486–7)), and in 1277 condemned a total of 219, in what turned out to be one of the most important doctrinal moves for the history of later medieval philosophy (*Chartularium universitatis parisiensis*, n. 473 (I, 543–55)). Simultaneously, in Oxford the Dominican Robert Kilwardby (1215–79), Archbishop of Canterbury, condemned 30 propositions, and this was reiterated by his Franciscan successor, John Pecham (*c.* 1230–92). A good flavour of the 1277 Parisian condemnation can be given if we look at part of one of the key sets of propositions condemned: those concerning the eternity of the world (here, I simply mention those that have some relation to the discussion of this issue that I offered above):

> 87. That the world is eternal as regards all the species contained in it, and that time, motion, matter, agent, and receiver, are eternal, because the world comes from God and it is impossible that there be something new in the effect without there being something new in the cause.
> 89. That it is impossible to refute the arguments of the Philosopher concerning the eternity of the world unless we say that the will of the first being embraces incompatibles.
> 99. That the world, although it was made from nothing, was not newly-made, and, although it passed from nonbeing to

being, the nonbeing did not precede in duration but only in nature.

101. That there has already been an infinite number of revolutions of the heaven, which it is impossible for the created intellect but not for the first cause to comprehend.

205. That time is infinite at both ends. For even though it is impossible for an infinitude [of things] to have been traversed, some one of which had to be traversed, nevertheless it is not impossible for an infinitude [of things] to have been traversed, none of which had to be traversed. (*Chartularium universitatis parisiensis* (trans. Hyman, Walsh, and Williams, p. 545))[2]

(In proposition 87, I assume that the point is that it is impossible to traverse an infinity of things if that involves traversing some one of the things *first*.)

But while these give a sense of what was going on, they are not, I think, articles with the most important consequences. The really significant claims have to do with the rejection of all forms of necessitarianism, and a consequent stress on the contingency and possible scope of divine activity:

52. That what is self-determined, like God, either always acts or never acts; and that many things are eternal.

53. That God of necessity makes whatever comes immediately from him. – This is erroneous whether we are speaking of the necessity of coercion, which destroys liberty, or of the necessity of immutability, which implies the inability to do otherwise.

58. That God is the necessary cause of the first intelligence, which cause being posited, the effect is also posited; and both are equal in duration.

147. That what is impossible absolutely speaking cannot be brought about by God or by another agent. – This is erroneous if we mean what is impossible according to nature.

(*Chartularium universitatis parisiensis* (trans. Hyman, Walsh, and Williams, pp. 542–3))

(Note proposition 58, against Avicenna's view on creation, outlined briefly above – an affirmation of contingency that was very important for John Duns Scotus (*c.* 1266–1308) later on.)

Among other things, the flexibility that this stress on contingency allowed did a great deal to undermine the basic insights of Aristotelian physics, almost as soon as those insights had been assimilated. Here are two examples, presupposing the falsity of the Aristotelian view that a vacuum is impossible:

> 34. That the first cause cannot make more than one world.
> 49. That God could not move the heaven in a straight line, the reason being that he would leave a vacuum. (*Chartularium universitatis parisiensis* (trans. Hyman, Walsh, and Williams, p. 544))

Now, this is not philosophically neutral: to make sense of what the condemnations ascribe to divine power, we have to reject the Aristotelian view that space is constituted relationally, by extended bodies and their mutual contact. No wonder that some philosophers and theologians felt that Tempier had radically overstepped the limits of his jurisdiction. Godfrey of Fontaines (*c.* 1250–1306/9) argues that Tempier's successor 'sins in his failure to correct certain articles condemned by his predecessor', since the condemnation 'impedes the progress of students, is an occasion of scandal, and is detrimental to useful teaching (*doctrinae*)' (*Quodlibet* XII, q. 5 (p. 100)). But whatever we might think about this, it seems to me that, curiously, the intellectual effect of the condemnation was almost wholly positive: it enabled – perhaps required – a degree of originality and imagination that had very significant philosophical results, particularly in the radically innovative thought of Duns Scotus. Doubtless, this was not what Tempier and the theologians behind the condemnation would have anticipated or wanted.

The institutional context

Much of the most important work in philosophy was done in the Middle Ages not by philosophers but by trained *theologians*. Part of the reason for this has to do with the nature of the academic institutions that grew up during the period. And part of it has to do with the nature of the discipline of theology, and ways in which it changed during the twelfth century. Indeed, to some extent the institutional structures are the result of the changes in the ways that theology was conceptualized during the period. So I consider here both this latter issue, and also what we need to know about the institutional and pedagogical structures that developed in the period.

Returning to our person living in 1100: he would have had good but limited options for what we would think of as higher education. (In what follows I rely in part on Evans, 1980.) Someone entering a religious order would attend the school attached to his monastery. He would receive a theological education, with a deeply practical goal: the formation of the monk's spiritual and religious life. This education cannot be said to have been a systematic organized academic discipline, and its aims were not primarily intellectual ones. Its pedagogical roots can be found in late antiquity and the early Middle Ages. For Augustine, back in the fifth century, 'doctrina Christiana' – Christian education or Christian culture – encompasses all important academic endeavour; according to Cassiodorus, in the sixth, the arts – i.e. the topics suitable for academic study – are merely a part of Christian culture, belonging to 'sacred literature' (Cassiordorus, *Institutiones* I, c. 27, n. 1), and they are only of interest in so far as they help us understand scripture (Cassiodorus, *Institutiones* I, c. 35, n. 1). The arts, on this view, are as it were reduced to theology.

In addition to these monastic schools, there were schools associated with cathedrals, from at least the ninth century onwards. These cathedral schools gained greatly in significance around the end of the eleventh century, and began to provide a real intellectual alternative to the monastic schools. The curriculum of these cathedral schools was the liberal arts, and the purpose was to produce not monks but men trained in manners and classical learning: court clergy and diplomats. During the early twelfth century, these kinds of more secular institutions proliferated, leading to schools founded independently of a bishop's see. And the schools themselves became *theological* centres, of a kind very different from the old monastic schools. Abelard, for example, saw no difficulty in writing works of theology, even from his rather secular background. When Abelard labelled one of his works *Theologia christiana*, the Cistercian Bernard of Clairvaux (1090–1163) mocked the 'arts master' for treating theology as a subject appropriate for academic study – as, in effect, an art (*Epistola* 190, c. 1, 1–2). So theology, here, is as it were reduced to the arts. Bernard's criticism was in some ways not unfair, but he was, in effect, fighting a rearguard action, and ultimately lost. I return to some of these issues, in particular the debate between Bernard and Abelard, in Chapter 2.

Thus the twelfth century saw an increasing sense of theology understood as an academic subject. The intellectual catalyst for the development was perhaps Boethius, specifically his account of the speculative philosophical 'disciplines' (i.e., academic subjects) in chapter two of *De trinitate*: natural science, mathematics and *theology*. The Boethian tradition here passed into the twelfth century via the commentaries of Gilbert of Poitiers (on which, see Chapter 2), Thierry of Chartres († after 1156), and Clarembald of Arras (*c.* 1110–*c.* 1187). By the middle of the twelfth century, we can claim that theology is firmly established as an academic discipline: it began to have a clear domain, and rational argument was accepted as an appropriate critical tool. Boethius defined 'theology' narrowly, to include effectively merely the divine nature and the Trinity, and it required something of a leap to extend the term to cover other doctrinal issues, or indeed the Bible. But this is precisely what happened, making theology the study, in effect, of Christian doctrines – a study that used the tools of philosophy in its service, and to which philosophy was subordinate. Hugh of St Victor (*c.* 1096–1141) has a grasp of this kind of relationship (*De sacramentis* I, prol., c. 6), which was to reach its apotheosis in the account offered by Thomas Aquinas some 100 years later. Clarembald of Arras, in his commentary on Boethius's *De trinitate*, is even clearer. Theology has two functions: it legitimately employs evidence and ratiocination; and it contemplates, the 'perception of the divine being [...] without the help of created matter' (*Tractatus super librum Boetii de trinitate*, § 14 (p. 70)). In both roles, reason is fully engaged, and in the first role it is so independently of, or prior to, revelation and faith.

Now, this approach to theology – this philosophical approach, the result of which was that most innovations and developments in philosophy took place in theological discussions – was ultimately reflected in changes in the structures of institutions of learning during the period. In effect, this growth of academic theology parallels the growth of the universities in the years between 1100 and 1200: the academic developments I have just been describing were institutionalized in the universities and their structures – the separation of theology from the old arts was important for the growth, in the early universities, of the theology faculty as a graduate faculty, separate from the undergraduate arts faculty. In effect, the old arts curriculum became the undergraduate curriculum of the new universities; the study of medicine, law, and theology, became professionalized in graduate schools. And this was of vital importance, since much of the best medieval philosophy springs from the work of such professional academic theologians, aiming first and foremost to develop advanced philosophical tools to understand the Christian faith. As in Abelard and other high calibre twelfth-century thinkers, we find in the later Middle Ages (thirteenth century and onwards) the serious application of philosophy to theology; but what we also find is an academic training in theology precisely as such, in principle divorced from (though of course not incompatible with) its spiritual context.

What initially happened was this. Around 1200 in both Paris and Oxford (the major theological universities during the period of interest in this book), an established group of masters, based at schools in those cities, evolved into a *corporation* of masters and students, governed by statutes. The precise circumstances and processes involved in each university are relatively obscure. In the case of Paris, the new corporation received its statutes from the papal legate, Robert of Courçon, in 1215. The teacher – the master – was officially recognized by his having received the *licentia docendi*: the licence to teach. And this was to be achieved by gaining a doctorate in one of the four faculties. Frequently, masters in the arts faculty were simultaneously students in one of the professional schools. In Paris, the formation of the university resulted from the need to clarify the respective powers of the chancellor of the cathedral school and the Bishop of Paris: the intervention of Innocent III ultimately deciding in favour of the masters by providing them with the relevant legal tools to ensure their structure and continued survival. Oxford developed analogously, and a large number of masters and schools existed in Oxford by the early thirteenth century. At any rate, for our purposes the key thing to note is the organization of the universities into faculties, in the way just outlined – for it is this institutional arrangement that most closely reflects the changes in philosophy and theology that I have tried to trace during the twelfth century.

All this explains, in a way, why the major later philosophical developments occurred in Theology faculties. Almost universally, the best thinkers were trained in the theology departments (John Buridan (1295/1300–1358/61) is the obvious exception).[3] Medieval philosophers lived in a world rather larger than ours: it contains God, angels, and souls – it contains, in short, immaterial beings, as well as material ones. And, like all good philosophers, the best medievals aimed at theories of maximal generality. So their theories had to take into account the kinds of entity that are typically the domain of theologians. And these kinds of entities served as the subject of complex thought-experiments, rather like the modern philosophers' brain-in-a-vat. How would angels move? How could God be numerically one thing but yet three persons? How can immaterial entities interact causally with physical objects? Again, this kind of way of thinking of theology is far removed from the kind of monastic approach that I identified in the early twelfth century: Abelard, we might say, definitively triumphed over Bernard, even if he was never in a position to know it.

Coincidental to all this – the institutionalization of learning in the universities, and the discovery of huge swathes of previously unknown philosophy – but crucial, albeit by accident, was a very important development in religious institutions at the beginning of the thirteenth century: the founding of the mendicant orders of friars, notably the Franciscans (by St Francis of Assisi, in 1209) and the Dominicans (by Dominic Guzman, in 1216). Friars are distinguished from monks by their lack of attachment to a particular religious house – they belong not to a place (a monastery) but simply to a network (the order itself). These orders were nimble, mobile, responsive in ways that monastic orders were not, or found it harder to be, and more unified and academically focused than the secular clergy. And their express purpose was preaching and teaching – functions that required global educational facilities. Much of the most significant philosophical work in the period from about 1230 onwards was done by members of these two orders. The old monastic schools were thus eclipsed not only by the universities but by the *studia* of the mendicant orders. For example, theology, following much the same *curriculum* as at the university faculties, was also taught at these *studia*, and some of the most important fourteenth-century theological works arose in this environment. William of Ockham's (*c.* 1287–1347) quodlibetal questions, for example, were disputed at the Franciscan *studium* in London. Adam Wodeham (*c.* 1298–1358) lectured on the *Sentences* a total of three times: once at the Franciscan *studium* at London, once at the house in Norwich, and once at Oxford. The most important *studia* in an order were the *studia generalia*, *studia* open to students from all provinces. We should not underestimate the importance of these in the theological formation of the medievals. In Bologna, for example, the Franciscan and Dominican *studia generalia* acted as something like an unofficial theology faculty until 1364. The mendicants also had *studia* at Paris, Oxford and Cambridge: originally just Franciscan and Dominican, but later also Carmelite and Augustinian. Since university functions were open to members of these *studia*, the *studia* enabled large numbers of the mendicant orders to receive a university education. Modelled along the same lines, it was possible to become a master in theology at the *studium generale* of the Papal Curia, founded in 1245.

Thus far, I have not spoken about the kind of curriculum which was followed in the arts and theology faculties. Above I discussed some of the requirements in the Paris Arts Faculty, and the extent to which Aristotle was alternatively forbidden and mandated. The basis of the curriculum in arts faculties (and, I take it, at non-university *studia* generally) was the old *trivium* (grammar, logic, and rhetoric) and *quadrivium* (geometry, music, arithmetic, astronomy). In grammar, everyone would have studied Donatus and Priscian; in logic, Aristotle (the *logica vetus* and *logica nova*) and some of the *logica modernorum*. Of the *quadrivium*, geometry was the most important area, and Euclid was a central component. To this, we can add – with the *caveats* noted above – Aristotle's key works (the *libri naturales*, the *Metaphysics*, and the *Nicomachean Ethics*). In theology, the major text remained in principle the Bible. After a brief flirtation with the *Historia scolastica* of Peter Comestor (died *c*. 1180), Paris soon established the *Sentences* of Peter Lombard (1095/1100–60), written 1154–6, as the other main text – probably following the lead of Alexander of Hales's (*c*. 1185–1245) *Glossa in libros sententiarum* in the 1220s. Oxford followed suit in the 1240s. The choice of the *Sentences* served two useful ends: it gave all students a rudimentary knowledge of the Church Fathers, above all Augustine; and it ensured, at least in principle, that systematic theology was studied by all. (I discuss the work in more detail in Chapter 2.)

In fact, by no means all of the teaching of the theology faculties was text-based. Coincident with the twelfth century development of theology as an academic discipline, an important heuristic change took place – the growth of the disputation. Disputations played an important part in teaching, and public disputations were a part of the statutory obligation both for qualification for the degree of master, and for a master officially engaged in lecturing – a Regent Master, a chairholder in the relevant faculty. And, more than that, the disputation structure formed the main literary model for lectures (e.g. on the *Sentences*) until the middle of the fourteenth century. The origin is the discussion of difficult points raised in a commentary by means of a series of *quaestiones*, interrupting the flow of the text, and dealing with intellectually difficult points separately. The most famous example from the theological literature of the twelfth century is the series of thirty such *quaestiones* raised by Abelard in the course of his Romans commentary, one of which I discuss in Chapter 2. We learn from a Boethian passage known to Abelard just what such a *quaestio* was: 'A question is a proposition that is open to doubt' (*In Ciceronis Topica* I (trans. Stump, p. 29)). Such *quaestiones* – just like those in Abelard's Romans commentary – were standardly part of a larger, textually based, work. But they became detached from this context, and the most significant works of our period were simply series of *quaestiones*. The first such was Abelard's *Sic et non*. The model is perhaps to be found in the collections of laws made by Bernold of Constance and Alger of Liège, and the origin is probably traceable to the *Digest* of Ivo of Chartres (1040–1115). Central to the purpose of these canonists was the task of reconciling conflicting legal authorities, making use of implicit hermeneutical rules. *Sic et non* turned out to be extremely influential as a model for the many theological textbooks which were produced in the twelfth century along similar lines: the most important one being Peter Lombard's *Sentences*. I return to these works in Chapter 2.

The separation of the *quaestio* from its text encouraged the development of its dialectical aspects. And the adoption of a basically dialectical method, opposing opinions against each other in a fundamentally confrontational manner in order to arrive at the true answer, proved to be an essential feature of scholasticism as it developed. What was originally – say in Abelard or the Lombard – a literary tool became an oral one as well, and one which assumed a certain pedagogical importance. As the universities developed institutionally, the disputation became one of the major features of a student's academic career. Examination by disputation was standard in the medieval theology faculties (as indeed it was in arts, medicine and law as well). Masters would hold regular disputations, and require their students to participate, extempore, defending or attacking a given view. The most well-known of these are the so-called 'quodlibetal' disputations held in Advent and Lent: disputations that would take as their subjects questions raised by anyone (*a quolibet*) in the audience, on any subject (*de quolibet*). The master and bachelors involved did not have prior warning of the topics that would be raised, though the master could refuse to debate any topic which he thought to be unsuitable. Equally, the master could himself raise questions for debate. *Quodlibets* are a kind of bell-weather for the interests and debates of a given year. The flourishing of the *Quodlibet* coincides almost exactly with the high-point of medieval philosophy (the thirteenth century and the first half of the fourteenth). For reasons I shall touch on in the Epilogue, the medieval universities never quite recovered after the devastating plagues of the late 1340s, and the abandonment of the *Quodlibet* is doubtless both a symptom and a partial cause of this.

Notes

1   It is not clear to me just how successful Aquinas is here. Causing is a transitive relation: if *a* causes *b* to cause *c*, then *a* causes *c*. But it is not clear that being a *total* cause is thus transitive: *a* in this sequence cannot be the total cause of *c*, because *b* is a partial cause of *c*, albeit that *a* is the total cause of *b*. And if creating requires being the total cause of at least one thing, then the producer of an eternal world is not a creator.

2   Note that the translation follows a twentieth-century numbering proposed by Mandonnet. For convenience and accuracy, I give the original numbering here.

3   Perhaps in addition to him we might mention in the second rank some of the members of the Paris Arts Faculty implicitly targeted in the 1270s condemnations (notably Siger of Brabant (*c.* 1240–82/4) and Boethius of Dacia (*c.* 1240–after 1277)); the Averroist John of Jandun (1280–1328); the logician William of Sherwood (William Heytesbury (before 1313–72/3), and some of the early fourteenth-century Arts Masters associated with Merton College in Oxford (on whom, see Chapter 8)). There are some logicians whose faculty affiliation we do not know about – Peter of Spain, and Lambert of Auxerre, for example. Some theologians are better known nowadays for the work they did in Arts: most notably, Radulphus Brito (*c.* 1270–1320) (though this seems just to be an accident of history: his theological works are unedited and have not been studied); also Nicole Oresme (*c.* 1320–82) (whose theological work is known but is far outshone by his contributions

in natural philosophy), and Francis of Marchia (Francis of Ascoli: *c.* 1285/90–1344) (though his theological works have recently appeared and will doubtless gather attention).

Part I

CONSOLIDATION

CHAPTER 1

Anselm of Canterbury (1033–1109)

The period from 1050 to 1200, the topic of my first two chapters, is best thought of as a period of consolidation: the sustained and systematic reflection on available material – much the same material as was in circulation 400 years earlier. As I outlined in the Introduction, the task of locating and translating new work began in the second part of the twelfth century, but its results did not really have an impact until the thirteenth. Even the *logica modernorum* sprang from material, both well-known and neglected, that was already available: the tremendously original contributions to logic made by the twelfth-century resulted fundamentally from consideration of Aristotelian and Porphyrian antecedents. But while it may be that the real philosophical genius of the twelfth century lies in logic, this was certainly not the only area to attract careful intellectual thought. And in any case, I avoid discussion of logic here, since it scarcely seems suitable for something intended as an introduction.

If we examine the intellectual achievements of the twelfth century in areas other than logic, we cannot fail but notice something immediately: that these achievements are really all *theological*, and philosophical only to the extent needed to make theological progress. This contrasts very strikingly with the thirteenth and fourteenth centuries, when strictly philosophical questions – questions discussed quite independently of their theological usefulness or relevance – begin to assume an importance all of their own.

Anselm of Canterbury is a stunning example of what a highly intelligent, innovative, and systematic philosopher might be able to make of a mixture of the dazzling but rather chaotic and uncontrolled heritage left by Augustine, the rather limited Aristotelian *logica vetus* inherited from Boethius, and the Latin Stoicism of Cicero and Seneca. Anselm himself was a Benedictine monk, belonging to the community at Bec, whose abbot he became in 1079. He was, for the last two decades of his life, from 1091, one of the first Norman Archbishops of Canterbury, a position that he did not much relish, and that required a degree of political compromise that he was unwilling and unable to manage. While we should not think of Anselm as springing up in some kind of intellectual vacuum – there was, after all, a tradition of monastic learning that was just beginning to take on a certain kind of philosophical discipline (e.g. in the work of Anselm's teacher, Lanfranc of Bec (d. 1089), who himself became Archbishop of Canterbury in 1070) – Anselm's original philosophical achievements place him in the very first rank of Western philosophers.

The most famous, and perhaps the best, example of Anselm's abilities can be found in his celebrated attempt to prove the existence of God, found in Chapter 2 of the *Proslogion*. Anselm argues that God is that than which nothing greater can be thought. And he reasons:

> That than which a greater cannot be thought cannot be in the intellect alone. For if it is in the intellect alone, it can be understood to be in reality (*in re*) also, and this is greater. If therefore that than which a greater cannot be thought is in the intellect alone, that very thing than which a greater cannot be thought is that than which a greater can be thought. And this certainly cannot be. Therefore without doubt there exists, both in the intellect and in reality, something that which a greater cannot be thought. (*Proslogion*, c. 2 (I, 101–2))

There is an Augustinian precedent (laid out in book II of *De libero arbitrio*, particularly chapters 6, 12, and 15), but it has nothing like the *prima facie* power of Anselm's argument.[1] The argument itself is an attempt to show that the denial of God's existence leads to a contradiction. It is what logicians label a *reductio ad absurdum*: a variety of indirect proof that attempts to show that the position opposed is contradictory. The idea is that positing that that than which a greater cannot be thought exists merely in the mind generates a contradiction, since in that case there would be something greater than that than which a greater cannot be thought: namely, that than which a greater cannot be thought existing both in the mind and in reality. Since it is therefore contradictory to suppose that than which a greater cannot be thought to exist in the mind alone, it follows that it is false that it exists in the mind alone. But, Anselm claims, that than which a greater cannot be thought exists at least in the mind. So it exists at least, but not merely, in the mind. Thus it must exist in reality.

The rest of the work makes good on the identification of God with that than which nothing greater can be thought (an identification made merely on the basis of faith in chapter 2), showing that that than which nothing greater can be conceived has the kinds of perfections that Christians traditionally ascribe to God.

Of course, Anselm's argument is the subject of much controversy. First, it seems to amount to a proof of God's existence, and Anselm states as much:

> I began to wonder whether perhaps it might be possible to find one single argument that for its proof required no other save itself, and that by itself would suffice to prove that God really (*vere*) exists. (*Proslogion*, preface (trans. Davies and Evans, p. 83))

But the work is cast in the form of a prayer, and Anselm calls his book *Faith Seeking Understanding* (*Proslogion*, preface). And, secondly, it is generally accepted that something is wrong with the argument. But what might it be? One standard criticism of arguments of this kind of form ('ontological' arguments), current since Kant, is that ontological arguments presuppose that existence is a kind of perfection that can be added to a concept. Does Anselm's argument presuppose this?

On the first of these issues, Anselm gives his own answer: he writes with the aim of raising his mind to God; but how he does that is to provide a proof that would be sufficient to convince the 'fool' – that is to say, someone denying God's existence; an atheist, as we would say. To raise his mind to God, in this case, involves providing a good deductive proof that by itself proves that God really exists. ('Really' in the Prologue is '*vere*': 'truly'; in Chapter 2, Anselm substitutes '*in re*': in reality, as opposed to (merely) in the mind. The aim is to show that God exists not merely in the mind, but also truly (*vere*), and that is what it is for him to exist in reality (*in re*).)

On the second issue – what might be wrong with Anselm's argument – there is a great deal that might be said. On the Kantian question, I think it is clear enough that Anselm is trying to establish the existence of something that (as he puts it in *Proslogion*, c. 3), 'cannot be thought not to exist': that is to say, a necessary existent, something that includes existence in its concept. If we do not think that existence could be built into a concept, then we are likely to be moved by Kant's worry. But the real point in Kant is that, however much we build into a concept (perhaps even including existence in a concept), it is always a further question whether or not that concept is realized. It is a feature of Anselm's argument that necessary existence is arrived at as a conclusion, not a premise. So, if effective, Anselm's argument would indeed provide an answer to the further question of whether or not the concept of that than which nothing greater can be conceived is realized. I do not think, then, that Anselm is obviously open to Kant-style critique.

Anselm certainly needs to presuppose that it is possible that there exists that than which nothing greater can exist – something that he does not explicitly state in chapter 2. But this presupposition crops up in Anselm's attempt to refute what looks like a specious objection to his argument raised by an otherwise unknown contemporary of his, Gaunilo of Marmoutiers. Gaunilo objects that, if Anselm's reasoning is correct, he should be able to construct a parallel argument in favour of the existence of a most-perfect island. If such an island lacked existence, its concept would not be a concept of the most perfect island (Gaunilo, *Pro insipiente*). The parallel argument clearly fails: there could not be any such thing as a most perfect island. But Anselm's argument is burdened with no such difficulty: it is not at all clear that there could not be a being than which none greater could be thought.

But this is not to say that his argument is free of defect. Quite the contrary, it seems to me that, for all its tremendous power, there is a crucial problem at its heart. Anselm's basic idea is that having a thought of an object involves that object's somehow existing in the mind. Given this, we can talk somehow of the same object existing in two different ways: in reality, and in the mind. And, given this, Anselm supposes, we might simply treat either of these two ways of existing as increasing the perfection of the object: existing in the mind *and* in reality is greater than existing merely in the mind (and, I suppose, conversely, existing in reality and in the mind is greater than existing merely in reality, though Anselm's argument does not require this). But this way of thinking of concepts confuses the *object* of a concept with its *content*. Cognitive acts have semantic or conceptual content, something that today we would naturally think of as propositional: that *x* is *F*, that (for example) centaurs have horns – irrespective of the thought's having an *object* – irrespective of their being centaurs or not. (I take the example from Fine, 1993, p. 123.) The case that Anselm has in mind requires contents with simple (i.e. non-propositional) semantic values, simple intensions: *centaur*, for example, or *God*. But while cognitive acts have to have contents, they do not have to have objects, things that they are about, or are directed at: there are no centaurs, and my thought that centaurs have horns, or even my thought *centaurs*, lacks any object. Failing to make this distinction leads Anselm into trouble. The fact that he has a thought with the content *that than which nothing greater can be thought* has no bearing at all on the existence of any *object* of that thought, and it makes no sense to add together the content of a thought and its object to increase somehow the perfection of the object. And, of course, if God does not exist, we can have a thought with the content *God*, or a thought with the content *necessary existent*, even though that thought lacks an object.

Still, for all its defects, Anselm's ontological argument remains a remarkable achievement, revealing an intellect of both astonishing power and great originality. But it is far from Anselm's only philosophical accomplishment. He got involved, in the 1090s, in a debate about universals. His opponent was the nominalist Roscelin, and the context Trinitarian theology. As a nominalist, Roscelin denies that there are any shared or universal substances, and Anselm maintains that an acceptance of the existence of (at least one) shared substance is a necessary condition for accepting the doctrine of the Trinity. Roscelin's theological view, as reported by Anselm, is that the three divine persons must count as 'three things (*res*) [...] intrinsically distinct like three angels or three souls', but that these persons are 'completely one and the same in will and power' (*De incarnatione verbi*, cc. 1 and 2 (trans. Evans and Davies, pp. 233 and 238)). And Roscelin attempts to show that denying this claim amounts to Sabellianism, the view that 'the Father and the Holy Spirit as well as the Son became flesh' (*De incarnatione verbi*, c. 1 (trans. Evans and Davies, p. 233)). Roscelin is clear that there are no extra-mental or, rather, extra-linguistic universals: he considers

universal essences to be merely vocal emanations (*flatus vocis*), and [...] can understand colours only as material substances, and human wisdom only as the soul. (*De incarnatione verbi*, c. 1 (trans. Evans and Davies, p. 237))

This is thorough-going nominalism; colours and dispositions, which might count as shared universals in a realist philosophy, are likewise reduced to particular substances. (There are no properties at all on this view: just particular substances.) So items that are 'intrinsically distinct like three angels or three souls' lack any common features. And the three divine persons likewise – their unity is extrinsic, unity of will and power.

Anselm is quick to diagnose Roscelin's nominalism as the root of his theological error:

> In what way can those who do not yet understand how several specifically human beings are one human being understand in the most hidden and highest nature how several persons, each of whom is a complete God, are one God? And in what way can those whose minds are darkened as to distinguishing their horse and its colour distinguish between one God and his several relations? (*De incarnatione verbi*, c. 1 (trans. Evans and Davies, p. 237))

Roscelin's metaphysics, according to Anselm, leads him into two distinct Trinitarian errors. The denial of universals forces him into tritheism (*De incarnatione verbi*, c. 4); and the denial of properties *tout court* allows him no account of the way in which the persons are distinguished from each other by distinct particular properties or relations (*De incarnatione verbi*, c. 2).

The first of these issues is, as Anselm acknowledges, a bit more complex than it seems. After all, the ways in which several human beings are 'one human being' and the several divine persons 'one God' cannot be just the same, otherwise orthodox Christians would (as Roscelin charges) have to affirm that there is just one human substance, just as there is just one divine substance. Anselm does not say much by way of clarification here, but he seems to fall into the Aphrodisian or Boethian tradition when he states that

> we surely do not predicate two angels or two souls of anything numerically one and the same, nor do we predicate anything numerically one of two angels or two souls, as we predicate

Father and Son of numerically one God, and numerically one
God of the Father and the Son. (*De incarnatione verbi*, c. 2
(trans. Evans and Davies, p. 240))

Here we seem to have, in the human and angelic cases, one
universal or shared nature, but one such that it is somehow more
than one distinct substance (it is not 'numerically one') – whereas
in the divine case the one shared nature is just one substance.
Elsewhere, again contrasting creaturely and divine cases, Anselm
talks about divisibility (in the creaturely case) versus indivisibility
(in the divine): universal substances are *divisible* into particulars;
the divine substance not so (*Monologion*, c. 27). What accounts for
this difference, according to the *De incarnatione verbi* passage just
quoted, is that divine persons, unlike created ones, are distinct from
each other merely by their relations to each other (the second of the
two points on which Anselm believes Roscelin's metaphysics leads
him into error):

> The Father and the Son are not two things in such a way that
> we in the case of these two things understand their substance,
> but that we understand their relations [...] [whereas] we
> speak of angels and animals as substances, not as relations. (*De
> incarnatione verbi*, c. 2 (trans. Evans and Davies, pp. 239–40))

And in this way Anselm tries to disambiguate Roscelin's language of
things: Father and Son are two things if 'thing' is construed generally
to refer to items distinct from each other, however minimally; but
they are not two things if 'thing' is construed as substance.

Anselm is noted too for his contribution to action theory and
moral psychology, and I mention just one component of that here:
his analysis of rational action in terms of two (possibly conflicting)
motivations in the will: the inclination to justice (*affectio iustitae*) and
the inclination to the advantageous (*affectio commodi*). (Here I follow
the penetrating and convincing account of these issues offered in
Visser and Williams, *Anselm*, pp. 178–85.) As Anselm sees it, free
action without motivation is impossible: a free action requires an
internal *inclination* to a certain kind of goal (*De casu diaboli*, c. 13).
But, he argues, the presence of such a motivation is not sufficient for
the freedom of an action – at least, of the first action performed by a
rational agent. If there were just one such motivation in the will, then

the action would be necessitated by whatever were responsible for establishing the motivation in the first place. And Anselm assumes that the initial fixing of motivations is the result of factors external to the agent. Thus if there were just one motivation, the initial action would be necessitated by something external to the agent, and thus not free (*De casu diaboli*, cc. 13 and 14). So for an initial action to be a free action, there must be a choice between alternatives – and given that choice requires motivation, the choice must be made somehow on the basis of two distinct motivations. Once the initial action is performed, motivation can be fixed on the basis of that action – for example, a choice for justice might result in the divine reward of perseverance in justice – in line with a definition of 'freedom', clearly derived from certain Augustinian claims, that Anselm endorses: 'Freedom is the power for preserving rectitude of will for the sake of rectitude itself' (*De libertate arbitrii*, c. 3 (trans. Evans and Davies, p. 179, slightly altered)); see e.g. Augustine, *De libero arbitrio* I, c. 15: 'The only genuine freedom is that possessed by those who are happy and cleave to the eternal law' (trans. Williams, p. 25)). Anselm holds that the *power* to act freely remains in the sinful agent, but that the fixity of motivation – merely for the advantageous – deprives the agent of the opportunity to exercise the relevant power, i.e. for justice (see *De libertate arbitrii*, c. 4).

The issue that Anselm's intellectual gymnastics here are designed to solve is the catastrophic first moment in the Christian drama – the Fall of Satan. Satan willed something he believed to be advantageous to himself against the interests of justice. Hence Anselm's stress on the first action of a rational agent. He means the *very first* action of any rational agent – the initial angelic choice, at the moment of creation. But the tools he uses, it seems to me, have their origins in a source quite external to the Christian revelation: in this case, again, Stoic – the contrast between the advantageous (*commodum*) and the just (*iustum*) that Cicero makes the heart of *De officiis*. Anselm's perspective is very different, as we have seen, and it is his Christian context, an account of the cosmic tragedy at the heart of the Christian religion, that makes all the difference. What in Cicero is a question of ethics is in Anselm a question about (human) motivation and the psychological explanation for wrong-doing.

If Anselm's account of the origin of sin is novel, so too is his account of its remedy – not, of course, the remedy for angelic sin, for according to Christians there is no such remedy, but the remedy for human sin. Christians associate notions of redemption with the life and death of Christ. The question Anselm sets out to answer is this:

> By what reason or necessity did God become man, and by his death, as we believe and profess, restore life to the world, when he could have done this through the agency of some other person, angelic or human, or simply by willing it? (*Cur deus homo* I, c. 1 (trans. Evans and Davies, p. 265, slightly altered))

Prior to Anselm, the standard answer went something like this. The result of human sin was that human beings are justly punished by Satan, and justly belong to his domain. God desired to redeem human beings from Satan's power, and offered an exchange: Satan could have the one sinless man, Christ, in exchange for some or all of those human beings held bondage by Satan. Satan agreed, and on Christ's death Christ descended into Hell. But (unknown to Satan) Christ was not only man but also God, and Satan was unable to keep hold of him. So by a rather slippery sleight-of-hand – by offering Christ as a bait on a fishhook (to use Gregory of Nazianzus's (329–89/90) striking image) – God managed to rescue human beings from the power of Satan while respecting Satan's rights. Anselm understandably thought that this view was absurd, and explicitly rejected it. He believes that it is just that humankind be punished, and that God permits Satan to punish humankind; but he believes too that 'the devil had no merit whereby he deserved to inflict the punishment' – and hence no rights (*Cur deus homo* I, c. 7 (trans. Evans and Davies, pp. 272–3)).

Anselm's own answer is very different. As he sees it, our sin places us in debt to God (*Cur deus homo* I, c. 11). We cannot pay this debt (*Cur deus homo* I, cc. 20, 23–4), and are thus justly punishable for our sin (*Cur deus homo* I, c. 12). But Christ as the sinless God-man is in a position willingly to pay the debt (*Cur deus homo* II, cc. 6, 14, 18) – i.e. to make satisfaction for sin (*Cur deus homo* I, c. 19) – and this satisfaction averts the punishment that would otherwise be due (*Cur deus homo* I, cc. 14 and 19). It is true that this whole mechanism removes human beings from the devil's power; but this removal is a consequence of the redemption, not its explanation or mechanism:

It is [...] not the case that God needed to come down from heaven to conquer the devil, or to take action against him in order to set humanity free [...] God did not owe the devil anything but punishment nor did man owe him anything but retribution – to defeat in return him by whom he had been defeated. But, whatever was demanded from man, his debt was to God, not to the devil. (*Cur deus homo* II, c. 19 (trans. Evans and Davies, p. 354, slightly altered))

One thing that is striking here is that Anselm, solidly in the monastic, Benedictine, tradition, felt himself able, indeed required, to propose a radically innovative doctrine on this point. Another monk from broadly the same tradition, Bernard of Clairvaux, reacted in a very hostile way to this kind of innovation: though apparently only when it was proposed by someone outside this monastic tradition – namely, Peter Abelard – as we shall see in Chapter 2.

As we saw above, Anselm proposes a novel proof for God's existence. But this is not the only part of Christianity that he attempts to prove. Anselm is extremely positive about the power of the human mind to come up with reasons in favour of the Christian faith – in general, the twelfth century seems to have been a more optimistic time in this respect than later centuries. In particular, Anselm develops his account of the atonement as part of an argument to show that, given human sin, it is necessary for God to become incarnate and die – just as the Christian religion teaches. Anselm is very serious about the probative force of his argument. The preface of *Cur deus homo* claims that the work 'proves by necessary reasons [...] that it is from necessity that all the things which we believe about Christ have come to pass' (*Cur deus homo*, praef. (trans. Evans and Davies, p. 262); see too II, c. 22). This is a remarkably ambitious project. The basic argument is that only a God-man could make satisfaction (book I and chapters 6–9 of book II); and that God's purposes require such satisfaction, given the reality of human sin (the rest of book II).

Underlying the argument is a very important assumption about divine action stated very clearly by Anselm:

I wish to come to an agreement with you: that no unfittingness where God is concerned – not even the smallest – shall be accepted by us, and that no reason – not even the smallest –

shall be rejected by us unless a more important reason conflicts with it. For just as, in the case of God, impossibility follows from any unfittingness, however small, correspondingly necessity follows from a small reason, if not defeated by a larger one. (*Cur deus homo* I, c. 10 (trans. Evans and Davies, p. 282, slightly altered))

And elsewhere Anselm's dialogue partner in *Cur deus homo* asserts, without contradiction from Anselm, that we can conclude the necessity of a certain divinely-chosen state of affairs merely from its being the 'more fitting and reasonable' of the possible alternatives (*Cur deus homo* II, c. 16). And, Anselm reasons, it is unfitting for God simply to forgive us; and unfitting for his purposes in creation to be frustrated as they would be in the case that we were punished for our sins (*Cur deus homo*, I, c. 14). This assumption about divine activity has a curious consequence: that God has alternative possibilities only in cases where two courses of action are equally fitting. Anselm does not spell out whether such a situation could arise, but given the standard medieval assumption that no two things are equally valuable, it may well be that Anselm has to be committed to the view that God only has one course of action available to him (albeit that human beings have alternatives, and thus that contingency might arise in God's activity in consequence of the different possible situations that different free human action might create).

Why introduce aesthetic considerations (of what fits with something else)? Anselm's purpose is to show that God's actions are just, and he elsewhere speaks of justice as giving a certain beauty:

If the divine wisdom did not impose these forms of recompense [i.e. punishment or satisfaction] in cases where wrongdoing is endeavouring to upset the right order of things, there would be in the universe, which God ought to be regulating, a certain ugliness, resulting from the violation of the beauty of order, and God would appear to be failing in his governance. Since these two consequences are as impossible as they are unfitting, it is necessary that either satisfaction or punishment follows upon every sin. (*Cur deus homo* I, c. 15 (II, 73–4; trans. Evans and Davies, p. 289, slightly altered))

From which we might infer that Anselm thinks that judgments about what is just or unjust are based or grounded on perceptions or judgments about what is beautiful; and this would explain the appeal to aesthetic considerations in the argument of *Cur deus homo*.

Further reading

The best introduction to Anselm's thought is Sandra Visser and Thomas Williams, *Anselm*, Great Medieval Thinkers (New York: Oxford University Press, 2009). Jasper Hopkins, *A Companion to the Study of St Anselm* (Minneapolis, MN: University of Minnesota Press, 1972) is still excellent.

Note

1   The decisive phrase in the argument – God is that than which nothing greater can be thought – occurs in Seneca, *Naturales quaestiones* I, praef. 13, describing God's magnitude (Seneca, as a Stoic, believed that all concrete objects were material) – but it is not clear whether or not a copy of this text was available to Anselm. My own view is that the phrasing is so strikingly similar that it is highly likely to have been.

CHAPTER 2

From 1100 to 1200

Peter Abelard

Peter Abelard is now one of the most well-known of medieval philosophers. But the situation was rather different in the later Middle Ages – at least, after Abelard's death in 1142. Abelard was certainly famous during his lifetime, much of which he spent teaching in northern France, both for his personal life and for his forays into theology. Highly intelligent, he clearly did not suffer fools gladly, and had an unerring instinct for generating the enmity of people whose paths he crossed. His contributions in logic are, perhaps, the most remarkable of the whole Middle Ages (possibly excepting Ockham). But he disappeared off the map, probably because of his theological speculations, for which he was twice condemned (once at Soissons in 1120, and once in 1141 as the result of proceedings at the Council of Sens in 1140 – something I return to below). He was barely known in the thirteenth century. One of his most notorious views in theology is that God cannot do other than he does, a view that was widely discussed and rejected in the twelfth century (both Hugh of St Victor and Peter Lombard discussed it, and in this guise it passed into the thirteenth century and even on to Leibniz, who considered it at some length). Aquinas knows that the view was held in the twelfth century, and notes that it was ascribed to 'Master Peter Almalareus' – the only reference to Abelard in his whole corpus, clearly second-hand and garbled (Aquinas, *De potentia*, q. 1, a. 5). It is a curious fact that Abelard was condemned for spelling out a belief that seems to be a clear implication of claims accepted by Anselm – as we have just seen. I mentioned above that I was not going to say much about logic in this introductory book. Were I to write with a greater focus on logic, it would be Abelard, not Anselm, who would have received a chapter to himself.

All of this is not to say that Abelard had no influence. Quite the contrary. Peter Lombard's *Sentences* engage constantly, though anonymously, with Abelard, whose *Sic et non* is the ancestor of the *Sentences*. David Luscombe puts the matter exactly:

> Peter [Lombard] [...] incorporated numerous [...] borrowings from Abelard's writings. In this way Abelard's thought and writing remained available to scholastic masters in later centuries and in this way too Abelard became, however much the fact lacked acknowledgement, one of the *fontes* of later scholastic teaching. (Luscombe, 1963, p. 263)

In *Sic et non*, Abelard presents conflicting Patristic views on a series of theological questions, but does not offer explicit comment on the correct interpretation of these opinions – he leaves that to his reader. But he provides a preface setting out hermeneutical principles that the reader might use in interpreting the texts he provides. There is, of course, something a little provocative in thus presenting Patristic teachings – as a set of conflicting texts, like problems to be solved – and clearly this was a factor contributing to Abelard's troubles at Sens. But in a way his preface is not particularly revolutionary: everyone knew that Patristic texts needed careful exegesis, and Bernard criticizes Abelard on substantive issues not for interpreting the texts, but interpreting them poorly. And, in any case, there is not much in the preface that cannot be found in Augustine's work on the interpretation of Scripture, the *De doctrina christiana*. The influence of Abelard on Peter Lombard's *Sentences* thus guaranteed him a place of considerable, if anonymous, importance in later scholastic theology.

Abelard's views on universals – magisterially formulated in his glosses on the *Isagoge*, part of the *Logica 'ingredientibus'* – take as their starting point three questions left unanswered in Porphyry's text:

> I shall beg off saying anything about (a) whether genera and species are real or are situated in bare thoughts alone, (b) whether as real they are bodies or incorporeal, and (c) whether they are separated or in sensibles and have their reality in connection with them. (Porphyry, *Isagoge*, n. 2 (trans. Spade, p. 1))

In this, Abelard expressly follows Boethius (*Glosses on Porphyry*, n. 3 (trans. Spade, p. 26)). Abelard basically adopts his teacher Roscelin's view that universals are words, though he works hard to show that this view does not lead to any kind of conventionalism on natural kinds. His primary opponent is another of his teachers and one of the foremost philosophers of the age, William of Champeaux (*c.* 1069–1122), Master at the School of Notre Dame. Abelard claims to have forced William into an embarrassing self-contradiction in public debate (*Historia calamitatum* (trans. Radice, p. 60)). Be this as it may, William's view is that a universal, the 'material essence', is 'one in itself and diverse [...] through the forms of its inferiors' (*Glosses on Porphyry* [= *Logica 'ingredientibus'*, pp. 7–32], n. 23 (trans. Spade, p. 29)), 'essentially the same [...] the same whole' (*Glosses on Porphyry*, n. 27 (trans. Spade, p. 30)) in different particulars. It 'becomes Plato [...] and Socrates' (*Glosses on Porphyry*, n. 27 (trans. Spade, p. 30)) through their distinct accidental forms (*Glosses on Porphyry*, n. 23 (trans. Spade, p. 29)). I assume that his view is supposed to be an exegesis of Boethius's Aphrodisian theory. But Abelard thinks that it is incoherent: one and the same whole (the universal) would have contrary forms in it (Socrates's accidents and Plato's accidents, for example), and this is impossible (*Glosses on Porphyry*, n. 29 (trans. Spade, pp. 30–1)). Equally, to the extent that the view claims that individuation is by accidents, it posits the explanatory priority of accidents over substances, and has the further consequence of making accidents *necessary* for the identity of a substance: 'Socrates cannot exist apart from his accidents, any more than *man* can exist apart from its differences' (*Glosses on Porphyry*, n. 39 (trans. Spade, p. 33)).

Abelard's proposed solution, like Roscelin's, is that the only things that are universals are words: specifically, those words that are 'apt on the basis of [their] invention to be predicated of several things one by one' (*Glosses on Porphyry*, n. 65 (trans. Spade, p. 37)). The key term in Abelard's exposition is 'predicated': predication here seems to be a relation that is instantiated only in *true* statements, and what makes statements true is the way the world is: 'a conjoining with respect to predication [...] pertains to the nature of things and to indicating the truth of their status' (*Glosses on Porphyry*, n. 72 (trans. Spade, p. 39)). A thing's status, mentioned in this last quotation, is its being such-and-such: a human being's status is its being a human being, and this status grounds the truth of relevant predications about that thing (*Glosses on Porphyry*, nn. 90–1 (trans.

Spade, pp. 41–2)). But, as Abelard makes clear, there is no reason to suppose that a status is a thing (*Glosses on Porphyry*, n. 92 (trans. Spade, p. 42)). Clearly, language is a matter of convention: it is a conventional matter that English-speakers use the word 'human being' to pick out only things with the status *being a human*: that is to say, only human beings. But it is not a conventional matter that the same word is predicated equally of all of them: the original imposer – the person who originally baptized human beings 'human beings' – Abelard maintains, was caused to do this by the fact that all human beings 'agree with one another': by the fact that he 'conceived a common likeness' of all human beings (*Glosses on Porphyry*, n. 92 (trans. Spade, p. 42)). And once human beings are thus baptized, the universal term 'human being' gives rise to a mental representation (*Glosses on Porphyry*, n. 98 (trans. Spade, p. 43)), or model, or likeness, of 'single men in such a way that it is common to all of them and proper to none' (*Glosses on Porphyry*, n. 103 (trans. Spade, p. 44)).

In accordance with this nominalist theory of universals, Abelard answers Porphyry's three questions by focusing not on any alleged universal thing (there is, he holds, no such thing) but on the signification of universal terms. And he is thus able to give positive answers to all three questions: universal terms signify real, subsistent things (i.e. individuals of the appropriate kind) (*Glosses on Porphyry*, n. 145 (trans. Spade, p. 51)); they (at least, some of them) signify corporeal things (*Glosses on Porphyry*, nn. 147 and 153 (trans. Spade, pp. 51 and 52)); and they signify things that exist 'in' sensibles (i.e. substance existing under sensible accidents) (*Glosses on Porphyry*, nn. 154–5 (trans. Spade, pp. 52–3)). Abelard had numerous twelfth-century followers on this issue – the so-called '*nominales*'. But, as we shall see, something like William of Champeaux's view of universals nevertheless predominated up to the time of Scotus; nominalism was not seriously revived until the fourteenth century and the thought of Ockham, and it was so without any direct knowledge of Abelard's writings, as far as I know.

Given his nominalism on the question of universals, Abelard is not able to give an account of the Trinity in the way that Anselm attempted to a few years earlier, and it is no surprise to find him developing a quite different model: not universals, but something akin to the sameness obtaining between a material constituent and the thing it constitutes (though note that Anselm himself at one point appeals to an analogous model – the river Nile: see Anselm, *De incarnatione verbi*, cc. 13–14). Abelard talks about things being the same in essence – where by 'essence' he simply means a particular thing – but differing by 'property or definition' – where by 'property' in this context he means *origin*. His example is a bronze seal. The substance of the bronze and of the bronze seal 'is the same', but their origins differ,

> for no one says: 'The material of the bronze seal is the material [thing] made from the bronze' or 'the material thing made from the bronze is the material of the bronze seal'. (*Theologia 'scholarium'* II, n. 147, in Marenbon, 2004, p. 248).[1]

The case of the three divine persons is the same: one substance, but different relative properties or origins: the orthodox view is that the Father is ungenerated, the Son generated by the Father, and the Holy Spirit produced by Father and Son. But what allows this to be an analogy for the Trinity, according to Abelard, is precisely *not* that the essence is universal (as in Anselm's argument); it is that essence is particular.

Abelard makes the view compatible with a strong account of divine simplicity by arguing that origin is not a form or property over and above the person himself. According to Abelard there are no forms in God other than the divine essence; so while there are differences in predication (we can make claims about the Father – for example, that he generates the Son – that are false of the Son), these differences are not grounded in any real difference of form (Abelard *Theologia christiana* III, n. 166). The differences in predication are grounded simply 'by the nature of the divine essence' (Brower, 2004, p. 251). Jeffrey Brower offers the following helpful critical assessment:

> The coherence of Abelard's account, and hence his solution to the logical problem of the Trinity, ultimately depends on the coherence of his assumption that the simple divine substance can ground the applicability of predicates such as 'father' and 'son'. For once we grant this assumption, it would appear that Abelard is justified in concluding that there is a disjunction among the persons that is both real and numerical. Now as far as I can tell, Abelard does not himself

give us any compelling reason to accept this assumption, or even to think it is coherent. (Brower, 2004, p. 251)

If the doctrine of the Trinity is to be compatible with divine simplicity, it would be hard to do better than Abelard (and it is very close to the kind of line taken later by Aquinas, for example: see *Summa theologiae* I, q. 28, a. 2 c). But other aspects of Abelard's Trinitarian theology got him into trouble at the hands of the meddlesome Bernard of Clairvaux. Abelard's genius in its way dominates the twelfth century; so I consider other aspects of his thought below, discussing Bernard and Peter Lombard.

Gilbert of Poitiers

Gilbert was a native of Poitiers, and ended up as its bishop. For a while he taught in Paris, and, rather like Abelard, attracted a highly intelligent and devoted student body. These followers, the *Porretani*, continued his work throughout the twelfth century.

Gilbert's thought is complex and difficult, though it well repays the effort that has to be put in. His readings of Boethius – in his commentaries on Boethius's theological treatises – were influential on the twelfth century more widely and thence, both directly and through writers such as Richard of St Victor (d. 1173), on the thirteenth and beyond, too. (Henry of Ghent (*c.* 1217–93) sometimes refers to him as the 'Commentator' – not on Aristotle, of course, but on Boethius.) In a famous aphorism (the second of the nine propositions preliminary to his treatment of divine goodness in *Quomodo substantiae*) Boethius states that 'being and that which is are diverse' ('*diversum est esse et id quod est*' (*Quomodo substantiae*, prop. 2 (Loeb, p. 40/41, l. 28)), and goes on, in the rest of the treatise, to argue, among other things, that the first being is such that 'it is not other than' what it is (namely, good) (*Quodmodo substantiae* (Loeb, p. 48/49, ll. 134–6)). This suggested to some later commentators – rightly, it seems to me – that Boethius's aphorism in fact amounts to the claim that, in beings other than God, there is a distinction between the being (*id quod* – that which is) and its properties – those things 'by which', or 'in virtue of which' (*id quo*) a thing is such-and-such). And this is precisely how the issue is formulated in Gilbert (see e.g. *De hebdomadibus* I, § 87), whose distinction between things and properties in terms of *id quod* and *id quo* becomes standard medieval parlance for substances and forms/essences, respectively. Abstract forms are paradigm cases of *id quo*s: whiteness, or wisdom, for example, in virtue of which a substance is, respectively, white and wise:

> [Boethius] says [...] '*esse*' – that is, the subsistence that is in a subsistent – and 'that which is (*id quod est*)' – that is, the subsistent in which is the subsistence – 'are diverse': e.g. bodiliness and body, or humanity and human being. (*De hebdomadibus* I, § 34 (p. 194))

Boethius understands immaterial entities such as God and angels to be pure forms: somehow both concrete (existent things capable of causal interaction) and yet abstract (lacking matter). Anything which is a pure form is 'that which it is' – that is to say, it is not in virtue of some other form that it is what it is. Neither can such a form be the subject of accidents: a form is a property, not a subject, and a pure form is just a (stand-alone) property (Boethius, *De trinitate*, c. 2). The notion was taken up in Gilbert in his discussion of divine simplicity. But Gilbert's thought on the issue was much misunderstood in his lifetime – as we shall see in a moment, parts of Richard of St Victor's work were silently directed against Gilbert; the whole issue provoked Bernard of Clairvaux's customary spleen, and he attempted to have Gilbert condemned at the Council of Rheims in 1148. The issue is this. Discussing Boethius's assertion that 'Every simple thing has its one *esse* and [its one] *id quod est*' (*Quomodo substantiae*, prop. 7), Gilbert claims God exists 'in virtue of (*qua*) the [divine] essence' – and this gives us *id quod* and *id quo* in God (*De hebdomadibus* I, § 58). Taken out of context (a favourite trick of Bernard's), Gilbert's words might indeed suggest disagreement with the following credal article formulated by Bernard for the purposes of the Council and read out in front of Pope Eugenius III, who was present at Rheims in 1148:

> We believe that the simple essence of divinity is God, and that it cannot be denied in any orthodox way that divinity is God and God divinity. And if it is said that God is wise by wisdom, great by greatness, eternal by eternity, one by unity, God by divinity and so on, we believe that he is wise only by that wisdom which is God himself, one only by that unity

which is God himself, divine only by that divinity which
is God himself; that is, that he in his own essence is wise,
great, eternal, indivisible God. (John of Salisbury, *Historia
pontificalis*, c. 11 (trans. Chibnall, p. 24))

As we learn from Bernard's discussion of the issue in *De consideratione*,
the underlying worry that he has with Gilbert's view that 'God exists
by his divinity (*divinitate*)' (Bernard, *De consideratione* V, c. 7, 15
(trans. Anderson and Kennan, p. 158)) is that it leads to a quaternity
in God: the three divine persons, and the divine essence, distinct
from them, in virtue of which they exist: and this essence is a 'fourth
divinity' (Bernard, *De consideratione* V, c. 7, 15 (trans. Anderson and
Kennan, p. 158)). But Gilbert's language is very careful – he notes
that God's essence is unknown, and that he is using creaturely words
to talk about the ineffable. And in the very next paragraph of his
commentary, he says things that suggest that the rogue passage is
indeed just a way of thinking or talking about God that does not
correspond to the metaphysical reality:

> And under this diversity of nouns there is in [God] such unity
> of a singular, simple and individual thing (I do not say such a
> union of things), that we can truly predicate of him not only
> 'God is, God is powerful, God is wise', but also indeed 'God is
> essence itself, God is power itself, God is wisdom itself', and
> such-like. (*De hebdomadibus* I, § 59 (p. 200))

This is, of course, more or less exactly the point that Bernard himself
defends ('the divinity by which God is said to exist is not distinct
from God' (*De consideratione* V, c. 7, 15 (p. 158)), and John of Salisbury
(*c.* 1115/20–80) reports that 'The Bishop [i.e. Gilbert] agreed' with
the article read out at the Council – unsurprisingly, since it simply
reflects his own view.[2] In fact, if we take together the two paragraphs
from the commentary on *De hebdomadibus* quoted above, we find a
very striking view indeed: that God's divinity is not ungrounded, but
is rather grounded in itself; and likewise, God's power is grounded
in itself and wisdom in itself. And since power and wisdom are
not distinct from God's essence, it turns out that all of these are
grounded in the divine essence. We might compare this with the
contrast between two other views: the view of the later schoolmen
that God is uncaused (a claim that, as we shall see, is central to the

structure of their proofs for God's existence), and the view of some of the seventeenth-century Rationalists that God is *causa sui*: the cause of himself. Gilbert's view seems to be an antecedent of this rationalist claim – a refusal to allow ungrounded facts. Clearly, if something like this is what is at stake, then Bernard's worries about a quaternity are wide of the mark.

I think that another crucial claim of Gilbert's that came under scrutiny at Rheims – the view that the relations between the persons of the Trinity are in some sense distinct from the divine essence – is rather different. If Gilbert is adamant that there is no distinction between concrete and abstract in the divine essence, he is equally adamant that the kind of divine simplicity defended by Peter Abelard – according to which the relations between the persons of the Trinity are nothing other than the divine essence itself – leads to modalism, the view that there are no distinctions *at all* between the persons.

To grasp his view, we need to see more of his general metaphysics, and also compare what he says to the rather different things that appear in his source – namely, Boethius. Gilbert makes a general distinction between a substance and its accidents: accidents are in some sense *extrinsic* to the substance – they are, in Gilbert's language, 'extrinsically attached' to the substance (*De trinitate* V, § 111). The class of accidents includes, of course, the category of relation (*De trinitate* V, § 5). One of the points of the extrinsicity claim, in the case of creatures, is that relations are such that

> they minimally confer *being something* on those things of which they are predicted, even though whatever is related by them cannot not be something. (*De trinitate* V, § 2 (p. 139))

And this is clearly appealing from the perspective of divine simplicity. But Gilbert seems to suppose that, if we are to be able to explain the distinction of the persons from each other, it is necessary to appeal to items in some sense distinct from the divine essence. Thus, in the case of creatures opposition of extrinsically attached accidents 'demonstrates that they are other' than each other (*De trinitate* I, § 42 (p. 148)). But in God, the situation is different:

> Divine persons, since they are one by the singularity of the thing by which they exist, and are by simplicity that which

they are, cannot be other than each other by the opposition of essences. Rather, they are other than each other, and are proved to be so, by the opposition of these extrinsically attached things. (*De trinitate* I, § 43 (p. 148))

Gilbert may be right about this – see Brower's comments on Abelard, quoted above – but it is clearly hard to fit the view together with a strong view on divine simplicity inherited from Augustine.

The language, of 'extrinsic attachment' comes from Boethius. But the meaning in Boethius is very different. For Boethius, it is relations and (generally) items in the last six Aristotelian categories that are extrinsically attached, and what Boethius means is that the relevant predications (in the last six categories) are grounded simply in *other* substances, altogether external to the item (see Boethius, *De trinitate*, c. 4 (Loeb, p. 24/25)).

At any rate, Bernard attacked Gilbert for his view – in effect, agreeing with Abelard in accepting a strong doctrine of divine simplicity. At Rheims, Bernard made the Trinitarian point as follows:

> We believe that only God the Father, Son and Holy Spirit is eternal, and that no things whatsoever, whether they are called relations or properties, singularities or unities or anything of the kind exist and have existed eternally in God, unless they are God. (John of Salisbury, *Historia pontificalis*, c. 11 (trans. Chibnall, p. 24))

I do not see how Gilbert could assent to this in any obvious sense – though perhaps his own view is sufficiently unclear that he had no difficulty with Bernard's formulation.[3] In any case, although Bernard does not make the point, his worries about a quaternity could well arise in this case: the divine essence grounds its own being; but if the persons are distinct from the essence or divinity, then it rather seems that their being is grounded in it: grounded, that is to say, in something distinct from themselves.

Bernard of Clairvaux

As we have seen, both Abelard and Gilbert ended up under ecclesiastical investigation. And, as we have likewise seen, the genius presiding over these processes was the first Cistercian abbot, Bernard of Clairvaux. Cîteaux, the order's mother house, is in Burgundy, on the road to Nuits-St-Georges, and the early Cistercians were responsible for cultivating the grape that still makes – uniquely, just in that part of France, and using some of the old vineyards first divided up by the Cistercians of Bernard's day – the most delicious red wine in the world. But whatever the merits and skills of the early Cistercians in viniculture, Bernard's attempts to resist the new, intellectual, approach to theological and doctrinal issues happily failed, and the result was the great flowering of Scholasticism that is the subject of this book. But he attempted, for all that, and his efforts had a devastating effect on the life of Abelard, a thinker of far finer calibre than Bernard himself.

Given all this, Bernard is probably best considered in terms of his negative contributions – his attempts to forestall the deep and innovatory insights of others. I have discussed at some length the failed process against Gilbert. A further very conspicuous example can be located in Bernard's treatment of Abelard, a few years earlier than the Council of Rheims. At Sens, in 1140, Bernard assembled a list of heresies, taken, as he supposed, from the works of Abelard, and managed to get the cardinals present to condemn these positions prior to the Council's meeting. Abelard denied that all of the positions were his, and appealed to the Pope. But the appeal failed, and Abelard was excommunicated. Through the good agency of Peter of Cluny (*c.* 1092–1156), the sentence was lifted, on condition that Abelard remain at the Abbey at Cluny for the rest of his life. In fact, Abelard was already ill, and known to be so; he died in 1142.

In relation to the list of alleged heresies, I will mention just two issues here. The first is Abelard's Trinitarian theology. I showed above that Abelard develops an account of the Trinity that is designed to be compatible with divine simplicity, and that a central component of this account is that the features that distinguish the persons are not forms over and above the divine essence. Bernard and Abelard agree about this. But Bernard ascribes to Abelard the view that the attributes of omnipotence, wisdom, and love are not to be ascribed to all three persons equally, but omnipotence merely to the Father, wisdom merely to the Son, and love merely to the Spirit (see *Epistola* 190, c. 3, 5). Now, Bernard misquotes Abelard on this point. He accurately repeats Abelard's words to the effect that talk of omnipotence is somehow a way of talking of the Father, but he adds to the beginning of his quotation the denial that all three attributes belong equally to all three persons (I put in italics Bernard's additional 'no', not found in Abelard's text):

> Power and many other attributes [...] are assigned to the Father and the Son in common, and not singly to each taken by himself. But [Abelard] says, '*No*; we find that omnipotence belongs especially to the *proprium* of the person of the Father, because he not only can do all things in union with the other two persons, but also because he alone has his existence from himself, and not from another, and as he has his existence from himself, so he has his power.' (*Epistola* 190, c. 3, 5 (trans. Eales, pp. 267–8), quoting Abelard, *Theologia 'scholarium'* I, n. 50, ll. 538–44 (p. 338))

This is misleading. Abelard is explicit that all three attributes belong in common to each person (see e.g. *Theologia 'scholarium'* I, nn. 43, 44, 47). His point is merely about the customary linguistic usage of the 'evangelists and apostles' (*Theologia 'scholarium'* I, n. 53): his aim, in other words, is exegetical – to explain Biblical usage (and Patristic and conciliar, for that matter: he cites, among others, Ambrosiaster and the Council of Nicaea, and the very passage that Bernard quotes so dismissively is in fact an exposition of the Patristic claim that 'God the Father is over all' (Ambrosiaster, *In epistolam ad Ephesios* IV, 4–5 (Corpus Scriptorum Ecclesiasticorum Latinorum, 81/3, p. 96, quoted at *Theologia 'scholarium'* I, n. 49, ll. 536–7 (p. 337))). Abelard's view is that these various writers sometimes use the word 'Father' to talk about divine power, 'Son' to talk about divine wisdom, and 'Spirit' to talk about divine love:

> I think it is clear from the above testimonies that divine power is, as we say, expressed by the word 'Father', the Son is understood to be divine wisdom, and the goodness of divine grace is named the 'Holy Spirit'. (Abelard, *Theologia 'scholarium'* I, n. 67, ll. 742–5 (p. 345))

This is an exegetical point, not a metaphysical or theological one, far removed from the opinion that Bernard ascribes to Abelard, and for which he attempted to get him condemned.[4] And Abelard's discussion, if it attests to anything, is evidence of the kind of hermeneutical sophistication expressed in the preface to *Sic et non* and learned from the Church Fathers.

The second issue is in its way more contentious – Abelard's theory of the atonement. I noted in Chapter 1 Anselm's innovations in this area. There is no direct evidence that Abelard had ever read *Cur deus homo*, but the connections between what he says and what Anselm said are so striking that it is hard to imagine that he had not encountered Anselm's highly novel take on the doctrine. And he then got into trouble for recounting more or less exactly Anselm's view on the matter. For example, here is how Abelard, in a very important question at the beginning of book II of his commentary on Romans (on Romans 3.26), raises the basic problem that motivated Anselm, in very similar words to Anselm's: 'Why was it necessary for God to take human nature upon him so that he might redeem us by dying in the flesh?' (*Commentarium in epistolam Pauli ad Romanos* II [3.26] (trans. Fairweather, p. 280)). Not to deliver us from the just power of Satan, since Satan had no such power, and since God could simply have deprived Satan of his *de facto* power:

> What right to possess humanity could the devil possibly have unless perhaps he had received human beings for the purposes of torture through the express permission, or even the assignment, of the Lord? [...] If the Lord should cease to grant this permission, no right whatever would be left to the tormentor. (*Commentarium in epistolam Pauli ad Romanos* II [3.26] (trans. Fairweather, pp. 281 and 282))

Abelard's considered answer to this question, found elsewhere in the Romans commentary, is I think an attempt to explain the position of Anselm:

> In two ways he [viz. Christ] is said to have died for our faults: first, because the faults for which he died were ours, and we committed the sins for which he bore the punishment; secondly, that by dying he might remove our sins, that is, the punishment of our sins, introducing us into paradise at the price of his own death. (*Commentarium in epistolam Pauli ad Romanos* II [4.25] (p. 153); in Quinn, 1993, p. 290)

It is a nice question whether or not this represents Anselm's view accurately: in particular, Anselm proposes a disjunction – either satisfaction or punishment – such that the wrong-doer is punished unless some other person, one who neither deserves the punishment nor receives it, perform some action that somehow restores to the wronged party what he has been deprived of (i.e. make satisfaction). Abelard, contrariwise, supposes that one person could be punished on behalf of or instead of another – something that Anselm's theory precludes. But the dynamic is similar: Christ's death, as punishment, averted our punishment, just as his making satisfaction averted our punishment.

Now, Bernard accepts the old ransom theory, and claims that, although the Devil's will was not just, his *power* was – which may or may not represent a claim stronger than Anselm's, namely that the Devil's activity was justly permitted (see *Epistola* 190, c. 5, 14). The Devil's unjustly claiming Christ as his own means that God can justly deprive him of his power over the human race (*Epistola* 190, c. 6, 15). Bernard occasionally uses Anselm's satisfaction language, though it is not clear to me whether this amounts to a covert acceptance of Anselm's innovative theory or not:

> He who owed nothing to death, lawfully freed him who was subject to it, both from the debt of death, and the dominion of the devil, by accepting the injustice of death; for with what justice could that be exacted from man a second time? It was man who owed the debt, it was man who paid it. […] As one bore the sins of all, the satisfaction of one is imputed to all. It is not that one forfeited, another satisfied; the head and body is one, viz., Christ. The head, therefore, satisfied for the members. (*Epistola* 190, c. 6, 15 (trans. Eales, pp. 279–80))

Here, the devil unjustly killed Christ, and in this way Christ – in virtue of the injustice of his death – paid the 'debt of death' or made satisfaction for us. His unjust death means that we no longer justly die. But the mechanism, I take it, is by depriving the devil of his right to inflict death – and if this is not what Bernard thinks, then he accepts the very theory found in both Anselm and Abelard.

On this showing, Abelard has much more in common with Anselm than Bernard does. In particular, both Anselm and Abelard deny that depriving the devil of a just power – or, indeed, of any power at all – can have any role in the explanation of redemption. But while Bernard says nothing about Anselm's theory, Abelard's provokes him almost to apoplexy. The problem is this. The Abelardian text that Bernard quotes – the *ex professo* answer to the atonement question raised in the commentary on Romans 3.26, discussed above – makes no mention of the penal theory, and rather focuses on the capacity of Christ's death to inspire heroic action in us. And, as Bernard points out rather vigorously, this seems to deprive Christ's death of any objectively redemptive component (see *Epistola* 190, c. 7, 17). Bernard should have read Abelard more closely.[5]

We have now seen something of Bernard's dealings with both Abelard and Gilbert; it is clear that he was not able, intellectually, to keep up with either of these two. John of Salisbury – himself a student of Abelard, and no mean philosopher, though admittedly a source more sympathetic to Gilbert than to Bernard – reports a story that nicely illustrates Gilbert's rather dismissive attitude to Bernard's intellectual achievements:

> I recall that I myself on behalf of the abbot [i.e. Bernard] entreated the bishop [i.e. Gilbert] to meet him in some religious house in Poitou, or France, or Burgundy, wherever he preferred, to discuss the writings of the blessed Hilary amicably and without rancour. He however replied that they had already disputed sufficiently on the matter, and if the abbot wished to reach a full understanding of Hilary he should first seek further instruction in the liberal arts and other preliminary studies. (John of Salisbury, *Historia pontificalis*, c. 12 (trans. Chibnall, p. 26)

Hilary, as it happens, is a writer whom Bernard never quotes – presumably, as Gilbert suggests, he found him to be rather too hard. It is difficult to resist the conclusion that, whatever his reputation as a spiritual writer, Bernard was simply out of his intellectual depth in these matters.

But despite all this did Bernard make any positive contributions to the development of medieval philosophy? I have already noted the importance of the will in Christian action theory – for example, in Anselm's two inclinations of the will, *motivations* distinct from our simple intellectual grasp of what should be done, or what is advantageous. Bernard plays a small but significant role in the development of an account of the will in action. The notion that Bernard has a role in shaping is that of *akrasia*, cases in which we do something we somehow know to be wrong. Bernard understands the defect here as *weakness of will* (*infirmitas voluntatis*) – indeed, he is the first thinker to use this phrase, as far as I know. The background is Augustine, who adopts from the Stoics a notion that I discussed briefly in the Introduction, that of *consent*, in effect intervening between deliberation and action. As Augustine sees it, we consent to the stronger of two different pulls – our reason, on the one hand, or, on the other, our (bad) emotional longings (*concupiscence*), longings in conflict with beliefs about what we should do (Augustine, *Confessions* VI, c. 11, 20). Sin consists in consenting to concupiscence (Augustine, *Confessions* VIII, c. 9, 21; VIII, c. 10, 24). On Augustine's view, then, it is possible both to act and to choose against better judgment, and even reluctantly so, in the sense that it is possible to consent to the stronger pull of emotion against the influence of reason (Augustine, *De spiritu et littera* XXXI, c. 53). (Indeed, Augustine's considered view is that human beings without the benefit of additional divine aid – without grace – cannot avoid consenting in this way, and thus choosing badly (see e.g. Augustine, *Contra duas epistolas Pelagianorum* III, c. 8, 24).) On this view, the sinful action is consented to, and thus *chosen*. The Augustinian claim that choice is not always in accord with reason, and can sometimes instead be in accordance with the pull of emotion, is developed by Bernard in a significant way. When agents find themselves in cases where reason and emotion are in conflict, they can consent to one or other of two options; weakness of will (*infirmitas voluntatis*) is exhibited in those cases where they consent to the emotional drive rather than the rational one (Bernard, *De gratia et libero arbitrio* XII, c. 38). Bernard explicitly holds that neither reason nor passion can necessitate this consent (Bernard, *De gratia et libero arbitrio* II, cc. 4–5). Here, then, we seem to have an account of freedom that amounts explicitly to liberty of indifference – in the exact self-same circumstances, we can do *a* or do not-*a*. Anselm, as we saw, has something like this notion, but only in the context of the two affections, not in terms of the more general conflict between reason and emotion.

We shall see in the later Middle Ages, incidentally, two distinct lines of thinking on the question of *akrasia*, one that fundamentally continues the Augustinian tradition of Bernard, and one that factors in Aristotle's view of *akrasia*, a view that does not have a place for the will, and tends to maintain that *ignorance* lies at the root of *akrasia*, and that akratic actions are not really chosen – both of which claims are of course problematic given a Christian (and reasonable) view that akratic actions are nevertheless sinful or blameworthy.

The Victorines

In late life William of Champeaux founded the Abbey of St Victor on the left bank of the Seine, a community living according to the Rule of St Augustine. The combination of tough educational standards and attention to the spiritual life seemed to capture perfectly the spirit of the early twelfth century, and the Abbey and school proved to be a great success.

The most well-known Victorine is Hugh, whom I mentioned briefly in the Introduction, above. But as far as I can see Hugh's discussions of substantive philosophical issues are all too brief and cursory to offer much of real intellectual interest (see for example his very brief proofs for the existence of God and the soul at *De sacramentis* I, pt. 3, cc. 7–10: barely a page of text in all).

Of greater philosophical interest is the thought of his *confrère* Richard. In his greatly influential *De trinitate*, Richard grapples with the Christian doctrine of the Trinity, and in the process introduces some very important notions into medieval metaphysics: in particular, individual forms and the notions of communicability and incommunicability. The work itself owes a huge amount to Boethius. But the key metaphysical insights are drawn not (as we might expect) from Boethius's own highly significant *De trinitate*, but rather from a more strictly philosophical source: Boethius's longer commentary on Aristotle's *On Interpretation*. And the language and ideas that Richard introduces turn out to form the major way in which the theological doctrine is conceptualized throughout the rest of the medieval period.

The easiest place to start is with Richard's well-known theological corrective to the definition of 'person' that Boethius offers in his Christological treatise, *De persona et duabus naturis*. There, in an attempt to clarify the theology of the Incarnation, Boethius defines 'person' as 'individual substance of rational nature' (Boethius, *De persona*, c. 3 (Loeb, p. 84/85)). Richard objects: God is a substance, and there is just one God: but God, the divine substance, is not a person, so Boethius's definition cannot be fully general (*De trinitate* IV, c. 21). Richard proposes some rather different terminology. Rather than 'individual', we should say 'incommunicable'; and rather than 'substance', we should say 'existence' (*De trinitate* IV, c. 23). The incommunicable is opposed to what is *common* – as the divine nature or substance is common to the three persons (*De trinitate* IV, cc. 16 and 20). And a thing's existence is its being (*sistere*) from (*ex*) something (hence *ex-sistere*): its having both an essence and an origin (*De trinitate* IV, c. 12). The first of these notions – the *incommunicable* – has its origin in Boethius's second commentary on Aristotle's *On Interpretation*. Boethius uses it to pick out that feature of a thing that individuates it by being unique to it: Boethius calls it an incommunicable 'property' or 'quality', and (as far as I can determine) the term 'incommunicable' is not used again in this sense until the middle of the twelfth century.[6] The incommunicable property is, I take it, an individual form, plausibly something with at least a family resemblance to what Duns Scotus will later term a 'thisness' ('haecceity') – on which, see Chapter 6. Boethius gives as an example *Platonitas*, the incommunicable quality that relates to one unique individual (Plato, in this case), and he defends his neologism by parallel with 'humanity': '*Platonitas*' is related to 'Plato' 'in the way that we call the quality of a human being "humanity"' (Boethius, *Commentariorum in librum Aristotelis Perihermeneias, editio secunda* II, c. 7 (p. 137): Boethius is followed here by Abelard, *Logica 'ingredientibus'*, p. 64). In his *De trinitate*, Richard of St Victor makes a similar point about his coinage '*Danielitas*', picking out the incommunicable feature of Daniel such that 'whoever will not have had it will not be able to be Daniel': '"*Danielitas*" is from "Daniel" like "humanity" from "human being"' (*De trinitate* II, c. 12 (trans. Coolman and Coulter, p. 235, altered)).[7] But the key point is that it is the talk of incommunicability that is relevant to the Trinity, since here (as Richard sees it) we have something individual (the divine essence) that is nevertheless communicable; hence the definition of 'person', using these analyses taken from Boethius's philosophical commentary, must include not 'individual' but 'incommunicable' – contrary to Boethius's own attempt at a theological definition of 'person'.

Why prefer 'existence' to 'substance'? Richard's thought is that something's existence is connected with its individuation: it picks out both the substance of a thing – what it is – and the thing's (unique) *origin* (*De trinitate* IV, c. 16). At some points in the discussion, Richard seems to suggest that a thing's incommunicable property is indeed just its origin – and this suggestion certainly suits his Trinitarian purposes, since (it turns out) that, just like creatures, divine persons are distinguished from other persons of the same kind by their differing origins (*De trinitate* IV, cc. 14–15). The picture is not entirely clear; what is clear, however, is that Richard is attempting to work out something of what we might want to say about the identity conditions of three persons who somehow share the same substance – a question that was taken with extreme seriousness by the medieval theologians. In fact, while there was some debate about whether the divine persons should be thought of as substances, Richard's language of existence, and the technical sense he proposes for it in his discussion, did not find much favour: 'existence' ('*exsistentia*') is used by and large in other senses, and, even when his definition of 'person' is quoted favourably, the use of 'existence' in this context is unique – something of a *hapax legomenon*.

All of this relates in a rather nice way to the discussion in Gilbert. Richard is often presented as someone who rejects the view that there is some distinction between *quod est* and *quo est* even in the divine case, and he presents himself in that way too. Thus, he explicitly adopts precisely Gilbert's Boethian language when he wants to emphasize this rejection:

> To say something more subtle, for the sake of those who are themselves more subtle: in natural and created things, *esse* and *id quod est* are diverse; in uncreated things, *esse* and *id quod est* are the same thing. (*De trinitate* IV, c. 19 (p. 183))

Gilbert, of course, is the 'subtle' one here. But in point of fact it seems to me that the two thinkers are not so far apart, and that Richard was perhaps influenced by Gilbert. Richard maintains that the divine essence exists 'from itself' (*a se*) – which seems to be precisely Gilbert's teaching. He clearly alludes to Gilbert in the next passage, too, but in a way that seems in accord with Gilbert's views about the divine essence, power, and wisdom (Gilbert's trio, it will be recalled):

> It is most certain that whatever is powerful is so by (*de*) power itself; whatever is wise is so by wisdom itself. Now we have

already demonstrated that the supreme substance has all that
it has only from itself. (*De trinitate* I, c. 13 (trans. Coolman
and Coulter, p. 221, slightly altered))

Here, divine power and wisdom are the same as the divine essence
or substance: thus God is powerful and wise in virtue of the divine
essence – just as Gilbert holds.

Richard even maintains, in the case of the Trinity, that the
divine persons, the same as the divine essence, exist *from* the divine
substance – they are 'that substance which does not exist from (*ab*)
any other substance but from itself' (*De trinitate* IV, c. 16 (trans.
Coolman and Coulter, p. 281)) – and *from* their personal properties:
'A personal property is that from (*ex*) which each one can be who he
is' (*De trinitate* IV, c. 17 (trans. Coolman and Coulter, p. 281, slightly
altered)). But I assume that part of the point of the 'subtle' language
Richard adopts is that a personal property, too – the personal *esse* or *id
quo est* of the person – is the same as the divine persons/essence. And,
unlike Gilbert's claim that the relations are *extrinsically* attached to
the persons, Richard claims that the '[personal] properties inhere
in the persons (*dicimus* [...] *proprietates personis inesse*)' (*De trinitate*
IV, c. 20 (trans. Coolman and Coulter, p. 285)) – which doubtless
represents an attempt to distance his view from at least the more
dangerous part of Gilbert's.[8]

I suggested above, discussing Anselm, that there is some sense in
which the twelfth century represents the height of optimism about
the possibilities for the rational exploration of the Christian faith.
Anselm claims that the Incarnation can be proved. Abelard goes
so far as to claim that something is not rationally believed unless
there are convincing reasons in its favour (see *Theologia 'scholarium'*
II, c. 46). Richard holds that it is possible to show that God is a
Trinity. Presupposed is the possibility that God's existence can be
proved. And this is precisely what Richard maintains. He offers two
distinct proofs, both rather subtle arguments that clearly take their
inspiration from Anselm, but go in different directions from Anselm.
The first argues that there must be a being that exists 'from itself',
otherwise

Nothing would be from eternity, and in that case there would
be no origin and succession of things [...] since no beings
would exist that draw their being from another and cannot

exist from themselves. (*De trinitate* I, c. 11 (trans. Coolman and Coulter, p. 220))

The assumption, made clear a little earlier, is that causes precede their effects, and thus that 'every being that is from another [...] follow[s] its origin' (*De trinitate* I, c. 9 (trans. Coolman and Coulter, p. 218)). Richard attempts, less than successfully, to show that this being – the being that exists 'from itself' – must be 'that than which nothing is greater' and 'that than which nothing is better'. He notes that such a being 'cannot receive the very thing that it is from a source inferior to it' (*De trinitate* I, c. 11 (trans. Coolman and Coulter, p. 219)). But this will not do: what Richard needs to show is not that a supreme being cannot be caused, but that a being that cannot be caused (that has its being from itself) must be the supreme being.

The second argument – a 'better' one, according to Richard – is altogether more ambitious, relying on some significant modal intuitions that Richard has. His crucial insight is that a thing's *possibility* requires explanation. This explanation is either internal or external: 'nothing can exist unless it either possessed the possibility of being from itself or received it from another source'. This source must be 'the power of being'; and since everything exists from this source, this source must exist 'only from itself'. Richard concludes: 'If every essence is from the power of being, then this essence must be the supreme essence' (*De trinitate* I, c. 12 (trans. Coolman and Coulter, p. 220)). But, again, there are problems here that Richard does not seem to have noticed. For example, why suppose that there is just one power of being – why could not (for example) each thing include the explanation of its own possibility? And why suppose that the power of being is something concrete rather than something abstract (e.g. a simple realm of logical possibility)?

What of Richard's proof for the Trinity? The argument takes as its starting point the claim that God is love, itself derived from the earlier demonstration that God is good (see *De trinitate* II, c. 16). A person's love requires an object – specifically, another subject – and supreme love thus requires a (second) divine person (*De trinitate* III, c. 2). But supreme love requires, too, that the same love be shared by two persons – that is to say, that the two are united in their shared love for a third (*De trinitate* III, c. 11): they 'share the pleasures of charity' (*De trinitate* III, c. 14 (trans. Coolman and Coulter, p, 259)). But these three persons cannot be three Gods or three divine

substances, because God is omnipotent and it is not possible for
there to be more than one omnipotent substance (*De trinitate* III,
c. 8; the argument that there cannot be more than one omnipotent
being is that an omnipotent being would be 'able to render any other
being powerless' (*De trinitate* I, c. 25 (trans. Coolman and Coulter,
p. 227))). Here we see, if nothing else, an optimistic and imaginative
rationality at the service of wholly theological ends.

Peter Lombard

Like *Sic et non*, Peter Lombard's *Sentences* consists of *quaestiones*
alone, unattached to any commentary, though Lombard adds
solutions (*sententiae*: opinions or judgments) worked out dialectically
via a discussion of *prima facie* conflicting Patristic claims. The crucial
difference between the later collections of *sententiae*, of which
Lombard's *Sentences* is representative, and Abelard's *Sic et non* is the
imposition of a clear structure: and what is more, a structure with
evident pedagogical functions. Abelard's work does show some signs
of treating of its various questions in some kind of order. But Peter
Lombard arranged his *sententiae* explicitly along clear systematic
doctrinal lines, set out explicitly in the prologue to the work. The
arrangement of the questions encouraged students to think of the
work as a self-contained and independent treatment of Christian
doctrine. It is perhaps no accident that such a useful book, forming
both a *florilegium* of Patristic sources and a primitive attempt at a
systematic theology, should turn out to be the major theological
textbook for the next 350 years.

Still, the work itself is an odd mix of systematic theological
summa and twelfth-century controversy and polemics. One result
of this is that, given the status of the *Sentences* as the main theology
textbook in the universities, many twelfth-century debates survive
into later centuries, but for the most part as mere academic
exercises and, ultimately, curiosities. We find these twelfth-century
discussion points mentioned only rarely in thirteenth-century
disputed questions, be they quodlibetal or regular: they are simply
no longer current theological topics. But Lombard was an able
controversialist, and the most intellectually engaging parts of the
Sentences are precisely these areas of twelfth-century theological
debate in which Lombard combats the theories of opponents, or

at least gives an account of the theological terrain in controverted issues of his times.

The most well-known of these controversial issues – and one which constitutes one of the longest single discussions in the *Sentences* – is Christological, and it is a question that Lombard does not resolve. In distinction 6 of the third book, Peter Lombard reports three possible ways of giving an account of the orthodox doctrine of the Incarnation, without deciding between them. I assume that the discussion is an attempt to represent exhaustively the state of play on the topic in the early and mid-twelfth century. The Christian doctrine on this question is this: that the second person of the Trinity, while remaining divine, became human, such that Christ, the incarnate divine person, is both fully God and fully man. Obviously, one difficulty with this doctrine has to do with the compatibility of divinity and humanity in one person. But it is not this issue that forms the focus of the Lombard's discussion. Rather, his concern is with different ways in which a God-man might be *constituted*: what parts or constituents he might have, what the relationship between these constituents is, and what the relationship between the constituents and the whole is. All three views assume that the second person of the Trinity genuinely is human. But they differ strikingly on the constitution question. The first view denies that the Incarnation could consist in the divine person's being constituted of divinity and humanity. If the divine person comes to have parts in this way, then there is no identity of person before and after incarnation: Christ is the divine person plus something else. Rather, according to the first opinion, Christ is the whole divine person, and vice versa (Christ and the divine person are *identical*); the only constituents in the incarnate divine person are human body and soul (*Sentences* III, d. 6, c. 2, n. 1). The second opinion maintains precisely what the first opinion denies: namely, that Christ is constituted of 'divine and human nature; that is [...] divinity, flesh, and soul' (*Sentences* III, d. 6, c. 3, n. 1 (trans. Silano, III, p. 26)). The third opinion agrees with the first, against the second, that Christ cannot be constituted of humanity and divinity. But it goes further, and denies *any* constitution relation at all: just as Christ is not composed of humanity and divinity, so too he is not composed of body and soul (as the first opinion maintains). Rather, the second person of the Trinity remains utterly simple, and has the body and soul like accidents – and probably accidents in the category of vesture or clothing (*habitus*), things that the divine person 'takes on' or 'assumes' (*Sentences* III, d. 6, c. 4, nn. 1–2).

Lombard finds Augustinian support for all three views. The first view is indubitably that of Hugh of St Victor (see *De sacramentis* II, pt. 1, cc. 9 and 11), and probably represents the closest to Augustine's genuine opinion; the second is distinctively that of the eighth century Greek theologian John of Damascus, and seems to me and others to be an attempt by the Lombard to represent the view of Gilbert of Poitiers (see Gilbert, *Contra eutychen* IV, §§ 37–50, where Gilbert affirms constitution from divinity and humanity). Identifying the third view is rather more complicated, but it is usually taken to be an attempt to represent Abelard's view.[9] Lombard seems to believe that all three views are orthodox – and I think the discussion is a good example of a theological pluralism that was regarded as wholly legitimate, and a good example of the Lombard's knowledge of the views of both Gilbert and Abelard, not the easiest of thinkers to grasp. The issue makes merely perfunctory appearance in thirteenth-century discussions, and is evidence of the changing nature of theological debate in the period. (For what it is worth, Aquinas seems simply to misunderstand the issues altogether, to judge from his discussion in *Summa theologiae* III, q. 2, a. 6 c.)

In his account of these three Christological opinions, Lombard does not find any error in the view that is plausibly ascribed to Gilbert. But he generally takes a dim view of Gilbert's theology. For example, he speaks in rather disparaging terms of Gilbert's claim that the divine relations in the Trinity are extrinsically attached to the persons. Lombard talks of Gilbert as having 'a malice "excited by the prompting of diabolical deceitfulness"' (*Sentences* I, d. 33, c. 1, n. 9 (trans. Silano, I, p. 183), quoting Hilary, *De trinitate* II, n. 5). Lombard's basic reason is that Gilbert's view is incompatible with the strong view of divine simplicity that he finds in various Patristic sources (Hilary, Jerome, Augustine, Boethius: *Sentences* I, d. 33, c. 1, nn. 2–5). But the details are rather complicated. As Lombard sees it, we should not want to say that the divine essence generates or is generated. And an advantage of Gilbert's view, according to Lombard, is that if we adopt it we will have no trouble giving an account of the falsity of these locutions: the Father generates, the Son is generated, and, in virtue of the fact that the relations are extrinsically attached to the persons, neither person is identical with the divine essence – so we can block the inference to 'the essence generates' (*Sentences* I, d. 33, c. 1, n. 9). Gilbert's view, in other words, presents a problem for Lombard, unless Lombard can show how someone denying that the relations are extrinsically attached to the persons could likewise deny the suspect locution. And this is what he attempts:

> Although fatherhood and sonship are the divine essence, since they do not determine it, it cannot be said that the divine essence both generates and is generated, or that the same thing is father and son to himself. For a property determines the person in such a way that by this property a hypostasis is the begetter, and by that property another hypostasis is begotten; and so it is not the same one who generates and is generated, but one generates another. (*Sentences* I, d. 33, c. 1, n. 10 (trans. Silano, I, pp. 183–4))

('Hypostasis' is a technical term for person; and note that 'to generate (*generare*)' and 'to beget (*gignere*)' are synonyms.)

But why should we not want to say that the divine essence generates or is generated? Earlier in book I of the *Sentences*, Lombard discusses exhaustively the various ways in which we might think of the essence generating or being generated. If the essence is generated, then either the essence is begotten by the Father, or it is begotten by itself; and if the essence generates, then either the essence begets the Son, or it begets itself. Clearly, the fourth of these cases is the same as the second (the essence's self-begetting). So there are three options: the Father begets the divine essence; the divine essence begets the Son; the divine essence begets the divine essence (*Sentences* I, d. 5, c. 1, n. 1). Lombard excludes all three options. The third one obviously violates worries, articulated in this context by Augustine, about the possibility of self-causation (*Sentences* I, d. 5, c. 1, n. 6). And, it turns out, the other two options do too. Both Father and Son are the same as the divine essence: if the Father begets the essence, then the same thing begets itself (*Sentences* I, d. 5, c. 1, n. 4); and if the essence begets the Son, then, likewise, the same thing begets itself (*Sentences* I, d. 5, c. 1, n. 6). (Note that these sameness claims are not supposed to entail that the Father and the Son are the same as each other: sameness in this context, whatever it be, is not supposed to be transitive – this is a commonplace if puzzling claim made in the context of Trinitarian theology, and not really sorted out until Scotus, as I discuss in Chapter 6.) The Lombard summarizes:

> Since the divine essence is one and the highest thing (*una et summa quaedam res*), if the divine essence generated an essence, then the same thing would generate itself, which is not at all possible. (*Sentences* I, d. 5, c. 1, n. 6 (trans. Silano, I, p. 31))

This view itself generated considerable controversy. Joachim of Fiore (*c.* 1135–1202) objected to it on the grounds that it entails a quaternity: the three divine persons and a further thing too, the divine essence. The most well-known reference to this is Lateran IV, which adjudicated between the two views, upheld Peter's and condemned Joachim's. But what precisely Joachim's own view was is a matter of some ambiguity. The Council accuses Joachim of seeing the unity of the divine persons as the unity of a collection with no real constituent in common (Lateran IV, const. 2 (p. 231)). The Council refers to a book ('libellum sive tractatum') that Joachim wrote explicitly directed against Lombard's view; but this is now lost. In the most extensive extant attempt to refute Lombard, found in his *Psalterium decem chordarum*, Joachim talks of the divine essence either as a fourth thing equal to the three persons, or as a fourth thing greater than the three persons, and finds both options (understandably) unacceptable. Presumably, the divine essence is not a *res*, not a thing, at all; God just is the three persons, and in the *Psalterium* Joachim compares the three persons to three coins – perhaps suggesting the collection view found in the Council (*Psalterium* fo. 277ra–b: for a translation of the whole passage, see Robb, 1997, p. 27). At any rate, Joachim does not want to countenance thinking of the essence as something in any way distinct from (one or all of) the persons. Fiona Robb provides perhaps the most sympathetic summary:

> For Joachim, any conceptualisation of the essence apart from its possession by the three Persons necessarily makes it a separate entity. (Robb, 1997, p. 28)

This is a very twelfth-century debate, albeit one that takes as its starting point the interpretation of various Patristic texts. In later *Sentence* commentaries, the focus is far more heavily on metaphysical and logical questions. Duns Scotus, for example, after repeating the standard claim that nothing causes itself, devotes most of his discussion to the reference of the term 'God' in this Trinitarian context, and includes considerable material on the metaphysical question of the constitution of, and distinction between, the various persons. In any case, the issue is cleared up at Lateran IV.

I noted above the considerable influence of Abelard on Peter Lombard. Indeed, the Lombard is by and large sympathetic to Abelardian positions. But on one key issue – one with which I opened this chapter – he strongly dissents: Abelard's view that 'God can only do what he has done', as Lombard phrases it (*Sentences* I, d. 43, c. un., n. 1). Lombard reports three crucial arguments, all of which have basically the same structure: God can do only what it is good (*bonum*), or just (*iustum*) for him to do (*Sentences* I, d. 43, c. un., n. 1), or only what he should (*debet*) do (*Sentences* I, d. 43, c. un., n. 3: the first of these is found roughly in Abelard, *Theologia 'scholarium'* III, n. 28; the second at n. 35). The point of Abelard's arguments is that it can be good/just/obligatory for God to do only what he has done, since otherwise he would fail to do what it is good/just/obligatory for him to do. Lombard's response in the first two cases is to disambiguate: it is true that God can only do what it is good or just for him to do, in the sense that whatever God does is good and just; but this does not entail that he can do only what he does (*Sentences* I, d. 43, c. un., n. 2). The ambiguity in the third case is slightly different: the word 'should' in this case does not imply an obligation, since 'God is not our debtor'; but whatever God does he should do in the sense that, 'he cannot do other than what, if he were to do it, would be truly suitable for him to do' (*Sentences* I, d. 43, c. un., n. 3 (trans. Silano, I, p. 235)).

Abelard adds a further consideration that Lombard does not discuss, and that makes Lombard's reasons rather less decisive than they would otherwise be: no two states of affairs are equally good – since if they were, God would have no grounds for deciding between them (Abelard, *Theologia 'scholarium'* III, n. 36). Of course, it is open to Lombard to claim that God's decisions do not have to be grounded in just this way: it is enough for God to choose the good. One way to establish this would be to claim that there is no maximum to the possible goodness of a created world (hence God, in making any such world, will always be such that he could have made a better world). Hugh of St Victor, discussing this problem, makes just the wrong move at this point, arguing against Abelard that if God makes the best possible world that world will be infinitely good and thus equal to God (Hugh, *De sacramentis* I, pt. 2, c. 22). His mind was in the right place, but he should rather simply have noted that there is no best of all possible worlds at all.

Further reading

On Abelard, the best recent study is John Marenbon, *The Philosophy of Peter Abelard* (Cambridge: Cambridge University Press, 1997). For Gilbert, a dense but rewarding read, that also covers Peter Lombard's Christology, is Lauge Olaf Nielsen, *Philosophy and Theology in the Twelfth Century: A Study of Gilbert Porreta's Thinking and the Theological Expositions of the Doctrine of the Incarnation during the Period 1130–1180* (Leiden: Brill, 1982). I do not know of anything general in scope on the philosophical contributions of Bernard of Clairvaux. For Richard of St Victor, see Nico den Bok, *Communicating the Most High: A Systematic Study of Person and Trinity in the Theology of Richard of St Victor* (Paris and Turnhout: Brepols, 1996). Peter Lombard is well served. The magisterial study is Marcia Colish, *Peter Lombard*, 2 vols (Leiden: Brill, 1994).

Notes

1 I rely on Marenbon's article for this interpretation of Abelard.
2 As Gilbert's modern editor, Nickolaus M. Häring, notes, on the basis of evidence provided by Bernard's minion and successor as Abbot of Clairvaux, Godfrey of Clairvaux, 'neither Gilbert nor Eugene put a correcting hand to the commentary' (p. 15) in the light of the proceedings of the Council. Here, Gilbert simply did not need to make any changes.
3 The fact that this teaching remains in Gilbert's text provides, I suppose, further evidence that no effort was made by Gilbert to bring his work in line with the decisions at Rheims.
4 We have to wait until Richard of St Victor, writing ten or more years after the death of Bernard, for a philosophical rationale for this scriptural and Patristic usage: just as the Father is presupposed to the Son's existence, and the Father and Son together presupposed to the Spirit's, so too power is presupposed to wisdom, and power and wisdom together presupposed to goodness: see Richard, *De trinitate* VI, c. 14.
5 For an excellent recent account of the atonement debate that is, in effect, more sympathetic to Bernard, see Thomas Williams, 'Sin, Grace, and Redemption', in *The Cambridge Companion to Abelard*, ed. Jeffrey E.

Brower and Kevin Guilfoy (Cambridge: Cambridge University Press, 2004), pp. 258–78.

6 Writing probably slightly earlier than Richard, we find it too one of the students of Gilbert of Poitiers, Peter of Vienna (see Nielsen, *Philosophy and Theology in the Twelfth Century*, p. 62, n. 106).

7 The other possible interpretation would be to see *Platonitas* as a collection of unique accidents. Boethius elsewhere thinks of individuation in this way – he does so in his *De trinitate* I, for example – but he does not speak in this way in the *On Interpretation* commentary, and talking of *Platonitas* as a quality (rather than a collection of qualities or accidents, as in the account of individuation in *De trinitate*) rather suggests the 'individual form' interpretation that I have proposed here. Another Victorine, Walter, does indeed interpret 'Platonitas' in this way, perhaps as a way of introducing some kind of consistency into Boethius's thoughts on these matters: personal features are those 'such as *Socratitas* or *Platonitas*, namely, the collection of all the properties composed of all the accidents of the parts, be they substantial or accidental [parts], that is to say, the form of unlikeness which makes him diverse from all others' (*Contra quatuor labyrinthos Franciae*, Patrologia Latina 199, 1133AB).

8 A note on the prepositions. As in English, there in Latin are various ways of signalling some kind of explanatory or 'in virtue of' relationship. Richard uses '*ex*', '*a(b)*', and '*de*' indifferently. Gilbert uses the ablative case. But these are all, I take it, semantically equivalent.

9 John of Cornwall's *Eulogium ad Alexandrum III Papam* (ed. Nickolaus M. Häring, *Mediaeval Studies*, 13 (1951), pp. 253–300), dating from 1179, identifies the first two views as those of Hugh and Gilbert, respectively, and ascribes the third to Abelard. Abelard's Christology certainly looks much like the third opinion: for example, he denies any composition claims, and claims merely that the two natures are 'associated' in one person (see *Theologia 'scholarium'* III, nn. 74–7). The clothing (*habitus*) metaphor is not, as far as I know, his. But it can be found in Augustine, and it is ultimately scriptural (Philippians 2.7, about Christ: 'Found in vesture (*habitu*) as a man); Augustine uses the term specifically commenting on this Biblical text at e.g. *De diversis quaestionibus*, q. 72, n. 2.

Part II

REVOLUTION

CHAPTER 3

From 1200 to 1277

The first three quarters of the thirteenth century are best characterized as an attempt to assimilate and process the huge number of new sources brought to the West in the second half of the twelfth century, and that continued to appear through the first half of the thirteenth century. (Hardly any additions were made to the *corpus* of Classical and Islamic texts after the translations of Aristotle and some of the Neoplatonic logical commentaries by William of Moerbeke in the 1260s and 1270s (notably Simplicius on the *Categories*), and the translations of Averroes's commentaries on the *Organon* around 1260.) This integrative work was largely completed by 1270 – Aristotle and Averroes had by this time become key sources in the philosophical conversations, and their central positions more or less clear to the participants in these discussions. After 1270, as we shall see, there was an explosion of highly original and speculative thought that presupposes the achievements of the first half of the century, but in many ways goes far beyond it in ways that would certainly have been very surprising to Aristotle, and probably to the thinkers I consider in this chapter and the next. But even in the first three-quarters of the thirteenth century, the sheer range of new ways of conceptualizing old problems, and of new problems to be answered, means that the period is perhaps best characterized in rather dramatic terms – hence the title of this part of the book.

Robert Grosseteste

The most well-known of the various early thirteenth-century thinkers, and with good reason, is the polyglot and polymath Robert Grosseteste. Grosseteste was the first Western medieval thinker to be able to make any coherent sense of Aristotle's *Posterior Analytics*, writing the first (Latin) commentary on it in the 1220s. And it would be easy to underestimate the importance of this. The *Posterior Analytics* is about the nature of, and systematization of, knowledge (*scientia*); and as Robert Pasnau notes,

> Inasmuch as scholastic philosophers take the goal of all their inquiries to be the achievement of [...] *scientia*, the strictures of the *Posterior Analytics* had an influence on virtually every area of scholastic thought, from theology [...] to metaphysics [...] and from grammar [...] to optics. (Pasnau, 2010, p. 357)

Grosseteste's commentary is notable for two things in this respect: first, it explains, though with a particular inflection, what is going on in the *Posterior Analytics*; and secondly, it already imports (from Themestius) an important relaxation on the requirements for *scientia*, relative to Aristotle's thinking on the matter.

On the first of these, Grosseteste repeats Aristotle's claim that *scientia* 'taken more strictly' is of necessary truths (see Aristotle, *Posterior Analytics* I, c. 5 (74b5039)); but he adds to this the claim that *scientia* 'taken strictly' includes contingent things that obtain 'always or most of the time' – an inductive twist to Aristotle's view. Aristotle himself makes a distinction between *explanatory* scientific inferences and other kinds of valid deductive inferences – those in which the premises do not explain the truth of the conclusions. The first sort of inference – an inference *propter quid*, in the medievals' Latin – starts from the essence of a kind, and attempt to derive from this essence, as from an explanation, the remaining necessary features of the kind – the *propria*. (I take it that, for Grosseteste, *scientia* in the two senses just outlined constitutes this explanatory project.) The second sort of inference – *quia*, in the medieval translation of Aristotle – reasons from an effect or derivative property of a kind to the explanation of the effect or property. For Aristotle, this kind of inference is not properly scientific at all. But Grosseteste notes that this is precisely how we come to infer the existence of God, and thus is a case of *scientia* 'most strictly' (*Commentarius in posteriorum analyticorum libros* I, c. 2 (p. 99)). This is the opposite of Aristotle's thinking on the matter: the properly scientific is the demonstration *propter quid*. Still, the whole set of issues is very Aristotelian in its general thrust.

On the second point: in addition to these three senses of *scientia*, Grosseteste adds a further one: any comprehension of truth

(*Commentarius in posteriorum analyticorum libros* I, c. 2 (p. 99)). This non-Aristotelian sense of *scientia* was in itself of little interest to the medievals generally, though they were, as we shall see, very interested in the psychological processes by which one might come by such *scientia*.

Now, of these, the second and fourth turn out to be extremely important in Grosseteste's innovative account of scientific induction, one that was later taken on by Roger Bacon, Duns Scotus, and Walter Burley. Grosseteste proposes that if we observe the constant or near-constant conjunction of two different events, we have grounds for supposing that the one is the cause of the other, thus allowing us to infer 'a universal principle' (*Commentarius in posteriorum analyticorum libros* I, c. 18 (p. 268)). Duns Scotus, later, makes the implicit assumption explicit: 'Whatever occurs in a great many instances from a cause that is not free is the natural effect of that cause', a principle that Scotus holds to be self-evident (Scotus, *Ordinatio* I, d. 3, p. 1, q. 4, n. 235 (trans. Wolter, *Philosophical Writings*, p. 109)).

Aristotle, of course, was very far from the only influence on Grosseteste. For example, in relation to his theory of knowledge, Grosseteste was not convinced at all of the possibilities for any kind of cognition not underwritten by divine illumination. In order to know the essences of things, we need some kind of access to the divine ideas of such essences. And the reason for this is that essences are modelled on such ideas: we can check the accuracy of our knowledge of an essence only by comparing it to the item on which it is modelled. The idea is not that we see the two things side by side, as it were (the essence and the idea), but that we see the idea 'only in a kind of conjunction and superfusion in the true things themselves' (*De veritate* (trans. McKeon, pp. 272–4)). This, of course, is a version of Augustine's teaching. But it nevertheless dovetails in with Grosseteste's views on the nature of *scientia* and induction. As Henry of Ghent later holds, it may well be the case that knowledge can get off the ground without illumination; but the scientific task in an Aristotelian universe is the discovery of the *essences* of kinds: and these, perhaps, cannot be recognized without illumination. (I discuss Henry's position in Chapter 5 below.)

Reflection on the nature of light leads to one of Grosseteste's most significant contributions to medieval science and mathematics: his account of the infinite. Grosseteste holds that the universe originated in a single, non-dimensional, point of light. The point multiplied itself into three dimensions; and since the point is itself non-dimensional, it must have formed three-dimensional space by *infinite* self-multiplication. One reason for making light the fundamental component in cosmology is that light seems capable of self-diffusion, and thus to explain the multiplication of objects by the extension of matter:

> The first corporeal form which some call corporeity is in my opinion light. For light of its very nature diffuses itself in every direction in such a way that a point of light will produce instantaneously a sphere of light of any size whatsoever. [...] Now the extension of matter in three dimensions is a necessary concomitant of corporeity [...] But a form that is in itself simple and without dimension could not introduce dimension in every direction into matter [...] except by multiplying itself and diffusing itself instantaneously in every direction and thus extending matter in its own diffusion. (*De luce* (trans. Riedl, pp. 10–11))

Now, this physical theory requires the possibility of actual infinites (actually infinitely many non-dimensional points) constituting a finite magnitude. This, of course, is profoundly anti-Aristotelian. But Grosseteste proposes a distinctive mathematics of the infinite:

> It is possible, however, that an infinite sum of number is related to an infinite sum in every proportion, numerical and non-numerical. And some infinites are larger than other infinites, and some are smaller. Thus the sum of all numbers both even and odd is infinite. It is at the same time greater than the sum of all the even numbers although this is likewise infinite, for it exceeds it by the sum of all the odd numbers. The sum, too, of all numbers starting with one and continuing by doubling each successive number is infinite, and similarly the sum of all the halves corresponding to the doubles is infinite. The sum of these halves must be half of the sum of their doubles. In the same way the sum of all numbers starting with one and multiplying by three successively is three times the sum of all the thirds corresponding to these triples. It is likewise clear in regard to all kinds of numerical proportion that there can be a

proportion of finite to infinite according to each of them.
(*De luce* (trans. Riedl, p. 11))

In line with this, Grosseteste maintains that taking any finite number of points 'does not shorten the line' (*De luce* (trans. Riedl, p. 13)). This all seems exactly right, though of course represented a strongly minority view in the Middle Ages. Grosseteste, in particular, does not consider what we might want to say about Aristotle's strictures on the impossibility of an actual infinite (Aristotle, *Physics* III, cc. 4–8), or of a whole's being equal to any of its proper parts (*Posterior Analytics* I, c. 11). In Chapter 8 I examine a few other theories of the actual infinite, though I do not know of any other thinker who makes so explicit the arithmetic of the infinite as Grosseteste does.

William of Auvergne

Robert Grosseteste and William of Auvergne (1180/90–1249) are the most significant thinkers of the opening decades of the thirteenth century: both were prolific, learned, open to the new learning, and highly capable (Grosseteste had been the first Chancellor of the University of Oxford, and spent the last 20 or so years of his life as Bishop of Lincoln; William spent the last 20 or so of his as Bishop of Paris: both dioceses of great size and importance). But their fates, both in the years immediately after their deaths and in later history, were very different: Grosseteste's work remained influential throughout the medieval period, and periodically attracted the attention of historians in later ages; William's vanished without trace almost immediately; he seems to have had no impact on thinkers as close to him in time as Bonaventure and Aquinas, and never to have generated any real interest. The contrast is not in style; both are rather difficult, prolix, and diffuse thinkers. Perhaps his lack of attachment to any religious order made his influence more diffuse. (Grosseteste had lectured to the Oxford Franciscans, and remained an important intellectual influence on the English Franciscans.)

William's approach to philosophy is rather open-minded, and Aquinas is very much in his mould. He has a clear grasp of the distinction between arguments from reason and arguments from authority, and seems to have believed – rather in the manner of

Anselm – that in principle the truths of the Christian religion could all be demonstrated by reason. William made informed use of the works of Avicenna and Averroes as well as the complete range of Aristotelian texts, and is clearly sympathetic to Peripatetic philosophy (interesting testimony to the state of Aristotelian study at Paris in the 1220s and 1230s). That said, the area of William's thought that has received the most sustained study in modern times – his theory of the soul – remains resolutely un-Aristotelian. (On this, see Moody, *Studies in Medieval Philosophy*, pp. 1–109, whose account I follow here.) A good example of this can be found even in the nature of William's argument in favour of the existence of the soul. He argues introspectively. The intellect knows that it knows things, and it knows 'that this act of its knowing is present to and in itself'. But a human being knows 'that the whole of him does not understand, that is, that neither his body nor part of it understands' – on the basis of which we can conclude that the subject of understanding must be something immaterial – and thus know inferentially that we have a soul (*De anima*, c. 1, pt. 4 (trans. Teske, p. 50)). Contrast the use of such introspective arguments in Aquinas (and even Duns Scotus), in which the purpose is to show that the soul is the form of the body, *not* that it is an immaterial agent of cognition.

Related to this argument is Avicenna's well-known and rather charming 'flying man' argument, that William also quotes in this context in favour of the incorporeality of the soul:

> Avicenna [...] says [...] that, if we put a man in the air who has his face covered and is without the use of any sense and who had not used any sense, there is no doubt but that it is possible that this man thinks and understands. Hence, he will know that he thinks or understands, and he will know that he himself exists. And if he asks himself whether he has a body, he will undoubtedly say that he does not have a body, and in the same way he will deny of himself each and every part of a human body. [...] He will grant that he has being, and he will deny, Avicenna says, that he has a body. [...] [Thus] it is necessary that he have being that does not belong to the body. (*De anima*, c. 2, pt. 13 (trans. Teske, p. 91), referring to Avicenna, *De anima* I, c. 1; V, c. 7)

And given that it is the *man* that is flying, William concludes further that Avicenna's thought experiment shows that the soul is the whole person (*De anima*, c. 3, pt. 11), again, against Aristotle.

In the light of this, it is perhaps no surprise that, although William uses Aristotle's language of form, he has no account of what this language might amount to. He rejects, for example, a proposal current at that time, probably deriving from Alexander of Aphrodisias, that the soul is the structure or organization of the body (*De anima*, c. 2, pt. 2), on the (mistaken) grounds that such a view would make the soul an accident of the body. (Aquinas later rejects the same view as insufficiently explanatory: substantial forms are supposed somehow to *account for* the structure of the body, not just *be* the structure of the body: Aquinas, *Summa contra gentiles* II, cc. 63, 64, 68.) The best William can manage is an analogy: as God is the source of life of the soul, the soul is the source of life of the body. The body is the *instrument* of the soul (*De anima*, c. 2, pt. 9): a view that Aquinas (for example) comes to regard as too Platonic, unable to account for the causal interactions between soul and body (Aquinas, *Summa theologiae* I, q. 76, a. 1 c).

Again, as we might expect, William's account of universals shows the influence of Avicenna pre-eminently. From Avicenna, William learns that (other than in cases of necessary beings) *esse* is not included in the essence of a thing, and is 'said accidentally' of created particulars (*De trinitate*, c. 1 (trans. Teske, p. 66)), even though it is not a categorial accident (*De trinitate*, c. 7). He learns too that the common nature is prior to particulars (*De trinitate*, c. 4), and that it is or includes a kind of potentiality – it is 'possible being' (*De trinitate*, c. 4 (trans. Teske, p. 77)). As such, it is 'receptive of actuality' (i.e. of *esse*) (*De trinitate*, c. 6 (trans. Teske, p. 83)), and an individual composed of essence and *esse* is composed of what are 'really two' (*De trinitate*, c. 7 (trans. Teske, p. 87)). Finally, William gives the whole position a distinctive theological basis: he holds that what grounds the potency is essence is divine power: it is because God can cause instances of such essences that such essences are possible (*De trinitate*, c. 8).

There are a number of claims here, and the entailments are probably not as secure as William thinks. In particular, seeing essence as some kind of potentiality does not entail that it enters into *composition* with actuality; and, furthermore, this composition claim does not entail that essence and *esse* are 'really two'. Still, the similarities with later thirteenth-century thinkers on some of these issues – particularly Aquinas and Giles of Rome (*c.* 1243/7–1316) – is quite striking. Equally, however, a number of things that one might have expected to have found taken from Avicenna are missing: in particular, any systematic discussion of the status of essence such as that found at the opening of book V of Avicenna's *Metaphysics*. But William gives a good sense of the ways in which Avicenna's thought was probably easier for Christians to assimilate than Aristotle's was.

Alexander of Hales

In some ways more standardly 'scholastic' than either Grosseteste or William, Alexander of Hales is notable not only for having made Lombard's *Sentences* the subject of his theological lectures, but also for the form which those lectures took, establishing the disputation style as the standard for later commentaries (at least until the second or third decade of the fourteenth century, when a more essay-like style took over). But despite his rather scholastic approach, Alexander remains in some ways a rather backward-looking figure. It is certainly true that he knows, and draws on, the *Physics* and *Metaphysics* of Aristotle. But Walter H. Principe's comment is apt:

> Alexander fails to rethink his philosophy radically under the impact of these works, but their presence and influence in his writings reveal the new outlook that was gradually penetrating the Faculty of Theology [at Paris] through the private reading and study of its professors. (Principe, 1967, p. 22)

Alexander became a Franciscan friar towards the end of this life. In some ways his thinking remained very continuous with the twelfth century, and this perhaps set the tone for distinctive later Franciscan intellectual developments, taking their lead from that century.

For example, Alexander structures his account of the nature of created (and uncreated) substance around the *id quod/id quo* distinction inherited from Boethius and Gilbert, paying little more than lip-service to Aristotelian metaphysics; and his preferred authority, even on metaphysical matters, is Augustine.[1] When discussing the view (accepted by Alexander himself) that the divine essence is shared by the three divine persons, Alexander appeals to a rough paraphrase of Aristotle, but in a way that is subordinated to an appeal to Boethius, and that is wholly ornamental (in the sense that he could just have well have restricted himself to the appeal to Boethius):

> The Philosopher seems to prove that the divine essence is neither universal nor particular in this way: universal and particular are in those things in which there is a two-fold nature, [the nature] of form, and that of matter. But in God there is entire simplicity: therefore neither universal nor particular. For Boethius says that 'God is form without matter'.
>
> And Boethius says [...]: 'In what is simple, *quod est* and *quo est* do not differ; in what is composite, they are distinct' [*Quomodo substantiae*, props. 7 and 8]. But the universal is that by which something is (*quo est*), differing from that which is (*quod est*); and the particular is that which is (*quod est*), different from that by which something is (*quo est*). Since, therefore, *quod est* and *quo est* do not differ in God, there is neither universal nor particular in God, and thus neither genus nor species. (*Glossa in quatuor libros sententiarum* I, d. 19, n. 21 (I, 200–1))

Alexander paraphrases a couple of Aristotelian texts here (*Metaphysics* E.3 (1028b34–1029a3) and *Physics* II.8 (199a30–1)); but the following from Boethius would have done better, the continuation of the passage from *De trinitate* that Alexander appeals to at the end of the first paragraph:

> Other things are not that which they are (*id quod sunt*), for each has its being from those things from which it is, that is, from its parts, and is this thing and that thing, that is, its conjoined parts; it is not this or that individually [i.e. it is not just this part or that part, but both of them together]. (Boethius, *De trinitate*, c. 2 (Loeb, p. 10))

And in any case the argument in the second paragraph is clearly more general, beginning from a distinction that obtains in the case of all created substances, not just material ones.

Another example: Alexander claims that the soul is the form of the human body; but has no account of what this might mean other than to claim that the soul moves the body:

God is not the life of the body in the way that the soul is. For the soul is life such that is vivifies the body, and brings about motion in it; and for this reason they compose one thing. But God is said to be the life of the body, not that he brings about motion there in the way that the soul does, but because he conserves it in being. (*Glossa in quatuor libros sententiarum* III, d. 21, n. 12 (III, 250))

In all, one has the impression of a kind of intellectual work-in-progress: the beginnings of an attempt to assimilate the new Aristotelian learning, but far from the completion of the process. The terminology begins to be adopted, but the fundamental structure of thought remains solidly Boethian. For the culmination of the process of assimilation, we need to wait until the next generation: Albert the Great, and pre-eminently Thomas Aquinas.

Albert the Great

Albert the Great (*c.* 1200–80) taught at Paris in the 1240s (where he taught Aquinas); in 1248 he and Aquinas went to Cologne, where Albert set up the Dominican *stadium* in that city. Although rather older than Aquinas, much of his writing overlaps with Aquinas's, either slightly predating it or being contemporaneous with it. For example, his *Sentence* commentary, very early in his career, dates from 1243–4 or thereabouts (compare Aquinas's, dating from 1252–6); and his Aristotelian commentaries probably span the years from the 1250s to the 1270s (compare Aquinas's, dating between 1267 and 1273). And he is thus able to interact with the teaching of his famous pupil, occasionally targeting it for criticism. For example, his views on universals seems to take something of a stand against Aquinas's in the early *De ente* of Aquinas (1252–6), a text that I discuss in detail in the next chapter. In *Super Porphyrium de universalibus*, written in the 1250s, Albert offers his own theory of universals. As we shall see, Aquinas takes Avicenna's views on the common nature as his starting point. But Albert proceeds rather differently, starting from a view not of (loosely) Aristotelian inspiration, but by the altogether more realist views of the Neoplatonists:

> We say that the universal can be considered in three ways: namely, as it is, in itself, a simple and invariable nature; and as it is related to the intelligence; and as it is in this or that through the *esse* that it has in this or that. [...] And this is what the ancients called 'three-fold forms': namely, *ante rem* (which are forms taken in themselves, existing as principles of things); *in re*, or with the thing itself (which are forms existent in them) [...]; and *post rem*, which are forms separated, by the intellect, from individuating principles. (*Super Porphyrium*, c. 3 (p. 24a–b))

(Note that the Aphrodisian tradition that I have described thus far simply dispenses with the first of these forms; Avicenna refers to such a form, but denies it has any being.) Albert's difference from Aquinas and Avicenna – apart from the appeal to the tradition of the Neoplatonists rather than to Avicenna's Aphrodisian view – is that the nature considered 'in itself' *exists*: as Albert puts it,

> The simple nature, which gives *esse*, and kind, and name [to particulars], exists most truly among all the things that are. (*Super Porphyrium*, c. 3 (p. 24a))

In another work, dating from 1259 – *De intellectu et intelligibili* – Albert makes the same point in rather different terminology (terminology that becomes important a generation later): the essence considered 'as a certain absolute thing, in itself' has 'the being [...] of essence (*esse* [...] *essentiae*)' (*De intellectu et intelligibili* I, tr. 2, c. 2 (Borgnet edn, IX, 493a)).

All this pushes in a rather more realist direction than Aquinas, and (as we shall see) is taken up in certain thinkers after Aquinas (particularly Henry of Ghent and Duns Scotus, in different ways). It is perhaps worth noting that, despite the appeal to the three-fold universal of the Neoplatonists, Albert's position bears scant relation to that. For the Neoplatonists, the universal 'in itself' is a Platonic form, separate from the particulars that exemplify it. For Albert, although the universal in itself has some kind of existence, this existence is never in fact separable from that of its exemplifications (see *De intellectu et intelligibili* I, tr. 2, c. 4).

Still, the reference to the Neoplatonists is notable: it is often thought that Albert pushes in a more Platonic direction than (say)

Aquinas, and there is a great deal in this rather simple generalization. For example, Albert's account of religious language and divine ineffability is far closer to that of Maimonides and the Neoplatonists than Aquinas's is. Albert holds that when we predicate things of God, we do so either negatively, excluding imperfections, or positively; and when we predicate things affirmatively of God, we mean to signify merely that God is the cause of the relevant perfection (*Commentary on Dionysius' Mystical Theology*, c. 1 (trans. Tugwell, pp. 139 and 153)). And Albert restricts the way in which analogy is applicable to God: God lacks anything even analogously in common with creatures, though he has 'something in common with creatures in the form of an imitative kind of analogy' (*Commentary on Dionysius' Mystical Theology*, c. 1 (trans. Tugwell, p. 152)). Albert at one point claims that properties that somehow 'preexist primarily in [God], such as wisdom, goodness, and so on' – are predicated 'essentially and [not just] causally of him' (*Commentary on Dionysius' Mystical Theology*, c. 1 (trans. Tugwell, p. 152)). But his standard line is that

> we affirm things of God only relatively, that is causally, whereas we deny things of God absolutely, that is, with reference to what he is in himself. (*Commentary on Dionysius' Mystical Theology*, c. 1 (trans. Tugwell, p. 153))

Given this, it is perhaps unsurprising that Albert is very circumspect about the nature of theology as a science. Aquinas holds that theology is a *propter quid* science, reasoning from first principles revealed by God (Aquinas, *Summa theologiae* I, q. 1, a. 2). Albert, contrariwise, vividly contrasts theology with natural and philosophical sciences. These latter proceed syllogistically, from first principles; theology, by contrast

> begins rather with a kind of divine light, which is not a statement by which something is affirmed; it is a kind of reality which convinces the understanding to adhere to it above all else. And so it raises the understanding to something which transcends it, and this is why the mind is left with something of which it has no clearly defined knowledge. (*Commentary on Dionysius' Mystical Theology*, c. 1 (trans. Tugwell, p. 139))

But, despite this Platonic stream in his thought, Albert was an innovator in a number of key ways: not least of which was his work, in the 1250s and 1260s, in commenting on the works of Aristotle. In particular, around 1250–2 Albert composed the first commentary on the complete *Nicomachean Ethics*. Among other innovations found in Aristotle's work was a discussion of the question of *akrasia* – weakness of will – developed in ways quite different from those found in Christian writers prior to Albert. I talked in Chapter 2 about Bernard's rather Augustinian account of the matter. The difference that Aristotle makes can be seen very strikingly if we compare that account with Albert's. For Aristotle, there is no further act or process – for example, an *appetitive* act, or an act of the will – between the reason's determination that such-and-such is to be done, and the act itself (see e.g. Aristotle, *Nicomachean Ethics* VII, c. 3 (1147b9–18)). *Akrasia*, then, cannot be explained in terms of any such additional appetitive act. Rather, *akrasia* according to Aristotle is the result of an emotional pull, such that people sometimes act against their choice, even while leaving choice (for the good) unaffected (Aristotle, *Nicomachean Ethics* VII, c. 10 (1152a15–17)). Specifically, the emotion can lead people to prefer a lesser good to the one that they choose by means of their deliberative processes. And it does this by causing some kind of temporary ignorance of the application of a good general principle to the particular case at hand, such that the *akratēs*, the incontinent or weak-willed person, whether or not he believes his action to be good, certainly fails to realize that the proposed action should not be done (Aristotle, *Nicomachean Ethics* VII, c. 3 (1147b1–5, 9–18); VII, c. 8 (1151a11–14)). Postulating this sort of ignorance allowed Aristotle to avoid the undesirable conclusion that reason is simply overcome by emotion, and thus allowed him to accept that akratic actions are blameworthy. Much like Aristotle, Albert persistently claims that both the akratic person and the wicked or malicious person are in some sense ignorant.[2] But the wicked acts from choice, that is, from his settled (bad) moral dispositions, and his ignorance about moral matters is culpable (Albert, *Ethica* III, tr. 1, c. 10), whereas the ignorance of the akratic person is explained by emotion (in the Augustinian guise of concupiscence), and his action is against his settled moral judgments and choices, such that the choice, though not the ignorance, is culpable (*Ethica* III, tr. 1, c. 14; *Super ethica* VII, lect. 3, n. 623). These emotions belong to the sensitive part of the soul

(Albert, *De bono*, tr. 3, q. 5, a. 1; tr. 3, q. 5, a. 3). Continence allows the agent to avoid the pull of concupiscence without the emotions themselves being ordered by the virtue of temperance (Albert, *Super ethica* VII, lect. 7.1, n. 600). The contrast with Bernard's will-based explanation could not be starker, and provides a vivid example of the way in which Aristotle changed the intellectual landscape of the thirteenth century.

One radical innovation brought by Aristotelian philosophy is an account of change in terms of potency, actuality, and privation: something which is not, but can be, φ, becomes actually φ: something with the privation of φ but the potency for φ becomes actually φ (see Aristotle, *Physics* I, cc. 7–8). As the more Aristotelian-minded medievals understood this, the case of substantial change – the production or destruction of a substance – is to be understood in just the same way, but the relevant subject – matter or prime matter – is just pure potency. (I examine this in more detail Chapter 4 below.) Albert does not quite make this move: while he believes that prime matter is the subject of change, and while he even asserts that prime matter is pure potency, he asserts too that this potency must have some kind of determination – it must be a potency for a certain set of (i.e. all really possible?) forms – and this kind of determination must itself count as a form or forms, somehow intrinsic to matter (see Albert, *Physica* I, tr. 2, c. 12).

According to one very influential modern commentator, Anneliese Maier, Albert is responsible for introducing an important distinction from the Islamic world's discussion of Aristotelian theories of change (see Maier, 1982, pp. 21–39). The distinction concerns the nature of gradual change. Does such change consist somehow in a succession of forms in the same category as the end term of the change? Or does such change consist in some kind of successive item, categorial or not, somehow supervening on a form in the same category as the end term? All of these views accept as an assumption the claim that motion is something that, as we would say, *perdures*: persists by having different parts at different times – by having temporal parts. On the first view, the perduring item is just the changing form, a process in the same category as the form. For example, consider a change from one shade of blue to a deeper one. On this view, the change is the form 'in process': perhaps the collection of forms of ever deeper hue. In later debates, probably drawing on terminological suggestions made by Albert, this analysis was seen as involving a *forma fluens* – a 'flowing form': blueness itself, becoming ever deeper. Albert ascribes this view to Averroes. On the second view, the perduring item is the 'route' (*via*) to the goal. And since category-membership requires being a fully-possessed form of such-and-such a kind, this route fails to count as anything categorial at all. Consider again the change from one shade of blue to a deeper one. The perduring item is simply the change itself. But the change is not itself any kind of form. In later debates, again probably drawing on Albert's terminology, this item is known as the *fluxus formae* – the 'flux of a form': something non-categorial, a 'deepening', supervening on blueness. Albert ascribes this view to Avicenna. The third view is very similar to this, but rather than claim that the supervening item is imperfect and non-categorial, the view maintains that motion is in fact a further form, belonging to some further category over and above the ten Aristotelian categories. Becoming bluer involves the inherence of a further, perduring form, over and above the blueness itself. Albert himself accepts the first of these views – the *forma fluens*. (For the whole discussion, see Albert, *Physica* III, tr. 1, c. 3.)

The debate on the nature of motion did not really take off, however, until the beginning of the fourteenth century (see Maier, 1982, pp. 30–3). William of Ockham holds the *forma fluens* view, but with the clarification (that perhaps Albert himself would be happy with) that there are no perduring items, and thus that the change just consists in the subject of change existing in different states at different times (Ockham, *Summulae in libros Physicorum* III, c. 6). His opponents are various Scotists (William of Alnwick (*c.* 1275–1333) and Francis of Meyronnes (*c.* 1288–1328)), who maintain that change is a *fluxus formae* to be located in the category of quantity. Curiously, something like this Scotist view was adopted too by the arch-Ockhamist, John Buridan, to explain the case of local motion (motion from place to place). Being in place, according to Aristotelian physics, consists in a relation to a surrounding body (Aristotle, *Physics* IV, c. 2 (209a31–b1)); but, according to Buridan, motion is something non-relational that 'exists in the moving body as a subject' (quoted in Maier, 1982, p. 33; for the whole extensive discussion in Buridan, see *Quaestiones super octos libros Physicorum* III, qq. 6–9). It is, I think, fair to say that the terminology in all this is not wholly clear.

At any rate, what we find in Albert is a range of issues far wider than that considered in the twelfth century, and a far greater range of conceptual and analytical tools available to assess these issues. To this extent, Albert is very representative of the revolutions of the thirteenth century.

Bonaventure

Bonaventure spent much of his life as an ecclesiastical leader and administrator – after his time as a Regent Master in theology at Paris, he was Minister General of the Franciscans from 1257 to his death in 1274 – and thus had little time (or perhaps inclination) to engage in philosophical writing in later life. And while he was no philosophical slouch, Bonaventure did not engage with Aristotle in the same systematic way that some of his contemporaries did. For example, as I show in the next chapter, one of the key teachings of thirteenth-century Aristotelianism is the status of prime matter as pure potency. Bonaventure's treatment of matter is quite different from this. In the thirteenth-century Aristotelian framework, prime matter is the pure potency underlying substantial change, just as substance itself is the qualified potency underlying accidental change. (I consider this issue in detail in Chapter 4.) Bonaventure does have a notion of matter as pure potency. But it is divorced from the Aristotelian disjunction between substantial and accidental change. Rather, Bonaventure identifies matter with the whole domain of the passively potential: anything susceptive of accidental change is composed of matter conceived as pure potency, even if that item is not susceptible to substantial change. Thus, in a rather elegant twist, Bonaventure adopts the so-called universal hylomorphism defended by the Jewish philosopher ibn Gabirol (Avicebron) (1021/1–*c.* 1057/8), whose *Fons vitae* was translated from Arabic by Dominicus Gundisalvi and Magister Johannes between 1160 and 1190. Universal hylomorphism is the view that all created substances include matter. So, as Bonaventure asserts, created non-physical items such as angels and souls must include matter, since such items are receptive of accidents (e.g. different thoughts, volitions, and activities) – the matter of such non-physical substances was usually labelled 'spiritual matter'. Of course, asserting that angels are receptive of accidents is very different from claiming that they are physical (*Commentaria in libros sententiarum* II, d. 3, p. 1, q. 1, a. 1 and a. 2). Conversely, the matter of physical objects – the matter associated with substantial change – is very far from Aristotle's pure potency, and owes more to certain insights of St Augustine's. Bonaventure adopts from Augustine the notion that matter includes *active* powers that are partial causes in matter's reception of different kinds of form – *rationes seminales*. These *rationes seminales* are *virtual* forms: they are active powers that somehow contain the fully-fledged form in some kind of restricted way, and have a causal role in the production of the fully-fledged form (*Commentaria in libros sententiarum* II, d. 18, a. 2, q. 1). The position, though not the Augustinian terminology, seems rather close to Albert's views on matter. Augustine uses the notion of *rationes seminales* to account for the universe's evolution from lesser to greater development, and Bonaventure expands on this evolutionary view to suggest that the initial state of the universe consisted of extended matter along with matter's active inclination for different kinds of elemental and animate forms.

This is a very different world from Aristotle's fully-formed eternal cosmos – I talked about this a little in the Introduction above. But it does not mean that Bonaventure was unacquainted with Aristotelian philosophy. Far from it: Aristotle is, of course, the Philosopher, and Bonaventure is comfortable using even difficult works like the *Posterior Analytics* as authoritative sources. But there is no attempt to develop a philosophy that *systematically* incorporates Aristotelian insights, and as often as not Bonaventure finds Aristotle wanting – as we shall see below, discussing Bonaventure's views about time.

Bonaventure frequently looked back to twelfth-century models. His proofs for God's existence are a good example. He reports with approval Anselm's ontological argument (*Disputed Questions on the Mystery of the Trinity*, q. 1, a. 1, arg. 23), and proposes an argument that clearly has a family resemblance to Richard of St Victor's arguments:

> If there is a being that exists from another, there is also a being that does not exist from another, because nothing can bring itself from non-being to being. Therefore there must necessarily be a first principle for bringing [things into being], and this is found in the first being, which is not brought from another. Therefore if that being which exists from another is called a created being, and that being which does not exist from another is called uncreated being, then every category of being implies the existence of God. (*Disputed Questions on the*

Mystery of the Trinity, q. 1, a. 1, arg. 12 (trans. Hayes, p. 110, altered))

But Bonaventure is quite happy to include arguments of loosely Aristotelian inspiration too, proposing two rather curious arguments to show that knowledge of God's existence must be innate to the human mind:

> The Philosopher says that 'it would be inappropriate for us to be in possession of the most noble [cognitive] dispositions, and yet to know nothing of them' [*Posterior Analytics* II, c. 18]. And since the truth of God's existence is the most noble truth and the one most present to us, it would be inappropriate that such a truth should remain hidden from the human intellect. (*Disputed Questions on the Mystery of the Trinity*, q. 1, a. 1, arg. 5 (trans. Hayes, p. 108, altered))

> Again, the desire for wisdom is implanted in the human mind, since, as the Philosopher says, 'By nature all human beings desire to know' [*Metaphysics* A, c. 1]. But that wisdom which is most desirable is the eternal wisdom. Therefore, there is implanted in the human mind a desire for such wisdom above all else. But [...] love cannot exist unless there is some knowledge of the object loved. Therefore, it is necessary that some knowledge of that highest wisdom be impressed in the human mind. But this is first of all to know the existence of God, who is that wisdom. Therefore [knowledge of God's existence is impressed on all human minds]. (*Disputed Questions on the Mystery of the Trinity*, q. 1, a. 1, arg. 6 (trans. Hayes, p. 108, altered))

Aristotle, I think, would have been surprised by the direction in which Bonaventure took his premises. But Aristotelian, nevertheless, the premises are. And note Bonaventure's ease with both the *Posterior Analytics* and syllogistic reasoning.

Bonaventure asserts rather more in this context than just that knowledge of God's existence is naturally innate in all human beings, however. Thinkers of the thirteenth century grappled with a question that Aristotle's *Metaphysics* forced them to think about: what is the primary object of the human intellect? A primary object of a cognitive power is a general feature in virtue of which those things that are non-inferentially cognized are cognizable. Aquinas holds that the essence or quiddity of material substance is the primary object of human cognition. In defence of his view, he appeals to the scholastic commonplace that the human intellect is naturally joined to a body. Aquinas argues that we can infer from the fact that the intellect is thus embodied that its proper object is something embodied too: as Aquinas puts it, its proper object is 'essence or quiddity existing in bodily matter'; and the reason for this is that 'a cognitive power is proportioned to the thing cognized' (Aquinas, *Summa theologiae* I, q. 84, a. 7 c). So we can conclude from the embodied nature of the power that its object is likewise embodied. Bonaventure disagrees fundamentally: we understand everything 'through being', and non-being likewise through *being* (only being – what is – can be understood; non-being is simply the negation of what is understood). Since potency is a kind of non-being, the thing through which we understand everything must be

> pure act. But this is not particular being, which is limited because mixed with potency; nor is it analogous being because that has only a minimum of actuality because it has only a minimum of being. It remains that the being in question must be divine Being. (*The Soul's Journey into God*, c. 5, n. 3 (trans. Cousins, p. 96))

Bonaventure is not suggesting, I think, that we have some kind of immediate intuition of the divine being, and that this grounds all other knowledge. But he clearly asserts some kind of implicit understanding of God here: the being that we grasp is the divine being, even if not explicitly so identified by us.

The question's Aristotelian ancestry can be found in a debate about the object of metaphysics (the most universal human science): is the object being as such, or God as first principle? Aristotle defends the first view at the beginning of *Metaphysics* Γ, and the second at the beginning of *Metaphysics* E; and (to make matters still more complex) Avicenna defends the first view, and Averroes the second. Aquinas defends the first view – though he identifies being-as-such as *esse commune*, the being under whose extension creatures, but not God, fall (Aquinas, *Super Boetium de Trinitate*, q. 5, a. 4), and thus adopts the view, eccentric by medieval standards, that God is not included in the subject-matter of metaphysics. Bonaventure's view is something of a compromise between the two Aristotelian views: metaphysics studies

> all beings according to their ideal causes, tracing them back to the one first Principle from which they proceeded, that is, God, in as far as God is the beginning, the end, and the exemplar. (*On the Reduction of the Arts to Theology*, § 4 (trans. Hayes, p. 43))

Bonaventure, then, makes God central to the nature of metaphysics and cognitive theory. He makes God central to human epistemology, too, in a way that later thinkers tended to reject. He accepts a version of the Aristotelian distinction between agent and possible intellects, holding that the agent intellect somehow processes sense data such that the possible intellect can know the relevant concepts. But he holds that the agent intellect cannot do this unless God moves it: 'If [the intellect] is to become intelligent in act, this must be brought about through someone who has actual knowledge of all things' (*Disputed Questions on the Knowledge of Christ*, q. 4, arg. 32) – I assume, by infusing into it the relevant conceptual content (see too *Commentaria in libros sententiarum* II, d. 24, p. 1, q. 2, a. 4).

So the intellect abstracts universal concepts. Bonaventure holds that such concepts correspond to something real: there must be extra-mental universals to ground the truth of claims about different individuals of the same kind. But Bonaventure does not have a great deal to say about such universals, merely noting a claim (that he ascribes to Avicenna) that essences are simply the 'quiddities of universals', and that universals are 'apt to be in many' (*Commentaria in libros sententiarum* II, d. 18, q. 1, a. 3).

If Bonaventure does not have much to say about the nature of universals, he has a good deal to say on a related question: the doctrine of the Trinity. As I have been presenting it, one of the central problems that the medievals found with the doctrine was how to reconcile it with divine simplicity. We saw divergent approaches in the twelfth century, with almost all thinkers lined up against Gilbert of Poitiers. Gilbert's view provides the occasion for Bonaventure's insights on the matter. Bonaventure notes that relations – unlike non-relational accidents – are not items inherent in a subject. They have 'minimal entity', since a relation 'arrives and recedes without any change in what is related' (*Commentaria in libros sententiarum* I, d. 26, a. 1, q. 2 arg. 1). Bonaventure does not mean that relational changes can be basic, but that a relational change in one of two *relata* might be wholly parasitic simply on a non-relational change in the other, and that such a merely relational change in the first *relatum* involves *no* real change in that *relatum* at all. There is, of course, a change in the things we can truly assert of this *relatum*; but what grounds this change is a real change in the other *relatum*. On this basis, Bonaventure argues that there is a sense in which the relation is the same as the essence: it is not anything added to the essence (against Gilbert). But still, relations require *relata*, and the *relata* are real enough. In this sense, the relations are real too: the persons are really related to each other (*Commentaria in libros sententiarum* I, d. 33, a. 1, q. 1 c).

Whether by chance or design, Bonaventure's account of relations here seems very Aristotelian, since he seems to suppose that relations are not things in any sense over and above the related extremes – something that I take Aristotle to assume in *Metaphysics* Δ, c. 15. But Bonaventure differs sharply from the Aristotelians on another philosophical question – again, one with theological ramifications. The issue is the nature of time. According to Aristotle, time is relative to motion, such that the existence of time requires – and is caused by – the existence of motion (see e.g. *Physics* IV, c. 11 (219b1–2)). The medievals tended to accept this definition. But it raises a problem: what should we say about the temporality of changeless things? For God, medieval theologians tend to affirm timelessness – existence with topological (i.e. structural) properties somehow analogous to those of an instant. But the medievals supposed that angels and disembodied souls might exist statically, and even that God could have made a universe that contained nothing other than changeless disembodied spirits. What should we say in such cases? The term for the durational measure of changeless creatures is '*aevum*', and accounts of the *aevum* fall into two groups: those that liken its topological properties to a temporal instant, and those that ascribe to it the topological properties of a temporal interval. The majority view is the first – as we might expect, given Aristotelian assumptions about time. But this majority view is very puzzling. After all, changeless angels might begin and cease to exist; and they might begin and cease in ways that are on the face of it temporally overlapping: Michael might be created prior to Gabriel, for example.

And none of this seems to make much sense on the majority view. Bonaventure is fully aware of these difficulties:

> If the whole existence [of an angel] is present, then 'being' and 'having been' are not different. Therefore, whatever does not now exist never existed; and whatever existed now exists. But God cannot make what existed not to have been. Therefore he cannot destroy an eviternal being [e.g. an angel]. But this is clearly false. Therefore [the whole existence of an eviternal is not now present]. (*Commentaria in libros sententiarum* II, d. 2, p. 1, a. 1, q. 3 arg. 7 (II, 62a))

And, on the second problem:

> If the whole existence of an eviternal is simultaneous, and its whole duration lacks 'before' and 'after', then there cannot be longer or shorter periods of existence in an eviternal. In this case, it follows that the soul of Peter is in glory neither before, nor for a longer period than, the soul of blessed Francis [of Assisi]. But this is clearly false. Therefore [the whole existence of an eviternal is not simultaneous]. (*Commentaria in libros sententiarum* II, d. 2, p. 1, a. 1, q. 3, arg. 8 (II, 62a))

These are serious problems for the defenders of the first view, because they concede that the conclusions that Bonaventure draws from their view are indeed false. For this reason, Bonaventure accepts the second view. But this raises Aristotelian puzzles all of its own. For how could there be time in the absence of motion, given that time is *defined* in terms of a necessary relation to motion?

The answer, of course, is simply to reject Aristotelian views of time, at least in reference to the *aevum*. So Bonaventure claims that we can talk of duration and succession even in the absence of any natural processes, or indeed any changes at all. (Thus his account of the *aevum* looks a little like the absolute time of Descartes and Newton.) There are two components to Bonaventure's theory, as far as I can see. The first is that succession does not require real change: as Bonaventure puts it, time properly so-called entails succession 'with variation, with aging and renewal' whereas the *aevum* entails succession while excluding variation or renewal (*Commentaria in libros sententiarum* II, d. 1, p. 1, a. 1, q. 3, c (II, 62b)). (I take it that the *aevum* might include simply getting older, not really varying; not undergoing any real exchange of forms.) And, secondly, an angel's *existence* (not the angel itself) is successive. Bonaventure construes something's existence as its relation to its primary cause. Presumably this relation is a perduring entity: the relations are different from period to period and moment to moment, and the whole collection constitutes the angel's one existence (*Commentaria in libros sententiarum* d. 1, p. 1, a. 1, q. 3 c (II, 62b–63a)). Bonaventure cannot have known Albert's *forma fluens* theory (Albert wrote his *Physics* commentary a few years after Bonaventure wrote his *Sentence* commentary), and I rather doubt that Albert ever read Bonaventure's commentary either. But the similarities between a creature's existence and Albert's *forma fluens* are striking (excepting, of course, that relations are not really forms for Bonaventure).

Given all this it is perhaps no surprise that Bonaventure is happy to label the *aevum* a sort of time. He distinguishes four senses of 'time': (i) taken 'most commonly' it is the 'measure of any created duration'; (ii) taken 'commonly', it is the measure of any mutation, whether from non-being to being, or from one being to another; (iii) taken 'properly' it is the 'measure of successive variation'; and (iv) taken 'more properly' it is the 'measure of motion or of successive variation that is continued and regulated according to the rule of the motion of the eighth [heavenly] sphere' – Aristotle's sense, according to Bonaventure. The first sense of 'time' here includes the *aevum* – so the *aevum* is a kind of time in the most general sense of time (*Commentaria in libros sententiarum* II, d. 2, p. 1, a. 2, q. 1 c).

Bonaventure's most astute follower on this question, Peter Olivi (1247/8–98), is more radical still. He concludes his account of the *aevum* by making the following observation:

> To the objection that every successive measure is time [such that if the *aevum* is a successive measure, it is time]: since no formal difference can be found between [time and the *aevum*], I confess myself not to know how to make such a formal differentiation [between time and the *aevum*]. (Olivi, *In secundum librum sententiarum*, q. 9 (I, 177))

I return to Olivi on this question below, since in thinking through some of the implications of a Bonaventureann position on the *aevum*, Olivi proposes a theory about how things *persist* through time – an issue that seems to us (and to Olivi) obviously to require some kind of account, but did not seem to strike most of the medievals in that way.

Roger Bacon

We know that Bacon received his earliest training in the Arts in Oxford. As I noted in the Introduction, he was lecturing in the Arts Faculty in Paris in the 1240s. At any rate, at some time in the late 1240s or early 1250s, he returned to Oxford. He was absurdly wealthy; when his money ran out (his family was ruined by their support of Henry III against Simon of Montfort), he joined the Franciscan order – probably in the late 1250s. This decision seems, in retrospect, to have been a mistake. The early Franciscans were plagued by debates about apostolic poverty. These debates became compounded by the radical apocalypticism that the Franciscans inherited from Joachim of Fiore, and Bonaventure, the minister general, dealt with these by censorship, making it against the order's rules for friars to keep or write books, or disseminate writings outside the order, without the permission of the Provincial Masters. Bacon's ally, Pope Clement IV, asked him in 1266 to produce what turned out to be in effect a summary of his philosophical doctrines. So, again in Paris, Bacon, in first of all writing, and then sending to the Papal court, his *Opus majus* and *Opus minus*, was disobeying an explicit mandate of the order. Equally, Bacon was seized by the Spirituals' apocalyptic visions, believing in the immanent return of the Antichrist. He explicitly linked his new scientific theories to this apocalypticism by claiming that they would provide the kind of accurate theories that the Church would need to oppose the Antichrist. We do not know what the consequences of Bacon's disobedience were, though a chronicle from 1370 reports that he was imprisoned. We know that he died sometime during or shortly after 1292.

There is a lot that could be said about Bacon's philosophy, but it seems to me that his most distinctive contribution – though one which wholly failed to be taken up by his successors – lies in a wonderfully generalized physical theory, replete with a very clear mathematical underpinning, that would allow for a genuinely quantitative account of the causal processes of nature – a rather modern approach. The starting point is Grosseteste's doctrine of light, which Grosseteste developed to explain the origination and physical extension of the universe. Bacon explicitly follows Grosseteste's lead, but develops it in a more metaphysical direction. For Bacon, species radiate out of all material objects: they are caused by the objects, and explain not only the fact that objects can be known and sensed, but also physical causation. All this is achieved by radiating species, which are 'generated out of the potentiality of matter' – the 'active potentiality of the recipient matter' (*De multiplicatione specierum* I, c. 3 (trans. Lindberg, p. 47)). Substances in this way generate substances, and accidents accidents. This represents a kind of fusion of the light metaphysics that originates in certain kinds of readings of Neoplatonism (particularly Plotinus, transmitted via Augustine and Proclus) with Aristotelian notions of generation and corruption. To make some sense of it, we should perhaps keep in mind that, in medieval Aristotelianism, effects are somehow *likenesses* of their causes; and that one sense of the medieval Latin word '*species*' is 'likeness' (as in 'intelligible species', for example). Substances and accidents multiply their *likenesses* in the matter of their effects. This might not seem to add much to standard Aristotelian accounts of generation and corruption. But Bacon hypothesizes that the same geometrical theories govern all these cases – light, cognition/ sensation, generation – albeit that the physical causal processes, and the active and passive powers involved, are different in nature. Hence, like Grosseteste, but in a far more radical fashion, he believes that the physics of light provides the key to the scientific understanding of all natural processes. And, unlike Grosseteste, Bacon had access to the most advanced and sophisticated optical theories from the Muslim world in the shape of the *De aspectibus* of Alhazen (Ibn al-Haytham) (965–*c.* 1040), translated sometime during Bacon's lifetime. This allowed Bacon to place his observations of natural causal processes on a firm geometrical footing; and given his view that these geometrical analyses are generalizable, Bacon thus possesses a theoretical tool that would unify all natural processes in the physical world – a medieval version of a theory of everything. Still, his fundamental orientation backwards to Grosseteste, his opposition to anything modern other than his own experimental theorizing, and his unhealthy interest (as his contemporaries saw it) in astrology, which he held to have a high degree of predictive success, perhaps guaranteed his intellectual marginalization. At any rate, this was a cast of mind out of step with the emphasis on radical contingency that resulted from the condemnations of 1277 and 1286. He was influential on Pecham, who shared his interest in optics, and on Witelo, whose importance for Kepler is well known.

The Paris Arts Faculty

Those theologians receptive to the new philosophical thought adopted a very particular hermeneutical strategy in their reading: expound theological and even philosophical authorities 'reverently': as Roger Bacon puts it, 'correcting Aristotle through a pious and reverential interpretation' (Bacon, *Opus majus*, p. I, c. 6 (p. 15)). The approach was quite different in the Faculty of Arts: simply to explain carefully the thought of a given philosopher, irrespective of the truth or falsehood of the philosopher's views. Key players were Siger of Brabant and Boethius of Dacia, and positions of both thinkers were targeted in the 1277 condemnation. I have already discussed the question of the eternity of the world. Perhaps an even more interesting case is the Averroist view that there is only one possible intellect for all human beings. Aristotle at times seems to suggest that there is just one *agent* intellect for all human beings, arguing that the intellect is 'separable [...] and unmixed' and 'immortal and eternal' (see *De anima* III, c. 5 (430a17 and a23)). And this teaching can be given a theistic spin by identifying the agent intellect as God. The view that there is just one *possible* intellect is an altogether different kind of claim. The possible intellect is the centre of human cognitive activity – it is the faculty that thinks, that introspects, and that is (as we would put it today) the centre of consciousness. The debate, as Siger recognizes, basically turns on a conflict between metaphysics and psychology. The Averroist position, motivated by a powerful metaphysical argument, is very simple:

> No nature existing per se, having its existence abstracted from matter (and thus being individuated of itself), can have many individuals differing numerically. But the intellective soul is a per se subsistent, having existence abstracted from matter, and is thus individuated of itself. Therefore it cannot have many individual instances in the one species. (Siger, *De anima intellectiva*, c. 7 (p. 102))

But there seems an equally compelling psychological argument against this view:

> If there were one intellect of all men, then, if I knew something, they would all know it, and so there could not be one learned man and one ignorant man. (Siger, *De anima intellectiva*, c. 7 (p. 107))

Aquinas makes this psychological argument a centrepiece of his refutation of the Averroist view (see e.g. *Summa theologiae* I, q. 76, a. 2 c: 'It would follow [...] that all human beings were one cognizer, with one act of cognition'). But he has tremendous difficulty dealing with the metaphysical argument. He accepts that the soul is the substantial form of the human body, and thus that it is naturally united to the body (Aquinas, *Summa theologiae* I, q. 76, a. 1). But he holds too that the soul, since it has an operation of its own (thinking) must have existence of its own too (Aquinas, *Summa theologiae* I, q. 75, a. 2). And he responds to Siger by resorting to the rather *ad hoc* claim that, although the soul exists *per se*, it is nevertheless in the natural run of things united to matter, and thus (unlike an angel) is individuated by matter (see e.g. Aquinas, *Summa theologiae* I, q. 76, a. 2 ad 1), or, in the case of a separated soul, by its 'inclination' for union with a particular chunk of matter (Aquinas, *Summa theologiae* I, q. 76, a. 1 ad 6).

Aquinas's position here can hardly be counted as particularly robust. And Siger sets about attacking the whole way in which Aquinas defends the view that the soul is the substantial form of a body. According to Aquinas, the soul is 'according to its essence' the substantial form of a human body, but has a power and an activity – namely, the intellect and cognition – that is independent of the body (see Aquinas, *Summa theologiae* I, q. 76, a. 1 ad 4 for the first claim and *Summa theologiae* I, q. 75, a. 2 c for the second). Aquinas believes that, if the soul were not essentially the substantial form of a human body, it would be impossible to ascribe the soul's activity to the whole human person – and an assumption here is that each embodied human being 'experiences that it is she herself who cognizes' (Aquinas, *Summa theologiae* I, q. 76, a. 1 c).

Siger subjects this view to devastating critique, in effect turning it on its head. For Siger, the union of soul and body takes place not at the level of the substances but at the level of the powers:

the soul is separate in essence, but united in power. Siger agrees with Aquinas's argument in favour of the view that the soul is the substantial form of the body. The whole human being understands, and this can be the case only if the soul is the form of the body. But thinking is, nevertheless, the function of something immaterial, and in this sense (as Aquinas agrees) the soul is separate from the body. But Siger does not see how thinking could be the function merely of a *power* without being the function of the *substance* (in this case the soul) itself. So, he reasons, if the intellect were united in its essence or substance to the body (as Aquinas affirms), then we should say that the body thinks (as Aquinas denies). Conversely, if thinking were the function of a power, then it would not be clear how we might want to claim that the substance (i.e. the soul) thinks; and if the soul did not think, then on the assumption that the soul is in its essence the substantial form of a human body, we could not say that the whole human person thinks (*De anima intellectiva*, q. 3).

Siger takes as the starting point for his own view the Aristotelian claim, accepted by Aquinas, that we cannot think without using the body: particularly, we cannot think without using the imagination and its images (the phantasm). So we must say that it is in its *power*, not its *essence*, that the soul is united to the body (*De anima intellectiva*, q. 3). (Siger's position changes on this slightly, as he got older: in the questions on book III of *De anima*, dating from around 1269–70, he claimed that the soul was united to the body in its operation, but not that it was the *form* of the body (*In tertium librum De anima*, q. 7 (pp. 22–4); q. 8 (p. 25)); in *De anima intellectiva* he shifts in a slightly more orthodox direction, claiming that the soul is united to the body as its form.) Locating the union in the soul's power, rather than its essence, allows Siger to make sense of the claim that the soul is separate from the body in the sense that (e.g.) it can survive the death of the body (*De anima intellectiva*, q. 4). And it allows Siger to claim that the whole person thinks: the soul is a part of the person, and activities of parts are attributed to their wholes (*De anima intellectiva*, q. 3).

So Siger's position seems to have some sensible metaphysical underpinnings. But how does Siger deal with the psychological argument against Averroism? The simple answer is that he does not know what to say:

Because of the difficulty of these things, and of certain others, I say that I have been doubtful for a long time which path of natural reason should be held in this problem, and what Aristotle thought about this question; and in such doubts we should adhere to the faith, which is above human reason. (*De anima intellectiva*, q. 7 (p. 108))

Note here that the agnosticism immediately leads to the claim that we should adhere to faith. Siger was once thought to subscribe to some kind of 'two truths' theory, according to which contradictory claims could be true, where truth is relativized to discipline (be it theology or philosophy: something might be true in theology and false in philosophy, or *vice versa*). Thus, the prologue to the 1277 condemnations includes the following claim:

They say that these things are true according to philosophy but not according to the Catholic faith, as if there are two contrary truths and as if the truth of Sacred Scripture were contradicted by the truth in the sayings of the accursed pagans (*Chartularium universitatis parisiensis* (trans. Hyman, Walsh, and Williams, p. 541))

But not so: here Siger is clear simply that natural reason can mislead. Note too that the whole of *De anima intellectiva* is presented merely as an attempt to explicate Aristotelian philosophy (*De anima intellectiva*, prologue). Here we see the Arts Faculty's hermeneutic in practice.

Further reading

The most thorough account of Grosseteste is James McEvoy, *The Philosophy of Robert Grosseteste*, second edition (Oxford: Clarendon Press, 1982). The best account of William of Auvergne is in Ernest A. Moody, *Studies in Medieval Philosophy, Science, and Logic: Collected Papers 1933–1969* (Berkeley, CA: University of Los Angeles Press, 1975), pp. 1–109. There is precious little on Alexander of Hales: for his metaphysics, see Walter H. Principe, *Alexander of Hales' Theology of the Hypostatic Union* (Toronto: Pontifical Institute of Mediaeval Studies, 1967). On Albert, the best monograph is in French, Alain de Libera, *Métaphysique et noétique: Albert le Grand, Problèmes et controverses* (Paris: Vrin, 2005); see also *A Companion to Albert the Great*, ed. Irven Resnick (Leiden: Brill, 2013). There is no worthwhile book-length study of Bonaventure's philosophy; for an introduction to his thought in general, see Christopher M. Cullen, *Bonaventure*, Great Medieval Thinkers (New York: Oxford University Press, 2006). For Siger of Brabant, the defining account is still Fernand van Steenberghen, *Maître Siger de Brabant* (Louvain: Publications Universitaires, 1977).

Notes

1   I think that much the same could be said of many other early thirteenth-century theologians. A good example is William of Auxerre (*c.* 1150–1231), author of a significant early *Summa* of theology, the *Summa aurea.* William's metaphysics draws heavily on Boethius; when he diverges – for example, in his frequent analysis of metaphysical issues in terms of *esse* – he largely seems to draw on Gilbert and other twelfth-century thinkers influenced by the Platonic tradition, such as they knew it. For an excellent summary of William's metaphysics, see Walter H. Principe, *William of Auxerre's Theology of the Hypostatic Union* (Toronto: Pontifical Institute of Mediaeval Studies, 1963); at pp. 175–6, n. 84 Principe makes suggestions about the background to William's thought.

2   For this account of Albert, I rely on Risto Saarinen, *Weakness of the Will in Medieval Thought from Augustine to Buridan* (Leiden, New York and Cologne: Brill, 1994), pp. 94–118.

CHAPTER 4

Thomas Aquinas (c. 1225–74)

Clearly, Thomas Aquinas is the most well-known of the medieval philosophers, and, given this fact, it is tempting to view the history of thirteenth-century philosophy in a way that sees Aquinas as the towering genius of the era, the person against whom other, later, thinkers defined their positions, and the most influential philosopher of his age. This, indeed, is just how he was viewed in much twentieth-century historiography. But it is not how things looked to his contemporaries. Quite the contrary: Aquinas was one of a large number of teachers of theology, and (outside Aquinas's own Dominican order) his works received no more attention than those of many of his contemporaries: he was not *primus*; he was not even *primus inter pares*. Scotus, for example, is far more interested in Henry of Ghent than he is in Aquinas, and of those thinkers, such as Aquinas, who are in some sense more recognizably Aristotelian than Henry, Giles of Rome and Godfrey of Fontaines feature far more strongly in Scotus's sights than does Aquinas. The situation was a bit different in the Dominican order: from an early date, the Dominicans issued a series of directives that by 1309 (at a meeting of the Dominican General Chapter in Saragossa) made the teaching of Aquinas's doctrine compulsory for all members of the order, and in 1313 the General Chapter at Metz made Aquinas's view the order's 'common opinion'. And, of course, this kind of directive does not exist other than in cases of real danger: presumably in this case the highly critical stance taken by the young and brilliant Dominican Durand of St Pourçain (*c.* 1270/5–1334), to whom I return in Chapter 8. At any rate, within his own order Aquinas achieved the kind of position that some twentieth-century historians of Catholic philosophy ascribed to him. But we go wrong if we generalize from that to elevate Aquinas above his peers in any way other than this.

That said, Aquinas's reputation as a philosopher is solidly deserved. Among other things, he did more than any other single author to attempt to understand Aristotle and show just how fruitful the engagement of Aristotelian philosophy and Christian theology could be. It is fashionable today to emphasize Platonic elements in Aquinas's thought, partly as a response to the stress placed on Aquinas's Aristotelianism in the first two-thirds of the twentieth century. But this modern emphasis on Aquinas's Platonism misses what is really distinctive about Aquinas within his own context. Platonic ideas were commonplace throughout the Middle Ages, and it would be astonishing if such ideas were not to be found in a theologian as capable as Aquinas (though it is worth noting that Aquinas is less receptive to ideas from the twelfth century than any of the other great thirteenth-century thinkers is). But what is genuinely remarkable is the extent – far greater than in any of his predecessors, and in most of his successors – to which Aquinas assimilates Aristotelian material into his thinking. Part of my aim in this chapter is to describe this assimilation, and show how it is modified by other influences too, notably Avicenna. And like Albert – and unlike any other of his contemporaries – Aquinas commented on almost all the major Aristotelian works, and several of the minor works too. And all the while, he was persistently involved in pastoral and academic duties: he was Regent Master in theology twice at Paris, and in between worked at the Dominican *studia* in Orvieto and Rome, and finally at Naples (close to his birthplace, and to the family that wanted him to become abbot of the wealthy Benedictine centre, Monte Cassino, not an impoverished but intellectually learned Dominican).

One of the first works that Aquinas completed, probably in the years 1252–6, is also one of his most important philosophical treatises: *De ente et essentia* (*On Being and Essence*). Aquinas here works out his own distinctive theory on universals, and it is one that retained its influence in subsequent debates (we have seen already how Albert the Great reacted to it; Ockham, some sixty years later, treats it, or something like it, as one of a sequence of four different views on universals – though admittedly his source might be not Aquinas himself but one of his early-fourteenth-century Dominican followers, Hervaeus Natalis (*c.* 1250/60–1323). The text is of great philosophical interest, in the sense that it shows how Aquinas weds Aristotelian accounts of matter, form, and individuation, to the Avicennian account of universals and essences. In the process the argument develops one of Aquinas's most distinctive philosophical positions – the real distinction and composition between essence and existence in an individual substance. As Aquinas sees it, we can consider an Avicennian nature or essence in two ways: absolutely, and 'as it exists in this or that'. The first of these comprises simply the definitional properties of the nature (e.g. *rational animal* in the case of human being), not including the conditions under which such a nature exists as or in one or more particular things. The second way includes such conditions, and is itself divided into two: really existing in one or more singular things, and existing in the soul. In the first of these (existing in one or more singular things), the essence 'has multiple existences' – it exists as many singulars. In the second, it is simply a universal concept (*De ente*, c. 3). Furthermore, with the exception of God, each singular thing is contingent, and thus is such that the defining properties of its essence do not include existence: we can think of such-and-such a kind of thing, as Aquinas reasons, while remaining in ignorance as to whether or not there *is* such-and-such a kind of thing. Hence each such singular is a composite of essence and existence.

It might be thought that the inference from contingency to composition is a bit quick: perhaps an essence's not including existence should lead us merely to posit a *rational* distinction between essence and existence, such that an essence can be *thought of* in abstraction from existence, without this requiring that a particular thing has two distinct constituents, as it were (its essence and its existence). But Aquinas buttresses his argument by considering the opposite case – that of a necessary existent. A necessary existent is such that its essence includes existence: in this sense (at the very least) a necessary existent is non-composite. And Aquinas takes this as equivalent to the claim that a necessary existent, a being whose essence includes existence, is pure actuality – is just its existence. So to secure contingency we need the complement of this non-composition: that is to say, composition of essence and existence, potency and actuality (*De ente*, c. 4; Aquinas repeats the argument on many occasions, most notably at *Summa theologiae* I, q. 3, a. 4).

Now, setting aside this claim about essence and existence, one important thing to take away from chapter 3 of *De ente* is that the nature considered absolutely does not include any kind of being. There is an odd sense in which it is a non-being (not, according to Aquinas, that it *excludes* being; but it does not in itself include it). This makes Aquinas's view on common natures and universals look like a kind of nominalism: common natures lack being, and universals are just concepts. This is precisely the view taken by Ockham later on. But, again, it would not be quite right as a reading of Aquinas: the nature – even the nature in itself – is supposed to do some kind of explanatory work. In particular, it is supposed to explain kind-membership: a nature F existing in an individual x is what makes predications of the form 'x is F' true ('The nature considered absolutely is what is predicated of all individuals': *De ente*, c. 3). This kind of explanatory claim is not open to genuine nominalists – so to the extent that Aquinas makes such a claim, he intends to distance himself from nominalism.

Running in tandem with this material on the nature of essence, and its relation to existence, is an extensive account of individuation. Clearly, as laid out thus far, individuals (and only individuals) actually exist. But while this makes existence a feature of individuals, it does not of itself make existence the *explanation* for individuation. In fact, Aquinas locates the explanation for individuation elsewhere. Basically, he adopts the standard Aristotelian view that what distinguishes individuals of the same kind from each other is their being constituted by different chunks of matter: what Aquinas calls 'designated matter', matter considered 'under determinate dimensions'. In fact, he conceives of individuation as something like a designation or determination of an essence, much as a species (such as *human being*) is some kind of designation or determination of a genus (in this case, *animal*). But what explains the relevant determination in the case of individuation is matter with determinate dimensions, splitting individuals of the same kind off from each other, as it were (*De ente*, c. 2). As Aquinas quickly notes, this account of individuation has no application in the case of immaterial substances (angels, God): since they lack matter, the only remaining explanation for their individuation is their belonging simply to different kinds or species: hence Aquinas's view that there can be no more than one angel of a given kind (*De ente*, c. 4) – something that fell foul of the 1277 condemnation.

If we were to find one philosophical claim that is the mark of the integration of Aristotelianism into a medieval philosophy, it might be the acceptance of the notion of form as having some general explanatory role across a variety of different domains. This might seem like a hopelessly vague claim, since all medieval philosophers use the notion of form, and they could have derived it from any number of sources known prior to the recovery of Aristotle. But a lot depends on how the notion of form is understood. We can begin to see something of this if we look at the notion with which that of form is supposed to contrast: namely, matter. It seems to me that one key innovation to come in with the recovery of Aristotle was a notion of matter as pure potency: of itself, it has no actuality, no determinate features, as it were: as Christopher Martin has nicely put it, 'there is not anything […] which [matter] is all the time' (Martin, 1988, p. 65). Just as substances can undergo accidental change, matter – prime matter, as it was known – can undergo substantial change, with literally no real features in common between the two states. The correlate of prime matter is substantial form: the features or structuring that result in a substance of a given kind. Here is the crucial bit: neither matter nor form, on this view, count as things *in their own right*, or even *things* at all: there is no sense in which they are concrete objects or existents, or concrete constituents that can be (as it were) set out alongside each other. Matter is just potency, and form is actuality – the explanation for structure. It is the composite substance – composite of prime matter and substantial form – that actually exists:

> Existence belongs properly to subsistents, whether simple, like separated substances, or composite, like material substances. Existence (*esse*) properly pertains to things that have existence – that is, to the thing that subsists in its existence. Forms and accidents, and other such-like, are not said to be beings as though they exist, but because something exists by them: as whiteness is said to be a being because by it a subject is white. So, according to the Philosopher, an accident is more properly said to be of-a-being (*entis*) than a being (*ens*). (*Summa theologiae* I, q. 45, a. 4 c)[1]

The simple or separated substances that Aquinas talks about are things like God and angels (and, in some sense, the human soul, to which I return in a moment). In relation to material substances, Aquinas makes it quite plain here that the things that exist are the substances, not their matter, substantial form, or accidents. Forms and accidents are that *in virtue of which* something is such-and-such (whiteness is that in virtue of which something is white).

And prime matter is the pure potency actualized in different substantial kinds.

The notion that matter is pure potency is very plausibly thought of as a distinctively Aristotelian claim. The situation is a little complex, because, although Aristotle talks of prime matter (*prōtē hylē*), he does not always use this term in the technical sense to refer to what is purely potential. If Aristotle himself rejected the notion of pure potency, he did so because he thought that the basic material constituents of the world are the *elements* (earth, water, air, fire) – and this, I think, was not accepted by any of the philosophers of the High Middle Ages. In fact, it seems to me that, if there is to be an account in Aristotle of prime matter as pure potency, we need to look elsewhere than in the occurrence of these technical terms to find it. It seemed that way to Aquinas, too.[2] His most important discussions of prime matter in the Aristotelian context occur in places where Aristotle is describing the nature of change, and doing so in a way that suggests precisely the pure-potency thesis. The most notable Aristotelian discussions can be found in *De generatione* I, c. 3, and II, c. 1. Aquinas never commented on the second book of *De generatione*. But he did so on book I. What Aristotle says in book I is not wholly clear, and perhaps the most plausible reading of chapter 3 is as a series of aporias – questions which remain unanswered. But Aquinas not unreasonably mentions the purely potential commenting on the following passage:

> Or it [viz. matter] is in some way the same, and in some way different. For that which is the subject [of contraries], whatever kind of being it is, is the same, but its existence is not the same. (*De generatione* I, c. 3 (319b2–3))

Aquinas remarks:

> He [Aristotle] adds that the matter of those things that are changed into each other is in some way the same, and in some way different. It is the same in subject – and this is what he means when he says that that which is subjected [to the change] is the same, in whatever sense it is a being (for it is not a being actually, but potentially). But it is not the same in existence (*esse*) or essence (*ratio*), for it has a different essence and a different existence as it exists under diverse forms,

and even insofar as it ordered to diverse forms. (*In libros de generatione et corruptione expositio*, I, lect. 9, n. 72)

Here we have the idea of something that is potentially such-and-such, and whose entire actual character is determined by the identity of the forms that inhere in it.

Aristotle is perhaps clearer at a passage in book I of the *Physics*, though again without using the term 'prime matter':

> The underlying nature (*natura subiecta*; *hypokeimenē physis*) is known according to analogy. For just as bronze is to a statue, or wood to a bed, or matter and the formless, before they receive form, are to anything which has form, so this [viz. the underlying nature] is related to substance, to the this or to the what is. (*Physics* I, c. 7 (191a8–12))

Here, Aquinas sees a clear reference to prime matter:

> He [Aristotle] says that the nature which is primarily subject to mutation, that is, prime matter, cannot be known through itself, since anything that is known is known through its form, and prime matter is considered as underlying every form. [...] Since therefore we see that that which is air sometimes becomes water, it is necessary to say that something existing under the form of air is sometimes under the form of water, and thus that is something beyond the form of water and beyond the form of air. [...] Therefore, what is related to these natural substances in the way that [...] any material and formless thing to form, we call prime matter. (*In octo libros physicorum expositio* I, lect. 13, n. 118)[3]

So Aquinas certainly takes Aristotle to accept the existence of prime matter as pure potency, and makes the notion central to his distinctive kind of hylomorphism. The most attentive and enthusiastic readers of Aristotle did likewise. But, as we shall see, many of Aquinas's opponents took a rather different view: Aristotelian matter underlies even the elements, but is not pure potency. For them, the question is not whether or not something underlies the elements, but just what the nature of that underlying subject must be (pure potency or not pure potency). For what it is worth, my view is that Aquinas's defence of pure potency, and his identification of Aristotle as the source of that theory, represents an attempt to integrate what he and others believed to be a very refined variety of Aristotelianism into the medieval world view – an attempt that many of Aquinas's contemporaries and successors rejected.

I said above that form, as the correlate of prime matter, is to be thought of as actuality. As Aquinas thinks of it, a substantial form actualizes matter's potency to exist as a substance of such-and-such a kind: 'Existence (*esse*) pertains of itself to form; so matter acquires actual existence (*esse in actu*) insofar as it acquires form' (*Summa theologiae* I, q. 75, a. 6). Given that Aquinas conceives of prime matter as pure potency, it might seem to follow that substantial form is pure actuality. But not so, according to Aquinas. After all, as we just saw, Aquinas holds that only a being whose essence is its existence is pure actuality – that is to say, only a necessary being is pure actuality. And those substantial forms that actualize the potency of prime matter are not like this. There are degrees of actuality, and substantial forms are not completely actual – they have some 'blending of potency (*permixtionem potentiae*)' in them (*De ente*, c. 4). Of course, it is one thing to claim that forms are not purely actual *beings*, and quite another to claim that forms are not pure actuality *tout court*; after all, on the account just sketched, substantial forms, those items that actualize matter's potency, are not *beings* at all, and *a fortiori* not purely actual beings. The argument, again, can be traced reasonably clearly in *De ente*. If there were no composition of essence (i.e. matter + substantial form) and existence in material substances, then such substances would be necessary existents. If forms were pure actualities, I assume, there would be no composition of essence and existence in material substances; entailing, absurdly, that they were necessary existents.

Now, on this conception of matter and form, it seems to follow reasonably straightforwardly that there can be no more than one substantial form in any substance of a given kind. The basic idea is very simple: once there is a form in matter, once there is an actualized chunk of matter, there is a substance. As Aquinas puts it,

> Nothing is simply speaking one thing other than through one form, through which the thing has existence (*esse*). For a thing is a being, and one, in virtue of one and the same feature. For this reason, those things that possess more than

one form (*denominantur a diversis formis*) are not one thing simply speaking, like a white man. (*Summa theologiae* I, q. 76, a. 3)

There are no chunks that are not kinds of thing, no units of matter and accident. And there are no complete substances that have (complete) substances as proper parts. After all, if there were such, then it would be hard to know what might explain the unity of a complete substance – hence the claim that unity of substance follows from unity of form, as Aquinas maintains. I label the thesis that there is no more than one substantial form in any substance the 'unicity thesis'; in Chapter 6 I consider the most sophisticated attempt to deal with the issue of substantial unity, given the assumption that the unicity thesis is false, and thus that there are complete substances that have other such substances as proper parts. (And I sketch too some of the reasons why philosophers were motivated to reject the unicity thesis – fundamentally to do with the apparent fact that the unicity thesis cannot explain the identity of living and dead bodies.) In line with this, Aquinas holds that the human soul is the substantial form of a human body – as I discussed in Chapter 3 above.

I just noted an important passage in which Aquinas denies that prime matter and substantial forms actually exist. The text makes just the same point about accidents, too: they are not existents, but, in the old tag, *in-existents*. This view, of course, makes very problematic one well-known medieval theological doctrine: transubstantiation. According to this doctrine, the bread and wine in the Eucharist are somehow 'converted' into the body and blood of Christ, such that merely the *accidents* of the bread and wine remain present. These accidents are supposed to be somehow 'free-floating'. In the usual run of things, accidents explain the truths of certain non-essential predications: the inherence of whiteness in a loaf of bread, for example, is what makes it the case that 'this loaf of bread is white' is true. Indeed, the inherence of the whiteness is supposed to the bread's *being white* (its *esse album*), and to this extent accidents have a curious sort of existence (*esse*): the kind of existence that explains a substance's being such-and-such. Of course, the only thing that there *is* on this view is the substance. Aquinas attempts to integrate this view into the doctrine of transubstantiation by the following two, not wholly consistent, strategies. First:

> Accidents of this kind [i.e. separated accidents] acquired individual *esse* in the substance of the bread and wine. But when this [substance of the bread and wine] is converted into the body and blood of Christ, the accidents remain, by divine power, in the individuated *esse* which they had previously. (*Summa theologiae* III, q. 77, a. 1 ad 3)

Secondly:

> While the substance of the bread and wine remained, accidents of this kind did not have *esse*, just as other accidents do not. Rather, their substance had *esse* through them, just as snow is white through whiteness. But after the consecration, the accidents that remain have *esse*. So they are composite of *esse* and *quod est*, as was said [...] about angels. (*Summa theologiae* III, q. 77, a. 1 ad 4)

In the first of these passages, Aquinas makes much the same point about accidents in standard cases as that which I just ascribed to him. Accidents always have their own *esse*. They get this *esse* 'in the substance of the bread and wine', which, I take it, is a way of saying that they somehow share in the existence of the substance (such that we might think of the whole as a composite of substance-essence and substance-existence, along with accident-essence and (the self-same) substance-existence). The move here seems to involve two distinct and questionable steps: first, that accidents do in fact have some kind of existence – the substance's existence, the kind of existence in virtue of which they are or can be independently existing entities – and secondly that they can retain this existence even in the absence of the substance. Note that both of these strategies tend to reify accidents in a way that Aquinas's 'official' or standard view does not allow (since on that view the only things there are are substances).

In the second of the two passages, Aquinas tries a rather different approach. Whiteness explains the snow's being white: it is that through or by which (*quo*) snow is white. To do such, accidents must be *abstracta* (the referents of abstract nouns such as 'whiteness'), and, Aquinas claims, *abstracta* 'do not have *esse*'. This is the basic Aristotelian line, expressed in terms of Aquinas's distinctive Avicennian philosophy of essence and existence. But Aquinas claims that, when separated, the accidents have *esse* of their own: they become composites of *quod est* and *esse*, which is another way of saying that they become concrete items (*quod est*, not *quo est*). The slippery claim here, it seems to me, is that we have to accept the possibility of something abstract somehow becoming something concrete.

On the whole issue, I take it, Aristotelian philosophy puts a severe strain on Christian theology – though since committed Aristotelians like Aquinas attempt to fudge the issue, and since the issue does not crop up in discussions in the Arts Faculty, the strain does not show up in the 1277 condemnations (since, I suppose the Bishop of Paris and the Parisian theologians at that time restricted themselves to issues that, as they suspected, thinkers were not prepared to fudge).

Accidents are, of course, forms, and as I indicated above, on the face of it one of the most powerful philosophical weapons in the Aristotelian conceptual armoury is the notion of *form*. Aristotle presses the notion into service to account for various perceptual and cognitive states, and (on some readings) for the nature of the human soul too, as I just indicated in the case of Aquinas. Forms are thought of as items *received* by subjects: substantial form is received by matter, and accidental form by substance. A key Aristotelian insight is that form can play different kinds of explanatory role depending on the nature of the item that receives it. I mentioned this in my discussion of Roger Bacon in Chapter 3 above. As Aquinas understands it, following Aristotle (see e.g. Aristotle, *De anima* II, c. 5 (418a3–4)), natural changes are those in which a form is received such that the recipient is made to be an instance of the relevant kind: reception of (say) blueness such that the recipient is made to be blue. But the same form received in the organ of sight makes someone *see* blue, and the same form again received in an immaterial soul makes someone *think* of blueness (see e.g. *De anima* III, c. 8 (431a20–8)). (These latter kinds of reception are often labelled 'immaterial' or 'spiritual', and the received form is often labelled a 'species'.) And – as the medievals thought of it, using insights from Alhazen – the same form received in the medium between an object and a sensor (the so-called '*species in medio*') conveys the relevant informational content from object to sensor.

Aquinas provides perhaps the fullest synthesis of this way of thinking of things. For example,

We sense or cognize intellectually as a result of our intellect
or sense being informed by a sensible or intelligible species.
(*Summa theologiae* I, q. 14, a. 2 c)

Aquinas talks about this immaterial kind of existence in most detail
when discussing sensation, and he contrasts it with natural existence:

There are two kinds of alteration: one natural, and the other
spiritual. The natural one obtains in so far as the form of
the changer is received according to its natural being in the
thing changed; the spiritual one in so far as the form of the
changer is received according to spiritual being in the thing
changed: as the form of colour in the pupil, which is not made
to be coloured by the reception. But for the operation of the
sense, there is required a spiritual alteration, through which
the form of the sensible object is brought about in the sense;
otherwise, if a natural change alone sufficed from sensation,
all natural bodies would sense when they are altered. (*Summa
theologiae* I, q. 78, a. 3 c)

In the case of sensation the spiritual change goes along with a real
one – the physical processes grounding sensation, to which sensation
nevertheless cannot be reduced:

Sensing, and the consequent operations of the sensory soul,
manifestly occur along with some alteration of the body – as,
in the case of seeing, the pupil is altered through the species
of a colour, and the same is evident for the other [senses].
(*Summa theologiae* I, q. 75, a. 2 c; in Pasnau, 1997b, p. 43)

Here, the 'alteration of the body' – clearly a natural or real change –
need not, I take it, be the natural reception of the form of the sensed
object (since the pupil does not become the colour of the object of
sight, for example); though it could be (since the hand really becomes
hot when a hot thing is touched). But clearly it is in every case some
kind of real reception of some kind of form, accompanying the
spiritual reception.

Intellectual cognition is different: it belongs to the immaterial
soul, and there is no corresponding physical process that it supervenes
on. But whereas, in sensation, the inherence of a species is, other

things being equal, sufficient for the sensation, the intellectual case is different. Aquinas supposes that intelligible species can exist in two states, as it were: dispositionally and actually, and occurrent cognition, actually consciously cognizing, is identified as the inherence of an *actualized* species in the relevant intellect. This is what Aquinas says, for example, about occurrent intellectual cognition:

> An intelligible species is sometimes in the intellect [...] according to the final completion of the act: and then [the intellect] actually understands. Sometimes it exists in a way intermediate between potency and act, and then the intellect is said to be in habit. And in this manner the intellect conserves species, even when it does not actually understand. (*Summa theologiae* I, q. 79, a. 6 ad 3)

Aquinas supposes that intellect itself actualizes the species:

> The intellect, formed by a species of the thing, by understanding forms in itself an intention of the thing understood, which is the idea (*ratio*) of the thing, signified by a definition. (*Summa contra gentiles* I, c. 53, n. 443)

Furthermore, still focusing on the generality of the notion of form, we find that the medievals use this notion to give an account of the existence of immaterial substances, all of which count as forms too. God, for example, is the simplest of all forms, and, in accordance with his general metaphysics, Aquinas holds that God lacks any kind of composition of essence and existence, as we saw. But Aquinas goes much further than this: God lacks any kind of composition whatsoever. God, for example, is the same as his various attributes (wisdom, goodness, etc.), and they are the same as each other. There is nothing unusual about this view: it comes straight from claims that Augustine makes, and I think represents the standard medieval view. As Aquinas sees it, this claim has striking repercussions on the question of religious language: how we talk about God. When we talk about God, our words pick out the 'one thing' which is God, and they do so by means of creaturely concepts that represent this one thing. These concepts, although they equally represent the one simple God, are distinct from each other, and the words that we use are thus non-synonymous, despite the non-complexity of the thing they pick out. But the creaturely concepts properly represent 'diverse perfections', so, given that they really do represent these perfections, the terms signifying them are not simply equivocal (*Summa theologiae* I, q. 13, a. 5 c): creaturely wisdom is really distinct from creaturely goodness (one can be good without being wise, and *vice versa*) (*Summa theologiae* I, q. 13, a. 4 c). So these concepts represent God in a very different way from that in which they represent creatures, and there is a corresponding difference in the meanings of the terms that we use in the two cases, divine and human: the words have different 'modes of signifying' (*Summa theologiae* I, q. 13, a. 3 c), and thus do not have the same sense in the two cases – they are not univocal (*Summa theologiae* I, q. 13, a. 5 c). Hence, Aquinas reasons, the words that we use of God and creatures are related 'by analogy'. The basic idea is that we know that God has these various perfections, and thus that we can truly predicate appropriate terms of him. And we know this on the basis of a general, Platonically-inspired, principle, that causes contain in a more perfect way the perfections of their effects, and thus that God contains in a more perfect way the perfection of his creatures:

> Whatever is said of God and creatures is said in accordance with some order of the creature to God, as to its principle and cause, in which all the perfections of things pre-exist in a more excellent way. (*Summa theologiae* I, q. 13, a. 5 c)

This gives us another instance of significant Aristotelian influence in Aquinas, since Aquinas's analogy – taking a focal sense of a word and making other uses parasitic on that one – is distinctively Aristotelian, and represents an innovation in thirteenth-century theology (for Aristotle, see e.g. *Metaphysics* Γ, c. 2 (1003a34–b6)). Still, to return to Aquinas's theory, because these perfections exist in God 'in a more excellent way', we do not know just what they are in the divine case; hence our creaturely concepts 'are deficient in representing him' (*Summa theologiae* I, q. 13, a. 2 c). But of course we know what grounds our legitimate analogical predications, and that is the resemblance relation that obtains universally between causes and effects. Aquinas holds that his position allows us to reason in theology while avoiding the 'fallacy of equivocation': drawing unsound inferences on the basis of semantic ambiguity (*Summa theologiae* I, q. 13, a. 5 c). It is not clear to me that he succeeds in this, and I return to the whole issue when considering Scotus's attempt to refute a position somewhat akin to Aquinas's.

One of the components of Aquinas's philosophy that is most well known today is his attempt to prove God's existence: particularly, the famous 'five ways' of proving God's existence found at the beginning of the *Summa theologiae*: the argument from motion or accidental change; the argument from efficient causation; the argument from necessity and possibility; the argument from degrees of perfection; and the teleological argument from finality. Of these, Aquinas claims that the first is the 'most manifest': presumably because, whatever we might say about the phenomenon of causation (bringing things into existence), it is evident that existent things change.

Nevertheless, the argument from efficient causation sets out the general pattern of Aquinas's arguments most clearly. Aquinas starts from a simple empirical observation: there are cause-effect relations, and these can exist in (transitive) *sequences*: x causes y to cause z. Such sequences, the argument goes, cannot extend back infinitely. Hence, each such sequence has a beginning: something that is itself uncaused, and that sets the sequence in train. Aquinas concludes with another observation, this time about the intellectual habits of his contemporaries: it is customary to label the first cause 'God' (*Summa theologiae* I, q. 2, a. 3 c). This was doubtless true; but in any case, Aquinas immediately goes on to show that the identification is correct, by showing that, whatever the first cause is, it has attributes that are uniquely associated with God. (Thus, his first step is to show that any such being must be wholly simple: (*Summa theologiae* I, q. 3): I have talked about this above.)

Clearly, the crucial step in the argument is the attempt to show that an infinite regress is impossible. As Aquinas presents the argument, this step fails. The reason he offers against the possibility of an infinite regress is this:

> In efficient causes it is not possible to go on to infinity, because in all efficient causes following in order, the first is the cause of the intermediate cause. (*Summa theologiae* I, q. 2, a. 3 c)

We know that an infinite sequence is impossible, because any sequence of efficient causes requires a first cause. Aquinas then uses the impossibility of an infinite regress to support his conclusion:

If in efficient causes it is possible to go on to infinity, there
will be no first efficient cause; neither will there be an ultimate
effect, nor any intermediate efficient causes; all of which is
plainly false. Therefore it is necessary to admit a first efficient
cause. (*Summa theologiae* I, q. 2, a. 3 c)

The gist of the first sentence is that an infinite regress is impossible;
from which, in the second, Aquinas infers that there must be a first
efficient cause. But it is precisely *this* claim – that there must be a
first efficient cause – that is the basis for Aquinas's conclusion that
an infinite regress is impossible. The argument, at least as presented,
is merely question-begging.

Setting all of this aside, perhaps Aquinas's single greatest
achievement in fact lies in the areas of moral philosophy and
psychology. In particular, Aquinas adapts an Aristotelian account
of the virtues into a remarkably sophisticated theory of natural
law – and in doing so fundamentally changes the character of the
Aristotelian theory. It is standard today to identify three basic ethical
theories: consequentialist (the goodness of an action is determined
by the goodness of its outcomes); deontological (the goodness of an
action is determined by its conformity to certain moral norms or
rules); and virtue-based (the goodness of an action is determined by
its being what a virtuous person, a person of good character, would
do – standardly called 'virtue ethics' in the literature). Aquinas says
things that, at first blush, seem compatible with all three of these
theories. For example, he seems very ready to provide cases in which
general rules should not be followed on the grounds that doing so
would produce harmful consequences:

It is right and true for everyone that they should act in
accordance with reason. And from this principle it follows as
a proper conclusion that things entrusted to another should
be returned. And this is indeed true for the most part (*ut in
pluribus*). But it can happen in some case that it would be
harmful, and consequently irrational, if what was entrusted
were returned: for example, if someone required it for fighting
against one's country. (*Summa theologiae* I-II, q. 94, a. 4 c)

But he is equally clear that there are certain norms that are necessary
and immutable:

If certain precepts were given which contained the conservation of the common good, or the very order of justice and virtue, these precepts contain the intention of the legislator, and are therefore indispensable. [...] The precepts of the Decalogue contain the intention of the legislator, namely, God. [...] Therefore the precepts of the Decalogue are utterly indispensable. (*Summa theologiae* I-II, q. 100, a. 8 c)

And, finally, he spends a considerable time – the whole of the massive *secunda secundae* of the *Summa theologiae*, 189 questions in all, subdivided into numerous articles (sub-questions) – discussing virtues and vices; and a good quarter of the *prima secundae* (qq. 22–48) discussing the emotions that the virtues regulate. As commentators have noted, Aquinas thus devotes *much* more space to a discussion of the virtues than he does to deontology. And of all of his achievements, this is surely the most astonishing of all, as an example both of comprehensive moral analysis and of remarkable phenomenological perspicuity.

Of course, the three theories are not on the face of it compatible with each other. And no one seriously supposes that Aquinas is a consequentialist (I will explain in a moment how to understand the kind of passage that I just cited in favour of consequentialism). But there is significant debate about the remaining two theories: is Aquinas a deontologist or a virtue ethicist? I believe that he is some version of the former. Basically, according to Aquinas, what makes an action good (or bad) is its conformity (or otherwise) with certain immutable or necessary moral norms, as the discussion of the Decalogue, just quoted, suggests. Virtues, for Aquinas, are what dispose human beings to act in accordance with those norms. While the discussion of the Decalogue gives a good account of Aquinas's normative ethical theory, we would be misled if we thought that what grounds these norms is a divine command or commands. Rather, Aquinas's deontology is of a *naturalist* kind. As we saw in the Introduction, theories of natural law can be found in the Stoics. Aquinas builds on Stoic theories in a crucial way: he grounds the whole legal edifice on Aristotelian teleology. From an ontological point of view, natural human goals – goals belonging to human *nature*, as it were – ground the norms; and, from an epistemological point of view, we can know the norms merely by correct analysis of, and inference from, natural human goals.

On the issue of ontological grounding, Aquinas argues straight-forwardly:

> Every agent acts for the sake of a goal, which has the character of the good. Therefore, the first principle of practical reason is what is founded on the nature of the good, which is: the good is what all desire. This, therefore, is the first principle of [natural] law, that the good is to be done and pursued, and evil to be avoided. And on this [principle] are founded all of the other precepts of the law of nature, namely, that all those things that practical reason naturally apprehends as human goods, belong to natural law as things to be done, or avoided. (*Summa theologiae* I-II, q. 94, a. 2 c)

And in this article Aquinas follows this line of argumentation very closely, regimenting particular human goals (individual life, family life, social life) to particular sets of precepts.

Epistemologically, Aquinas seems to think both that many of these goals are obvious, and that the relation of specific precepts to the particular goals is obvious too; and that, in cases where the relations are not obvious, they are still evident to those who consider the matter carefully:

> There are some things connected with human actions that are so evident that they can be approved or disapproved immediately, with minimal reflection, from common first principles. There are some things for judging which much consideration of diverse circumstances is required, and this diligent consideration can be done not by everyone but by the wise: just as the consideration of the particular conclusions of a science do not pertain to everyone but merely to philosophers. (*Summa theologiae* I-II, a. 100, a. 1 c)

What should we make of Aquinas's claim that the natural law requires a legislator? On the one hand, Aquinas is clear that God is the legislator in natural law. But, on the other, he does not understand this to mean that the goodness of the precepts or norms of natural law derives from its being so legislated. It is rather hard to keep together all the things he says on the matter, but it looks as though the law is natural in the sense that it is naturally known to us, and the goodness of the actions it prescribes (and badness of the actions it proscribes) likewise, without any kind of revelation (since its goodness is grounded in human teleology, and this is known to us). But its *binding* or (better) *coercive* character derives from God's promulgation (which he does simply by giving us natural knowledge of its contents) (see *Summa theologiae* I-II, q. 90, a. 4 c and ad 1). In terms of the *content* of the law, this is empty, in the sense that God's giving human beings reason is a necessary consequence of his creating human beings: being rational is part of what it is to be human. We saw above evidence to show that the ontological grounding of natural law lies in human teleology. And when defending the goodness of the precepts of the Decalogue, Aquinas does not appeal to any kind of divine revelation to explain human knowledge of the content of the natural law. Rather, he proposes the following rather naturalistic syllogism:

> The judgments of human reason in relation to good behaviour are derived from natural law.
> The precepts of the Decalogue are in accordance with the judgments of human reason.
> Therefore the precepts of the Decalogue pertain to natural law. (See *Summa theologiae* I-II, q. 100, a. 1 c)

Aquinas is not claiming here that the judgments of human reason ground the Decalogue. But he is making an epistemological point that we can discern the rightness of the Decalogue by noting its conformity with our *prior* understanding of natural law.[4]

Above I drew attention to a passage in Aquinas that seems to admit of a consequentialist interpretation. This was, of course, something of a joke on my part, since there is no plausible reading of Aquinas's ethics that would make him a consequentialist. But what should we make of the discussion of the morality of loans and trust in the text I highlighted? As we have seen, Aquinas talks about certain norms that express 'the will of the legislator' – the preservation of the common good. He distinguishes between these – the first principles of natural law – and norms that are such that, 'if the letter of the law were observed, it would be contrary to the intention of the legislator' (*Summa theologiae* I-II, q. 100, a. 8 c). The Decalogue is all of the first kind (see *Summa theologiae* I-II, q. 100, a. 8). The second kind are those that hold *ut in pluribus* – for the most part – and Aquinas characterizes them as 'conclusions' that (in some sense) follow from the first principles – viz. those that do not admit of exceptions (*Summa theologiae* I-II, q. 94, a. 4 c). His example is returning what is owed: there are exceptions to this norm, in cases where we are impeded, through a clash of conflicting norms, from following it:

> The [principle that one should return what is owed] is found to fail the more we descend to particular cases: for example, if it were said that things deposited should be returned with such-and-such a guarantee, or in such-and-such a way: for as more particular conditions are added, the principle can fail in more ways, such that it may be not right to return, or not right not to return. (*Summa theologiae* I-II, q. 94, a. 4 c)

In no sense does Aquinas think that the rightness of the action is determined by its consequences. Some norms are inviolable; and others obtain only in the absence of any clash of norms.

What, finally, of the role of virtue in all this? I claimed above that, for Aquinas, virtues are what dispose human beings to act in accordance with the norms of natural law. Virtues are dispositions or inclinations: someone with such a disposition does not just happen to follow the relevant norms; she is independently *motivated* to follow these norms. Aquinas makes his point most clearly when discussing the virtue of prudence, the intellectual virtue that enables us to grasp what we should do in a given situation. As Aquinas puts it,

> In practical reason there pre-exist certain naturally known principles, and these are the goals of the moral virtues. [...] And in the practical reason some things exist as conclusions, and those things which are directed towards the goal, and which we derive from those goals, are of this kind. And prudence pertains to these, applying universal principles to the particular conclusions of practical matters. (*Summa theologiae* I-II, q. 47, a. 6 c)

Here, Aquinas straightforwardly identifies the goals of the moral virtues as the principles and conclusions of natural law. Norms expressed as conclusions from the first principles are, according to Aquinas in this passage, norms that pertain to the means to our final goal or goals; prudence is required to enable us to deliberate about these norms. More precisely, prudence is the virtue that allows us correctly to apply universal principles (viz. of natural law) to particular circumstances: to work out under which principles the relevant acts are to be subsumed. All of this is wholly compatible with Aquinas's views on natural law – indeed, it shows that he believes his account of the virtues to be dependent on his account of natural law. But it rather confirms the view that his ethics are basically deontological in thrust – the goal of the virtues, the thing that they help us to do, is follow the norms, the principles and conclusions, of natural law.

It might seem odd for someone with Aquinas's strongly Aristotelian inclinations to prefer deontology to virtue ethics. I have already indicated above one way in which Aquinas pushes his deontology in an Aristotelian direction: he grounds the norms of natural law on human teleology in a way that his Stoic predecessors did not. And, in any case, there is another very strong driving force in Aquinas's intellectual life that pushes towards deontology, and that is Christianity. The New Testament may have much to say about virtues (St Paul), and much to say about acting in an unspecified loving way (Jesus). But the Hebrew Bible – part of divine revelation, according to Christians – is fundamentally deontological, with its stress on moral and ritual rules, the former of which are encapsulated in its key theophany: Moses's reception of the Decalogue. Aquinas's discussion of natural law is part of a general discussion of law that has the Decalogue at its very heart.

Aquinas's account of the moral virtues itself highlights another aspect in which Aquinas follows Aristotle in a way that many of his contemporaries do not. As Aquinas sees it, the fundamental role of the moral virtues is to reintegrate the emotions, and Aquinas is explicit that some of the acquired moral virtues belong to the sensitive part of the soul, not to the rational will (*Summa theologiae* I-II, q. 56, a. 4). This means that the sensitive part of the soul is able to cooperate fully in rational, moral, human activity (*Summa theologiae* I-II, q. 59, a. 5 c): the rule of reason over the sense appetites is, as Aquinas puts it, following Aristotle, not despotic but *political* (*Summa theologiae* I-II, q. 58, a. 2 c). The contrast is with thinkers of a more voluntaristic stripe, who tend to place all moral virtues in the (rational) will (the classic example is Scotus, but we can find the view in Bonaventure and Henry of Ghent, too, among others: see e.g. Scotus, *Ordinatio* III, d. 33, q. un., nn. 44–5). The reason is that virtues are supposed to have a causal role in good choice, and thus should inhere in the faculty responsible for choice. Aquinas's view makes it clear how the emotions can be cooperative dispositions in good action; for the voluntarists, the emotions belonging to the sensitive appetite are simply tamed by the good inclination and virtues of the will.

A further way in which Aquinas decisively moves away from the Augustinianism of the twelfth century, and towards the new Aristotelianism, is in the domain of action theory – as my discussion of virtues and the emotions will have suggested already to the reader sensitive to these things. As I mentioned in Chapter 3, Aristotle holds that a dictate of practical reason – a judgment that such-and-such *ought* to be done – is sufficient for action provided there are no external blocks preventing the action (and, perhaps, provided that there is no intervening passion). As we saw earlier, Augustine rejects any such view: for him, there is a power to *choose* which has a function distinct from that of reason and intellect: namely, the *will*. Although Aquinas keeps the Augustinian terminology, his account of the will minimizes the role of the will in choice. For Aquinas, the will is basically the executive power, putting into action the dictates of practical reason. He treats human action as proceeding equally from intellect and will, using the analogy of matter (will) and form (intellect) constituting a substance (i.e., in the analogy, an action) (see e.g. *Summa theologiae* I-II, q. 13, a. 1 c). Reason or intellect is the form: it gives the action its *content*. But Aquinas does not quite hold that a dictate of practical reason is sufficient for execution. While the content of a given activity is fixed by reason and knowledge of the object of a proposed action, the will can somehow place a block on the action, for example by refocusing reason on some other object (by means of some mechanism that Aquinas does not specify: see e.g. *Summa theologiae* I-II, q. 10, a. 2 c). As Aquinas puts it, the specification of an action comes from its object; but its exercise (doing it rather than not) comes from the will.

And Aquinas's account avoids determinism in a further way too: contingency can enter in at the point of the *reason's* deliberation:

> Reason has a power to opposites in relation to contingent things, as is clear in dialectical syllogisms and rhetorical persuasions. But particular operations are contingent, and

therefore the judgment of reason is related to diverse things and is not determined to one. (*Summa theologiae* I, q. 83, a. 1 c)

The role that Aquinas allows to the will, small though it be, moves Aquinas slightly out of the Aristotelian ambit. But the basic contours look Aristotelian, and the strong bias in this direction is confirmed by Aquinas's treatment of the question of *akrasia*. For Augustinians, these cases are dealt with easily: the choice of a weak will is for what is known to be the lesser good. (I say 'easily', but, of course, the challenge for such views is showing how the choice is not simply irrational or arbitrary: I return to this in Chapter 6 below.) For Aquinas – much as for Aristotle – such cases are explained simply by intellectual error. The intellect, under the influence of emotion or passion, produces a dictate that such-and-such ought to be done even given a settled belief that the opposite is the case (that such-and-such ought not to be done) (*De malo* III, q. 9; *Summa theologiae* I-II, q. 77, a. 2). The settled belief, however, fails to be occurrent, and the opposite of that belief is the one that is assented to. And this, of course, is a case of intellectual or rational malfunction. Cases of weakness are cases of error: culpable error, admittedly, since the occurrent belief is contrary to a habitual intellectual disposition of the agent, and thus should not have been assented to – the agent had both the means and the ability not to assent (*Summa theologiae* I-II, q. 76, a. 3). As we shall see in the next chapter, this view of Aquinas's fell foul of the 1277 condemnation.

Further reading

There is a huge bibliography on Aquinas. For a general and wide-ranging introduction to his philosophy, see Robert Pasnau and Christopher Shields, *The Philosophy of Aquinas* (Boulder, CO: Westview, 2004). The most recent intellectual biography is Jean-Pierre Torrell, *Saint Thomas Aquinas. Volume 1. The Person and His Work* (Washington, DC: Catholic University of America, 1996).

Notes

1   See too e.g. *Summa theologiae* I, q. 6, a. 3 ad 3.
2   Among other places where Aristotle uses the phrase *prōtē hylē* are *Physics* II, c. 1 (193a29), *Metaphysics* Δ, c. 4 (1015a7–10), *Metaphysics*

Θ, c. 7 (1049a24–7). In each of these cases, Aquinas, probably rightly, does not take the passages to be about prime matter (see *In octo libros physicorum exposistio* II, lect. 2, n. 150; *In duodecim libros metaphysicorum Aristotelis expositio* V, lect. 5, n. 821; IX, lect. 6, n. 1841). At *Metaphysics* E, c. 4 (1044a23), the phrase crops up again, and Aquinas here assumes, without comment, that there is a genuine reference to prime matter (see *In duodecim libros metaphysicorum Aristotelis expositio* VIII, lect. 4, n. 1729 ('prime matter, of itself having no form')).

3   See too Aristotle, *Metaphysics* Z, c. 3 (1029a12–19), and Aquinas's commentary, *In duodecim libros metaphysicorum Aristotelis expositio* VII, lect. 2, n. 1283.

4   Aquinas goes on, in the same article, to deal with certain very specific exceptions – for example, the prohibition on graven images. But these exceptions do not affect my overall argument. What does on the face of it challenge this interpretation is a possible inconsistency in Aquinas's own presentation. Under force of Biblical authority, he has to explain God's command to Abraham to sacrifice Isaac. He argues that this command is not contrary to the Decalogue's prohibition on murder, since a killing commanded directly by God does not count as murder (see *Summa theologiae* I-II, q. 100, a. 8 ad 3). This is perhaps problematic for Aquinas's view, since it now looks as though God could command any action, provided that action is suitably described – or at least, that the descriptions of moral status of various actions would have to include an entirely *ad hoc* exclusion (e.g. 'unless commanded by God') which would push Aquinas strongly in the direction of a divine command metaethic; but in fact the very move is designed *not* to threaten the relationship between the Decalogue and natural law: murder is always wrong, but the killing of Isaac, given divine command, would not have been murder.

Part III

INNOVATION

CHAPTER 5

From 1277 to 1300

Aquinas, along with some of the thinkers I consider in this chapter, represents the most consistent attempts to integrate the insights of Aristotle into a Christian world view. But the debate quickly moved on, partly because the immense originality of the leading philosopher in the decades between Aquinas and Scotus – Henry of Ghent – forced philosophers to look at a whole range of issues in both metaphysics and action theory in a radically new way. (The condemnation of 1277 was more a sign of the dissatisfaction that philosophers felt with the integrative attempts of the Aristotelians than a cause of it: Henry, after all, was one of the theologians involved in drafting the relevant articles.) Aristotle, it was felt, certainly raised some interesting questions, but his answers did not really find common assent. In this chapter, I try to outline something of the huge variety of approaches in the decades after the condemnation, leading up to Duns Scotus, who is the topic of Chapter 6. We will see, I think, both change and continuity – and reference back to the twelfth century as much as to the work of the earlier thirteenth century.

Correctorium *literature*

One of the Thomist positions of broadly Aristotelian inspiration that most of his contemporaries rejected is his view that there cannot be more than one substantial form in any given substance. The view was formally condemned by Robert Kilwardby, the Archbishop of Canterbury, in 1277, a condemnation reiterated by his successor, John Pecham, in 1286 (*Chartularium universitatis parisiensis*, I, 559). Opponents marshalled a number of arguments against Aquinas's view. Here I will pick out one that has both philosophical and theological forms, and that seems to me very hard for unitarians such as Aquinas to refute.

The earliest systematic attempt to rebut the views of Aquinas can be found in the Franciscan William de la Mare's *Correctorium fratris Thomae*, written in 1279. William assembled and 'corrected' some 117 theologically and philosophically objectionable articles taken from the *Summa*. The Franciscans quickly adopted the work, and in 1282 a meeting of the General Chapter at Strasburg made the *Correctorium* its official stance on Aquinas's teaching and required that no copies of the *Summa* should be made without the *Correctorium* appended to it. One of William's worries about Aquinas's unicity thesis is that it offers no way of preserving the identity between a living and a dead body: my corpse is not my body, or the body that was mine (a. 31 (p. 130)).

Of course, Aquinas would concede this consequence, and simply hold that there is no such identity. But his view raises a very sharp theological problem, which is William's real concern. If there is no identity between a living body and a dead one, then Christ's body in the tomb is not his body. Aquinas, of course, does not accept the theological consequence. But his way of defending the post-mortem identity of Christ's body is, to say the least, rather *ad hoc*:

> The body of Christ dead and alive was simply speaking numerically the same. For something is said to be numerically the same simply speaking since it is the same in hypostasis (*supposito*). But the body of Christ, alive and dead, was the same in hypostasis, since it had, dead and alive, no other hypostasis than the hypostasis of the Word of God. (Aquinas, *Summa theologiae* III, q. 50, a. 5 c)

The idea is that in the case of Christ the identity of the body is fixed not by its relation to its form but by its relation to its person – that is, the second person of the Trinity. But this is a unique case: standardly, loss of form results in the generation of a substance of a different kind (here, at any rate, something that is only 'equivocally' a human body: Aquinas, *Summa theologiae* III, q. 50, a. 5 obj. 2, a standard Aristotelian view on the identity of dead bodies and detached body parts); the thought is that, uniquely in the case of Incarnation, there is a person with two natures, and that this somehow requires that the identity of the body (a component of the nature that it is merely contingent that the divine person have) is secured by the divine person (Aquinas, *Summa theologiae* III, q. 50, a. 5 ad 2), But this is *ad hoc*, since Aquinas makes no attempt to explain just how the mere appeal to the fact of the Incarnation is supposed to make a difference. He just asserts that it does.

Among Franciscans, the rather combative Pecham seems to have found this doctrine particularly offensive: he calls it 'worthless and empty (*frivola et inanis*)' (Pecham, *Quodlibet* IV, q. 11 (p. 198)), and 'foolish (*stultum*)' (*Quodlibet* IV, q. 11 (p. 199)). His main argument against it is that Aquinas's *ad hoc* principle about the identity of bodies in the Incarnation would lead to a rather counterintuitive result:

> Although the numerical unity of a nature follows from the unity of a hypostasis that is caused by the principles of that nature, it does not follow from the unity of a hypostasis of a different nature. For example, if Christ were to assume two different human natures in the identity of hypostasis, those human natures would not be one human nature. (Pecham, *Quodlibet* IV, q. 11 (p. 198))

Here, the thought is that identity of soul and body (the 'principles of a nature') does indeed depend on hypostasis in the case that the hypostasis is constituted by the nature; but there is no reason to accept the principle in a case in which this constitution relation does not obtain. The counterexample Pecham gives, however, does nothing much to strengthen his case, though it perhaps picks up on an ambiguity in Aquinas's account. The instance that Pecham has in mind is one in which the second person of the Trinity becomes incarnate in two distinct human natures. Aquinas elsewhere considers such a case, and concludes that we would say that there is one human being in two human natures. His reason is that, as a matter of linguistic fact concrete nouns (such as 'human being') pick out hypostases and their concrete parts, not natures (Aquinas, *Summa theologiae* III, q. 3, a. 7 ad 2). Likewise, the term 'body' ought to refer to the incarnate divine person, or a part of that person, just as 'human being' does. In *this* sense, of course, the identity of the body is parasitic on the identity of the person, since the body just is a part of the person. If this is what Aquinas means in claiming that the body of the dead Christ is the same as the living body, then his position makes complete sense. But it is not clear that Aquinas would want to say that the body is the same as, or identical to, the divine person, or that he wants to use the term 'body' to refer to the divine person, rather than to a part of his human nature.

The *Correctorium* led to something of a pamphlet war, with Dominican response and Franciscan counter-response, throughout the 1280s. The Dominicans produced more than one 'correction of the corruptor' (*Correctorium corruptorii*), some known by their *incipit*s: the most significant, Richard Knapwell's *Correctorium 'quare'* (1282–3); in addition, Robert Orford's *Correctorium 'sciendum'* (1282–3); William Macclesfield's *Correctorium 'quaestione'* (before 1284); and John Quidort's *Correctorium corruptorii Thomae* (before 1284). On the theological topic just discussed, none of them has any more to say than Aquinas, and by and large they do not advance the debate much. I return to the matter in Chapter 6.

Henry of Ghent

Henry of Ghent, secular theologian and Regent Master in Theology at Paris from 1276 to 1293, is arguably the most important philosopher in the years between Aquinas and Scotus. He is certainly the most influential, since his work became the starting point – and target of criticism – for much of Scotus's thought. And Scotus learned a great deal from him, as we shall see. But for all his originality, Henry himself owed much to his predecessors. Like Aquinas, though not perhaps to such a degree, he was a wide and attentive reader. For example, Henry has often been presented as continuing the kind of 'Augustinian' tradition supposedly found in Bonaventure. While we need to be cautious about such labels, it is certainly true that Henry sometimes builds on insights from Bonaventure, invariably providing them with rather more philosophical support, and always thinking through their consequences more systematically. A good example is Bonaventure's claim that God is the primary object of the intellect. Henry claims that there is a sense in which Bonaventure is right: the intellect knows being indeterminately; but to know being indeterminately includes necessarily first knowing being in its greatest degree of indetermination – that is, the subsisting being that is proper to God (*Summa quaestionum* XXIV, qq. 7–9)).

Although Henry occasionally suggests that it would be possible to construct some kind of *a priori* argument for God's existence, and cites passages from Augustine's *De trinitate* VIII that make some gestures in this kind of direction (*Summa quaestionum* XXII, q. 5), his *ex professo* arguments for God's existence in fact owe far more to Aristotle and Aquinas than they do to Augustine and Bonaventure. While imposing a novel structure on the series of arguments he proposes – dividing the arguments into those from causality (efficient, formal, and final) and those from degrees of perfection or eminence (a structure that will turn out to be followed closely by Scotus) – the basic contours of each argument are similar, in every case relying on the impossibility of an infinite regress, and in most cases concluding with a phrase such as 'and this we call God'. Like Aquinas, Henry describes the argument from motion as 'the first and most manifest […] way' of proving God's existence, and in two of the arguments from efficient causation even appeals to the Aristotelian claim that 'everything that moves is moved by another' – a claim that Henry rejects for immaterial substances but accepts for material ones (in this context simply on the basis of Aristotle's arguments in favour of it in *Physics* VIII (*Summa quaestionum* XXII, q. 4)).

Henry gives a rather nice theological spin to the question of universals, making an obvious theological move that was not made by his contemporaries. Basically, what he does is identify Avicenna's essences with divine ideas. But in the process, he develops Albert's talk of *esse essentiae* in a way that was almost universally rejected by his contemporaries and successors. In his discussion of Avicenna's three-fold consideration of the nature, Henry, holds that existing as a universal – with *esse rationis*, in the mind – and as a particular – with *esse exsistentiae*, in extramental reality – are extrinsic to the nature in itself. But he goes on to assert nevertheless that the nature in itself has some kind of being – *esse essentiae*, somehow distinct from the *esse exsistentiae* that it has in things and from the *esse rationis* that it has in the mind. His reason is to distinguish possible things, things of which there are divine ideas, from *impossibilia* – things of which there is no coherent concept, and thus no divine idea (Henry's examples are *chimera* and *goat-stag*). Things of which there are divine ideas have *esse essentiae*, and this distinguishes them from the nothingness of *impossibilia*.

Now Henry, at least as I read him, is clear that *esse essentiae* as such is not any real kind of being: it is the being that attaches merely to the content of a divine idea. This being is 'in a divine concept (*intentione dei*)', and it is not in any way external to the divine mind (for the whole discussion, see *Quodlibet* III, q. 9; for the claim that *esse essentiae* is nothing external to the divine mind, see *Quodlibet* IX, q. 2). Henry's opponents understood him to be pushing in an unacceptably realist or Platonic direction, ascribing some kind of extramental *esse* to an essence considered in itself. But in a way Henry is moving in a more conceptualist or nominalist direction, since what has *esse essentiae* is simply a concept – a concept in the divine mind. His opponents are perhaps right, nevertheless, to think that something odd is going on in Henry's view, since Henry maintains that items with *esse essentiae* can be actualized in extramental existence, and it is odd to think of a divine idea being somehow actualized – gaining *esse exsistentiae* and becoming something real (on this, see again *Quodlibet* IX, q. 2). Perhaps it was for this reason his opponents were tempted to think of Henry's essences as real, and existent in two states: possible, and actual.

Henry explicitly ties his account of essences into his account of individuation (see *Quodlibet* V, q. 8 for the *ex professo* discussion, in the context of individuation, of Avicenna's view of essence). *Esse essentiae* is common; what is responsible for individuation is a thing's actual existence (its *esse exsistentiae*: see *Quodlibet* II, q. 8; XI, q. 1). Furthermore, real things, as instantiations of an essence, have some sort of *esse essentiae*: they have, as Henry thinks of it, a relation to God as formal cause (recall that *esse essentiae* is the content of a divine idea; this content is then somehow realized in the particular). The formal feature of an existent thing that accounts for its existence is its *esse exsistentiae*, and this *esse* consists in the thing's relation to its efficient cause. Hence, as Henry puts it, a substance's 'individuation is efficiently caused merely by the thing that produces [the substance]; and is formally merely through this *esse*' (*Quodlibet* XI, q. 1 (Paris edn, fo. 439rV)): a thing's *esse exsistentiae* is thus *identified* as its relation to its efficient cause. The distinction between *esse essentiae* and *esse exsistentiae* is more than merely rational, since the relation to a formal cause and the relation to an efficient cause are two relations. And if there were merely a rational distinction between the two kinds of being, then the substance itself would be a necessary existent, essentially including its own existence. But the distinction is not real, since real distinction, for Henry, requires separability, and clearly a thing cannot exist without these two relations, just as they cannot exist without it. And in any case, if *esse exsistentiae* were itself a thing, then either it would explain its own existence (and thus be a necessary existent, like God), or its existence itself would need explaining, and so on to infinity. Henry asserts instead that the distinction between *esse essentiae* and *esse exsistentiae* is 'intentional' – extramental, but not a distinction between *things*, between items that are realizations of divine exemplars (*Quodlibet* X, q. 7; XI, q. 3).

In tandem with this view of the role of *esse exsistentiae* in individuation, Henry also maintains that individuation consists simply in a two-fold negation: indivisibility (into subjective parts) and non-identity with anything else (see particularly *Quodlibet* V, q. 8 and XI, q. 1). (I propose a way to integrate the two theories in a moment.)

All of this is important in the light of 1277, relating, as it does, to a series of condemned propositions:

> 81. That God could not make several intelligences of the same species because intelligences do not have matter.
> 96. That God cannot multiply individuals of the same species without matter.
> 191. That forms are not divided except through matter. – This is erroneous unless one is speaking of forms educed from the potency of matter. (*Chartularium universitatis parisiensis* (trans. Hyman, Walsh, and Williams, pp. 543 and 546))

The target here is the view of Aquinas (and others) that angels are distinguished by their species. And the basis of this view is the Aristotelian claim – rather common-sensical, on the face of it – that intraspecific individuation is by matter, or chunks of matter. (I outlined this view in Chapter 4 above.) But Henry's view has some common-sense appeal too. His basic view is that any (creaturely) essence is such that it can be instantiated multiple times. Essences, after all, are not individuals, but are akin to universals. As Henry thinks of it, there is a distinction between a particular and its essence even in the case of angels. (And, although Henry is too kind to point it out, even Aquinas agrees about this, since Aquinas holds that an angel includes both its essence and its existence, and that these are distinct: see Aquinas, *Summa theologiae* I, q. 50, a. 2 ad 3.) On Henry's view, what it is for individuals to exist is for essences to be (as we would put it) *instantiated*. Simply being an instantiation is sufficient for having a unique identity as an individual, and thus it seems not unreasonable to take the distinction between instantiations as a kind of primitive fact, much as Henry seems to. Question 8 of Henry's second *Quodlibet* – one of his central discussions of the issue – dates from Advent 1277. The discussion is thus about as philosophically current as one might hope. Rather nicely, Henry presents the articles of the condemnations as the *conclusions* of his kind of philosophical reasoning. Having laid out his view and supported it with philosophical argumentation (including appeals to Aristotle), he notes, '*Therefore*, this position [that there cannot be more than one angel of a given kind] is condemned, among the erroneous articles recently condemned by the Bishop of Paris': and Henry goes on to quote the three articles given just above (*Quodlibet* II, q. 8 (Leuven edn, VI, 45)).

Henry does not explain precisely how his two theories on individuation – existence and negation – are to be held together. At one point, he expounds the existence view, and laconically remarks, 'We have explained elsewhere how individuation is brought about negatively' (*Quodlibet* XI, q. 1 (Paris edn, fo. 419rV)). The most philosophically plausible view would be that Henry takes *esse exsistentiae* to be the formal explanation of individuation, and the two-fold negation just to amount to a description of what individuation consists in (as I hinted above). On this reading, the fact that something is indivisible and non-identical with anything else is what needs explaining; and it is explained by the *esse exsistentiae*. In his reading of Henry, Scotus understands the two-fold negation to be an explanation of individuation, and thus thinks that Henry's account fails, since in fact the two-fold negation is no more than a description of the problem to be solved (Scotus, *Ordinatio* II, d. 3, p. 1, q. 2). In fact, Henry talks of the two-fold negation as the *ratio individuationis* – and '*ratio*' could mean '(formal) explanation' of individuation, or 'meaning' of 'individuation'. Scotus reads Henry in the first way – imagining that the two-fold negation is supposed to *explain* individuation – and ignores Henry's material about *esse exsistentiae* in this context. He thus finds Henry's theory wanting. But the second reading of '*ratio*' is possible, and would allow us to integrate what Henry says into one coherent theory, in the way just outlined: the two-fold negation is a description of the fact that needs explaining, and *esse exsistentiae* is the explanation. (It is still not a theory that Scotus would accept: he rejects the view that actual existence could individuate for different reasons, however, that I return to in Chapter 6.)

Henry's treatment of these matters was extremely important. And it is no mean achievement: more than any other thinker, he provided a way to tie together issues of individuation, universals, essence, and existence into one clearly-articulated system, and his formulations of these topics constituted the starting point for all of Scotus's reflections on the same issues – reflections that resulted in theories that proved highly influential and philosophically insightful.

Another of Henry's key positions was of signal importance for Scotus too, and that is his line on the freedom of the will. Henry follows the Augustinian emphasis on the will – particularly in the version proposed by Anselm, maintaining that the will is indeed the subject of different and possibly conflicting inclinations. Henry uses this insight to give an account of the will's freedom. As he sees it, the intellect acts deterministically, and if the intellect, or the cognized object, caused the will's activity, then the activity of the will would be deterministic too. Now, Henry construes freedom as a power to act otherwise in the self-same circumstances – what we call 'contra-causal' freedom. Hence, Henry reasons, the will's being determined by the intellect, or by its object, would be incompatible with the will's freedom. Rather, the will causes its own act, such that it could cause other than it does; the activity of the intellect, presenting an object to the will, is merely a necessary condition for this (*Quodlibet* XII, q. 26).

As Henry sees it, the principal threat to his position is the Aristotelian claim that self-motion is simply impossible. After all, the will's activity must be caused by something, and if it is not caused by anything extrinsic to the will, it must be caused by the will itself. Henry's opponent is Godfrey of Fontaines, who (as we shall see) is strongly wedded to the Aristotelian impossibility of self-motion. Henry argues that this impossibility obtains only in the physical world, in which cause and effect need to be spatially located, and in which there needs to be spatial distinction between cause and effect. But this requirement for spatial location cannot obtain in the world of immaterial entities (souls, angels, and so on); neither can the requirement for spatial distinction. Rather, we can see from the activity of the intellect that immaterial objects are able to cause effects in themselves: they are capable of *reflexive* activity (e.g. the intellect is able to cause abstract conceptual content in itself, by abstracting

from phantasms – that is to say, from images in the imagination).
(On the reflexivity of immaterial substances, medieval philosophers
often appeal to the *Liber de causis*, prop. 13.) Likewise, the will can
cause its own activity. (On all of this, see *Quodlibet* IX, q. 5, and X,
q. 9.) Of course, allowing for the possibility of self-motion, and for
its applicability in the case of the will's activity, does not of itself
establish the possibility of the will's contra-causal freedom: perhaps
the will could be a self-mover that can produce merely one kind of
activity in any given set of circumstances. But the Anselmian claim
that the will has conflicting inclinations allows Henry to argue that
the will is precisely not such a power – namely, one that can produce
merely one kind of activity in any given set of circumstances. Rather,
it has an inclination to the beneficial, and an inclination to the just,
and, this latter inclination, far from being such that the Fall renders
it inoperable (as Anselm supposed), is what explains the fact that the
will can will other than it does (e.g. the just rather than the beneficial,
or the beneficial rather than the just). Of course, all appetites are or
include inclinations to the beneficial; so it is the inclination to the
just that is the mark of a free appetite (*Quodibet* XIII, q. 11). Again,
this crops up in Scotus too, though in rather different form.

    One of the key areas in which Scotus criticized Henry is on the
question of epistemology. Henry attempts to combine Aristotelian
and Augustinian epistemological insights. While his views did
not remain wholly stable (and have thus been the subject of some
controversy in the recent literature), the basic contours seem
reasonably clear. The epistemology is linked with Henry's views
on the psychological mechanisms of cognition, so I start with an
account of these. Throughout his life he accepted the importance and
necessity of abstraction in intellectual cognition, and he explicitly
distinguishes two kinds: *imaginative* abstraction (resulting in
phantasms), and *intellectual* abstraction (see e.g. *Quodlibet* V, q. 14
(Paris edn, fo. 176vO)). The early Henry believes that intellectual
abstraction results in an intelligible species (see e.g. *Summa
quaestionum*, a. 1, q. 2, for abstraction, and a. 3, q. 1 for intelligible
species). Later, he rejects such a view: intelligible species would be
(he avers) real accidents impressed by their objects, and cognition
cannot consist in the inherence of such a real accident; neither can
real accidents be the bearers of conceptual content. Rather, the form
of the external object is received 'intentionally': an *expressed* species,
received 'as the known in the knower' – to use Henry's Aristotelian

jargon. The point is that there is merely a 'spiritual' reception of the form in the intellect, with no accompanying real inherence of any real accident, no species 'impressed' on the intellect (see *Quodlibet* IV, q. 21). Occurrent cognitions, according to Henry, themselves cause habits – dispositional cognitions in virtue of which conceptual content can be recalled (see *Quodlibet* IV, q. 8, and V, q. 16). (Such habits are, of course, real accidents; so it is hard to see how, by Henry's lights, they could be the bearers of conceptual content; so, in turn, it is hard to see how they can dispose someone to an occurrent cognitive act with no further conceptual input. But let that pass.)

So far, so Aristotelian (at least, in Aristotle's medieval incarnation). But Henry does not believe that this mechanism is sufficient for knowledge. After all, there are plenty of ways in which the abstractive process can be inadequate for purposes of knowing (for example, abstraction from mutable objects cannot strip off all mutability; and it cannot distinguish between dreams and waking: see *Summa quaestionum*, a. 1, q. 2 (Leuven edn, XXI, 43–5)). So he posits, rather in the Augustinian manner of Grosseteste and Bonaventure, that the accuracy of our cognitions is underwritten by some kind of divine illumination: once we have abstracted universal content, God offers to those whom he chooses 'the standards (*regulas*) of eternal light', enabling them to have 'unimpaired (*sincera*) truth' (*Summa quaestionum*, a. 1, q. 2 (Leuven edn, XXI, 62–3)). In the early Henry, this kind of cognition is propositional: divine illumination guarantees that beliefs formed on its basis are true (*Summa quaestionum*, a. 1, q. 2 (Leuven edn, XXI, 50–2)). Later, Henry seems to believe that divine illumination secures, rather, the accuracy of our simple concepts: that, for example, I can correctly abstract the concept *cat* from the cats that I encounter in the world (see e.g. *Quodlibet* IX, q. 15). At any rate, Augustinian illumination seems in some form or another to be a constant feature of Henry's epistemology as much as Aristotelian abstraction does of his theory of cognition.

Peter Olivi

Petrus Ioannis Olivi – Peter, the son of John Olivi – was without a doubt the best philosopher, the most intelligent and most creative, in the period between Aquinas and Scotus: and probably by quite a considerable margin. But Olivi is something of a wild, Janus-type figure. He spent half his time teaching and writing scholastic philosophy at the very highest level, and half his time preaching the imminent apocalypse to the peasants of Provence. He was one of the more extreme of the so-called 'Spiritual' Franciscans, portrayed so vividly in Umberto Eco's *The Name of the Rose* – following the vastly speculative apocalyptic account of history proposed by Joachim of Fiore, and adhering to a life of absolute poverty.

Olivi was often in some kind of trouble, partly as a result of internecine Franciscan controversies about poverty, and partly because of a suspicion, probably rather unjust, that some of his teachings were influenced by the Catharism of southern France. Some of his positions were condemned at the Council of Vienne in 1311–12, most notably his views on the human soul.[1] Olivi believes that the human soul consists of a collection (*collegium*) of powers, each inherent in one and the same spiritual matter (for the first claim, see *Quaestiones in secundum librum sententiarum*, q. 54 (II, 259); for the second, see q. 54 (II, 256–7)). Among these powers are sensory and intellective powers. And Olivi holds that, while the sensory part of the soul is the form of the body, the rational soul is not. His reason is that we do not ascribe intellectual cognition or free choice to the body:

> If the intellective part is the form of the body, then, since all matter is actualized by its form, it follows that just as a human body is truly sensory and living through the sensory soul, so that body will be truly intellective and free through the intellective part. (*Quaestiones in secundum librum sententiarum*, q. 51 (II, 104–5) translation in Pasnau, 1997a)

That we should not ascribe intellectual cognition or free choice to the body was not a controversial assertion. As Olivi argues, if the intellect were a bodily form, its operation would be organic, and thus restricted to the cognition of material objects. Equally, the intellect is capable of self-knowledge, by introspection: and material objects are not capable of any kind of reflexivity (for these claims, see *Quaestiones in secundum librum sententiarum*, 51 (II, 112)). From all of this, it follows straightforwardly that it cannot be the case that the soul's 'intellective and free part is, of itself and considered as such, the form of the body' (*Quaestiones in secundum librum sententiarum*, 51 (II, 104)). Olivi does not believe that this blocks the inference to the claim that the soul itself is the form of the body, since the fact that a part of the soul informs the body is sufficient to secure the claim that the whole soul informs the body. As Olivi puts it, the whole *essence* of the soul informs the body, even though it is not the case that all of its powers do (see *Responsio ad Litteram magistrorum*, ed. in Laberge, 1935, p. 128). This is not just an unprincipled assertion; Olivi has a reason for it, at least in the case of the intellect:

> Although [...] the powers are parts of the soul, nevertheless by their names are named the whole substance of the soul. [...] For it is customary that the name of the whole form or whole being is taken from the ultimate difference or formal nature. (*Quaestiones in secundum librum sententiarum*, q. 54 (II, 258))

Be all this as it may, in 1283 the Franciscans censured Olivi for maintaining that the rational soul is not the form of the body (see the so-called *Littera septem sigillorum*, written by seven Franciscan theologians, including the talented Richard of Middleton (*c.* 1249–1302/3), and sent to every Franciscan house in Olivi's province); and the Council of Vienne condemned the view that 'the rational or intellective soul is not truly and *per se* the form of the human body' (Decretum [1] (*Conciliorum oecumenicorum decreta*, p. 361)). Whether or not Olivi was rightly condemned, the view gives some sense both of his originality and of his talent for spotting what kinds of answers need to be given through the stages of a philosophical argument.

In fact, much of Olivi's work exhibits this skill. For example, according to Aristotle, both sensation (of particulars) and conceptual thought (of universals) are *passive*: they consist in the reception (in a certain way) of the form of an external object: the senses and mind are *acted upon* by their extramental objects, and sensing and thinking are things *done* to the cognizing subject by the object (see e.g. Aristotle, *De anima* III, c. 4 (429a13–15, b22–5)). Olivi takes a diametrically opposed view. Olivi agrees that sensation requires the passive reception of sensible species. But he does not believe that any case of such reception is sufficient for sensation. After all, we can be distracted, such that, while the physiology of sensation functions in just the normal way, we do not consciously sense anything at all (*Quaestiones in secundum librum sententiarum*, q. 58 ad 14 (II, 484)). Olivi therefore maintains that actual sensation requires the sensor's active attention to the object. And this attention is caused solely by the sensor; the object is a non-causal necessary condition, something to which the attention is directed without being a cause of that attention. Intellectual acts arise too merely from such attention (to the external object), and other than cases of memory do not require any kind of species in the intellect at all (for a discussion of all this, see Pasnau, 1997b, pp. 131–4, 169–74). (Olivi holds, incidentally, that there are intelligible species, but that these are caused simply by prior occurrent cognitive acts, or by the soul, with the acts as something akin to the relevant causal power – and thus what thinkers such as Henry label not species but habits (Olivi, *Quaestiones in secundum librum sententiarum*, q. 73 (III, 37); q. 74 (III, 114 and 121)).) The reason is that material objects, including sensible species and acts of sensation, cannot cause any effect on an immaterial substance. The agent intellect, were there such a thing, could not help, since (Olivi maintains) there is nothing in the phantasm sufficient to explain the conceptual content of a cognitive act – and hence not enough prior conceptual content for the agent intellect to work with, as it were. Hence, again against Aristotle, there is no agent intellect (Olivi, *Quaestiones in secundum librum sententiarum*, q. 73 (III, 27–30)).

Still, according to Olivi, cognitive acts are caused wholly by the intellect (*Quaestiones in secundum librum sententiarum*, q. 72 (III, 9 and 17); q. 58 (II, 462)). The fundamental reason for this, in line with a consideration just mentioned, is that thinking is an *animate* function, and thus that nothing inanimate can have a role in causing it (*Quaestiones in secundum librum sententiarum*, q. 58 (II, 412)). Robert Pasnau summarizes:

> [Olivi] proposes an account based on what he calls virtual attention. Cognizers obtain information about the external world not by receiving physical impressions through the sense organs but by virtually extending the soul's cognitive attention to particular features of the external environment. (Pasnau, 1997b, p. 168)

Of course, Olivi does not wish to deny that cognitive acts have objects. But he does want to deny that the object can ever have any efficiently causal role in the production of the act. And he denies that anything in the mind – other than the mind itself – could be a partial cause of a cognitive act. So he maintains that an object of cognition is necessary for the existence of a cognitive act – the act is about something – but denies that the object has any kind of causal role in the production of the act. Basically, the object cannot do this, because powers such as the intellect 'could not be moved or provoked by [their objects] unless they were already converted on them' (*Quaestiones in secundum librum sententiarum*, q. 58 (II, 476)).

On this view, our cognitive powers in relation to sensation and occurrent thought are entirely active: their objects have no causal role in their activity. Perhaps unsurprisingly, Olivi holds that the same is true of the will:

> It is necessary that the free choice has the feature of being a first mover and such that it can impel, move, and avert both itself and the other active powers and virtues subject to it, and it can do this not merely when there is nothing impelling to the opposite, but even when there is present something impelling to the opposite. (*Quaestiones in secundum librum sententiarum*, q. 58 (II, 411))

So the will has, as we would say, both the liberty of spontaneity and the liberty of indifference. Olivi argues for this latter feature in a number of ways – by considering various human affects (aversion, mercy, friendship, boastfulness and shame, gratitude, feelings of subjection and domination, hope and diffidence, fear (*Quaestiones in secundum librum sententiarum*, q. 57); and by considering the ways in which human beings can choose and change both their goals and the means to those goals, and choose between two equally desirable options. This last argument is rather striking:

> When many things hold equally, and are equally useful, there is no reason why the will chooses one of these other than its liberty by which it can tend equally to this or to that, as is clear in the case of two apples or two human beings like each other and equal in all and through all, but such that the will can still choose one and reject the other. (*Quaestiones in secundum librum sententiarum*, q. 57 (II, 326))

Here the will can pick between two objects in identical circumstances, and what explains its picking is just the will itself.

Olivi intends us to understand some kind of introspective argument for this conclusion, and that the assumption is that we perceive that we have these options such that we really could, in just the same circumstances, choose a different object. Olivi makes the introspective point explicitly when considering our freedom to act or refrain from acting in just the same circumstances:

> A human being senses indubitably that he has in himself a certain power which is not determined to acting when it acts and to not acting when it does not act, such that, when it acts, it could not act, and when it does not act, it could act. (*Quaestiones in secundum librum sententiarum*, q. 57 (II, 327))

This gives us the power to choose to act or not to act, and to choose to do this or that, in precisely the same circumstances. And our knowing that we have this is phenomenally grounded: it seems to us that this is how it is.

Part of Olivi's genius lies in seeing exactly where an argument needs to go next; sometimes, however, he does not know just what to say. He sees that he needs an argument about other minds here, to the effect that what seems to me to be the case about myself is the case for other people too – we are *all* free in this way. Here, Olivi sees the need for the move, and he makes a couple of linked proposals:

> We sense in a certain wonderful (*miro*) way that this is in other human beings as in ourselves, and on that account we find ourselves to have an ability such that, according to combinations of the above-mentioned affects we can join ourselves to other human beings and not to animals or to things lacking reason. (*Quaestiones in secundum librum sententiarum*, q. 57 (II, 327))

We might think that the inference would go the other way round: we infer from the fact that we form distinctively human kinds of relations with other human beings that other human beings are free in the way that we ourselves are. But Olivi here grounds our desire to form such relationships on a (non-sensory) perception that others are like us, and he takes this perception to be something obvious.

Another move that needs to be made in this context has to do with the apparent absence of such freedom in non-human animals. Olivi considers the issue by discussing the case that we now know as Buridan's ass, and showing how random animal activities are not cases of liberty at all:

> If it is said that the same is true of an animal who chooses one of two things that are equally desirable to him and equally distant from him: it is clear that the case is not the same, because animals do not deliberate about the equality of the desirability of those things, neither do they judge with full affirmation, as human beings do. (*Quaestiones in secundum librum sententiarum*, q. 57 (II, 326–7))

By itself this is not enough, since deliberation seems to be an intellectual operation, somehow picking out features more desirable in one than the other. But Olivi has something rather specific in mind: our reflecting on the fact that we could indeed equally choose either one, and that our decision is precisely *not* made on the basis of the greater desirability of the one over the other. And on the basis of this reflection, we 'sense that we choose from the mere liberty of our will' (*Quaestiones in secundum librum sententiarum*, q. 57 (II, 327)). And the animal case is different: animals lack this reflective capacity, and thus lack freedom, and act in the case described 'as it were from nature, moved by continuous impulse, since [they] are in continuous motion or continuous agitation' (*Quaestiones in secundum librum sententiarum*, q. 57 (II, 327)).

The allusion to Buridan's ass is perhaps another rather subtle dig at Aristotle. Aristotle considers in passing the case of a person who

> though exceedingly hungry and thirsty, and both equally, yet being equidistant from food and drink, is therefore bound to stay where he is. (Aristotle, *De caelo* II, c. 13 (195b34–5))

Clearly, the case fails, and this is Olivi's assumption. But I say 'perhaps' this is another dig at Aristotle, since the context of Aristotle's discussion makes it rather unclear whether the example of the starving man is supposed to be ironic: Aristotle appeals to it as an illustration of Anaximander's view that what explains the earth's remaining at the centre of the universe is its 'indifference' – its being equidistant from every extreme point in the universe. And this reasoning Aristotle finds absurd.

Olivi maintains that the will has power over our cognitive faculties and moral dispositions. But the voluntary control of thought seems to raise a problem. On the face of it, the will requires objects, and free will seems to require objects of which the subject is conscious. (In the old tag, nothing is willed unless it is first known: *nil volitum nisi praecognitum*.) If the will can control *all* thought, then it seems that it can reach out to an object that is not consciously known. I am not sure precisely what Olivi thinks about this. But at one point he seems to suggest just this: the presence of the object is clearly somehow required, but there are two possible ways in which an object can be present to the intellect: really present, or present merely in an intelligible species. And presence in the second of these two ways would involve the will's choosing an object *unconsciously* – perhaps parallel to the intellect's reaching out to an object *prior* to occurrently thinking of the object. Thus, in response to an objection to the effect that the will is moved by its object, he asserts that 'the will is free to focus itself and the other powers on their objects, and hence on their acts' (*Quaestiones in secundum librum sententiarum*, q. 58 (II, 476)), and the context suggests that the will seems to be responsible for focusing the intellect on its objects prior to any occurrent intellectual act.

As I have just tried to show, Olivi's accounts of the cognition and the freedom of the will are profoundly anti-Aristotelian, and, in the case of the will, I think deeply original. Indeed, whatever we make of the details of his discussion, the whole provides a wonderful example of Olivi's philosophical intelligence and perspicacity. His account of time, drawing on some insights from Bonaventure that I discussed in Chapter 3, but developing them in a powerfully original way, illustrates his anti-Aristotelian attitude very nicely. It shows, too, that we go badly wrong if we think of those thinkers who were less enamoured of Aristotelianism to be fundamentally backward-looking, 'Augustinian' in orientation. All the medievals were influenced by Augustine. But hesitation about aspects of Aristotelian thought is often coupled with profound philosophical originality, and Olivi is a good case in point. The trend is illustrated even more vividly in the towering genius of Duns Scotus, as I show in Chapter 6.

Olivi basically agrees with Bonaventure's line on the *aevum* and absolute time. He distinguishes a substance from its duration, and maintains that, while the substance lacks temporal parts, its duration is temporally extended and has temporal parts. And the duration – the 'continuation' of the substance – consists in the 'repetition' of one and the same substance at different times without any change in form (recall Bonaventure's identification of a substance's duration or existence with its constant causal dependence on God). The continuation or repetition is temporally extended, even though the substance is not (*Quaestiones in secundum librum sententiarum*, q. 9 (I, 174)). The term 'continuation' clearly alludes to Bonaventure. But the repetition claim is new in Olivi, and represents a significant attempt to give a philosophically satisfactory account of the persistence of eviternals (items whose existence corresponds to the *aevum*), and presumably of any object that lacks temporal parts. The idea is that numerically one and the same object is repeated in any instant at which it exists, such that the whole object exists at each instant – there are no parts that it lacks at any instant at which it exists. And this view allows Olivi to deal with the worry that eviternals are changeless and thus atemporal. There is a change in the duration of the substance, since this duration consists in the temporally extended repetition of the substance. The repetition of an eviternal is not a standard case of motion, involving any real exchange of forms. The duration of an eviternal is an accident; but it is *one* accident, composed of temporal parts, and hence talking about duration does not in itself entail the real exchange of forms. But there is change in the parts of this duration: presumably, the duration itself is continuously amassing more parts (*Quaestiones in secundum librum sententiarum*, q. 9 (I, 176–7)). And this gives us Olivi's account of persistence: an object endures by being continuously diachronically repeated. Olivi spots that this theory of persistence can be understood in terms of an analogy to the existence of the divine nature in the divine persons, repeated synchronically, as it were:

> The most beautiful image of the personal production existing in God lies in the fact that these *rationes* [viz. the repetitions of one and the same individual] pertain both to becoming and to existing, such that there can be said in some way to

be many becomings and many existings, or many makings and existences, without diversity of essence, just as in its way there are [in God] many productions and existences with the maximal identity of essence; and just as there in a certain way production is the basis of the plurification of existence, rather than *vice versa*, so it is in the case at hand. (*Quaestiones in secundum librum sententiarum*, q. 9 (I, 186))

Olivi uses this account of duration to solve a long-standing *aporia* in Aristotle's account of time. On the face of it, we need an account of how it is that time flows: of how future and past are related asymmetrically, and how it is that only the ever-changing present moment, the flowing *now*, actually exists. Aristotle, notoriously, did not know how to give an account of this, giving three paradoxes in *Physics* IV, c. 10 designed to show that (flowing) time cannot be real. But Olivi has a suggestion:

I do not believe that a 'now' should be posited as the flowing thing in successive duration. Rather, the enduring thing [(i.e. the substance) should be posited as the flowing thing in successive duration], the flux of which thing is nothing other than its continuous conservation or becoming, or its quasi-continuous repetition. (*Quaestiones in secundum librum sententiarum*, q. 9 (I, 178))

Time does not presuppose change, and its reality is not explained by the flow of the present moment. Time presupposes the repetition of one and the same object – not an instant but a substance – and its reality is explained by this repetition.

At one point, Olivi identifies too strong a reliance on pagan philosophy as the cause of his opponents' difficulties: 'The path [...] of pagan philosophers, as I believe, deceived them' (*Quaestiones in secundum librum sententiarum*, q. 9 (I, 175)) – though the pagan belief that Olivi has in mind is the belief in everlasting and indestructible creatures, not specifically the sorts of Aristotelian problem I have been discussing here. Nevertheless, it is clear to me that Olivi does provide satisfactory answers to the problems about this that his contemporaries inherited from Aristotle, and that – unlike any of his contemporaries – he has a satisfactory account of what it is for a substance, something that has all its parts at once, to persist. The whole treatment is unique in medieval philosophy, as far as I know, though there are related discussions of the same issue rather later in Buridan (*Super octo libros physicorum* I, c. 10) and Marsilius of Inghen (*c.* 1340–96).

Giles of Rome

My next two philosophers – Giles of Rome and Godfrey of Fontaines – represent attempts to be far more faithful to Aristotle, and to be sympathetic to some of the core views of Thomas Aquinas too, whose Parisian lectures were probably audited by Giles of Rome. Unlike Henry, they would both, in effect, find themselves on the wrong side of the 1277 condemnations – in the case of Giles, in a way that had a direct impact on his theological career. Godfrey was in Paris by the early 1270s, and was intimately acquainted with the on-going debates between Arts masters and theologians at the time: he kept a small notebook in which he copied important works in the controversy. And one of his *Quodlibets* from the mid-1290s subjects some of the condemnations to severe criticism, not only substantively (as we saw in the Introduction), but also because of the damage that they do to the teachings of Thomas Aquinas: the condemnations are 'detrimental […] to the teaching, very useful to students, of the most reverend and excellent doctor, brother Thomas' (Godfrey, *Quodlibet* XII, q. 5 (p. 102)).

Twelve seventy-seven was a significant year not merely in the life of the University of Paris, but also in the life of Giles of Rome. For just weeks after the Condemnation of 219 propositions on 7 March, 51 propositions taken from Giles's work were condemned, and Giles was forced to leave Paris. He returned again in 1285, having recanted certain portions of his teaching. But Giles led an active life as much outside the academy as within it. He was prior general of the Augustinian Hermits from 1292 to 1295, and Archbishop of Bourges from 1295 – and thus, incidentally, had as his episcopal seat the most remarkable and beautiful of all Gothic buildings. But he spent little time enjoying his architectural treasure, and was largely to be found at the papal *curia* at Rome and then Avignon, where he died in 1316. He was also the theologian charged at the Council of Vienne with drawing up the list of suspect articles from the work of Olivi.

Perhaps the feature of Giles's thought that has been the subject of the most attention in twentieth-century scholarship is his view that essence and existence are distinct as *thing* and *thing*, and thus that there is a real distinction between them. Commentators have, by and large, found his view either incoherent or at least unfortunately expressed. It seems to me that – while the view is doubtless false – it suffers from neither of these defects. But to see why, we need first of all to be very clear on what the view actually amounts to – and I do not think it has been fully appreciated in the literature.[2] Basically, Giles's metaphysics includes the view that (as we would say) property-tropes (abstract particulars, particular properties or property-instances) coalesce to constitute particular substantial and accidental wholes. But as he conceives of this it involves a curious kind of 'doubling' of properties. For example, for matter to be extended, a quantity-trope (a quantity *res*, as Giles puts it) must be united to matter. But *matter* is genuinely extended by quantity. So matter must, as a result of its union with a quantity *res*, be quantitatively modalized: it must have (it must receive from the quantity *res*) a quantity *mode*. It is easy to see how one might arrive at this position: we want matter itself to be extended, and this seems to require that its extension be somehow intrinsic to it. But the explanation for its extension is extrinsic (matter is not of itself extended), and this seems to require an extension to be added to it.

But while it is easy to see how we might arrive at the position, the position itself looks remarkably implausible: instead of one extended item, we have two; and the same for other accidents too (instead of one blue item, we have two: the blueness *res*, and the bluely modalized substance) – hence my worry about the doubling of properties: two extended things, and two blue things, when in each case we would want and expect just one. So something, it seems, must have gone wrong with the original reasoning. Be this as it may, this view is the background to Giles's celebrated belief that essence and existence are distinct as *res* and *res*. His basic position is this. No created essences can include existence, since no creature is a necessary existent. Thus, for something contingent (something whose essence does not include existence) to exist it must be united to an existence *res*, one that explains its being modalized as an existent, just as a substance is modalized by its accidents (Giles makes all these points most explicitly – though at great length – including the analogy to extension, at *Quaestiones de esse et essentia*, qq. 8–10; for a summary, see *Theoremata de esse et essentiae*, th. 5–8 and 19–20 (trans. Murray, pp. 35–50 and 94–103)).

Medieval critics of Giles's view took a number of different routes. Henry of Ghent agreed that there is some kind of distinction between essence and existence, but held that it is misleading to talk of essence and existence as *res*, or that there is a real distinction between them, since *res*, the kinds of thing that can be really distinct from each other, are *concrete* items, items that are realizations of divine exemplars, and even if essence is such an item, existence certainly is not – I discussed Henry's view above (for his initial criticism of the view, from a date even earlier than the first written evidence we have for the view from Giles, see Henry, *Quodlibet* I, q. 9). Giles, in turn, found the intentional distinction that Henry posited between items that fall short of being *res* unintelligible (*Quaestiones de esse et essentia*, q. 9). There are some very deep disagreements in ontology that neither man managed quite to articulate in his discussion of his opponent. Godfrey of Fontaines maintains, against both Giles and Henry, that there is no kind of distinction between essence and existence: identifying something involves identifying something existent, and it makes no sense to suppose that we need to pinpoint two distinct components in an individual – the individual and its existence (see Godfrey, *Quodlibet* III, q. 1). I return to Godfrey's view below.

Giles's position on essence and existence has nothing much explicitly to do with Avicenna's claims about common natures – which was the context for the teaching of both Aquinas and Henry on the question. Giles, in fact, is a committed nominalist on the question of universals. He denies that there are common natures, or that the nature in abstraction from particulars is anything other than a concept. He thus denies the explanatory role that Aquinas allows to common natures in his theory of substance. Giles gives Avicenna's account of essence, explicitly ascribing it to '*aliqui*' – some people, but not to Giles himself, as it turns out: and, clearly enough, the opponent is Henry of Ghent. As the opponent understands the matter, essence has *esse naturae* – being in various individuals – *esse rationis* – being as a universal concept – and *esse essentiae* – the being that essence has in itself, abstracting both from real being and conceptual being. Giles objects to the last of these: *esse essentiae* is just *esse rationis*, the being that the essence has as a universal concept: it is nothing real at all (*Quodlibet* II, q. 6). So Giles's claims about the real distinction between essence and existence are to do with *individual* essences and their existences: an existent substance is a composite of an individual essence along with (its individual) existence: the individual essence *res* receives from the individual existence *res* its existence mode.

It might be thought that adopting nominalism would render otiose discussions of individuation. But, as Giles sees it, this is not the case. As we saw above, medieval thinkers distinguish two distinct questions pertinent to individuation: what it is that separates one substance from another, and what it is that renders each substance indivisible – that is, such that it is not itself shareable in the way that some maintain common natures to be shareable. On the face of it, nominalists deny that anything is really shareable in this way, and thus might well deny that lack of shareability requires explanation: it might just be the way that things are, and are as a matter of necessity. (Generally, nominalists regard the relevant sense of 'shareable' as unintelligible.) But the first question might still need answering. Consider the case of two qualitatively identical substances, for example: on a plausible thesis about identity (the identity of indiscernibles), there could not be two such qualitatively identical substances, even if nominalism is true. And it is this distinction question that Giles sets himself to answer, in the context of the thorny question problematized in 1277: the individuation of angels of the same kind, a possibility affirmed in the 1277 condemnation, which Giles quotes at the beginning of his discussion of the matter. As Giles sees it, the crucial question to ask is about the individuation of property-instances – a patch of whiteness, to use his example. White patches are qualitatively identical, and what standardly distinguishes two white patches is the fact that they inhere in distinct chunks of matter. And this distinction results in the distinction of the *esse* (the *esse exsistentiae*) of such forms. But Giles adds another step, one designed to deal with the question of angelic individuation. One function that matter plays in the whiteness example, according to Giles, is to *restrict* the perfection of whiteness. Unrestricted forms are complete, such that there can be at most one instance of them – they are sufficiently expansive, so to speak, that they fill out their one possible instantiation. Instances of restricted forms lack some degree of actuality, such that there can be many of them. God can create appropriately unrestricted forms, and if he does so he cannot make more than one of the kind. And this, Giles claims, is what he did in the case of angels. But restriction does not have to be the result of materiality: the restriction could be internal to the form; and if God had made angels in this way, there could have been more than one in any given species. (Note that the condemnation explicitly rejects only the view that the singularity of angelic substances is explained by their immateriality, though a natural reading of it, I think, takes it as condemning the whole Thomist view on angelic individuation. Giles knows that he is on weak exegetical grounds, and asserts that he 'does not fully endorse this evasion, since it is not entirely clear how an angel can have perfect or diminished being in the way outlined' (*Quodlibet* II, q. 7 (p. 69a)). The idea in this latter case, in which the restriction is internal to form, is that plurality of *esse exsistentiae* leads to plurality of substances: and such plurality of *esse exsistentiae* is possible since the imperfection of the substance means that it does not attract the full weight of the kind-relevant *esse exsistentiae*, as it were (*Quodlibet* II, q. 7).

Does this discussion not covertly commit Giles to Avicennian natures (after all, in trying to explain Giles's view I spoke just now of the *instances* of a nature)? I do not think so. Giles is talking about (as we might say) qualitatively or formally identical substances, and his thought is that there could not be more than one of such substances in the case that the substance were perfect or unrestricted relative to its kind. The assumption is that it is an imperfection in a kind of substance for there to be able to be more than one substance of the relevant kind. It must be said that the whole discussion has more than a hint of the *ad hoc* – trying to preserve the Thomist view that there cannot be more than one angel of a given kind along with the view of 1277 that the opposite is the case – and I cannot think of any reason to agree with Giles that solitariness in a kind is a perfection.

For much of the twentieth century, commentators have thought of Giles as someone whose role was fundamentally that of an expositor and adapter of the thought of Thomas Aquinas. After all, his thought was involved negatively in the condemnations of 1277 in much the same way as Aquinas's was. But while it is true that Giles's early work (pre-1277) is indebted to Aquinas, it is clear that his work ultimately developed along lines rather different from those found in Aquinas. What I have just had to say about Giles's views on essence and existence should make that abundantly clear. And it is true too for much of Giles's distinctive thought. For example, one of the most curious features of the 1277 condemnation of Giles of Rome is just how part of it fits in with the extensive condemnation of 219 propositions a month earlier. Among the 219 propositions condemned are the following:

> 129. That as long as passion and particular science are present in act, the will cannot go against them.
> 130. That if reason is rectified, the will is also rectified. – This is erroneous because contrary to Augustine's gloss on this verse from the Psalms: 'My soul hath coveted too long', and so on [Ps. 118.20], and because according to this, grace would not be necessary for the rectitude of the will but only science, which is the error of Pelagius. (*Chartularium universitatis parisiensis* (trans. Hyman, Walsh, Williams, p. 548))

Giles of Rome, in book I of his *Sentence* commentary, dating from 1269/70 defends something like the following view: 'There is no malice in the will unless there is error or some ignorance in the reason.' Now, the masters responsible in 1277 for drawing up the list of propositions to be condemned from Giles's work expressly endorsed this claim – not at all what we might expect, given the more significant condemnation earlier in the year. The difficulty was quickly perceived, and the claim became known as the *propositio magistralis*: the proposition defended by the assembled Masters in Theology (*magistri*). The point, of course, has to do in general with action theory (the interrelations between the intellect and will in human activity), and more particularly with ethics (the possibility of *akrasia* – weakness of will). The conflict was seized on with some joy by Godfrey of Fontaines, who in any case was displeased by the 7 March condemnation. But Godfrey is probably not quite correct, at least in the sense that the *propositio magistralis* can be plausibly taken as a hermeneutical lens through which to interpret the earlier condemnation: article 129 was interpreted as making a strong *causal* claim: the intellect and/or passion cause the will's activity, and the *propositio magistralis* makes no such causal claim. And the condemnation of article 129, of course, puts considerable pressure on Aquinas's action theory – another case in which Aquinas's Aristotelianism was seen as incompatible with the kind of account of human freedom that, it was believed, was required by Christian doctrine.

Now, Giles's position on the question of freedom might best be thought of, in fact, as navigating a middle path between the intellectualism of Aquinas and the voluntarism of Henry (and if there is any ambiguity about Aquinas's view, there certainly is not about the determinism that Godfrey of Fontaines espouses – as I show in a moment). On the one hand, like Henry, Giles allows to the will a real role in choosing between different actions. As he puts it, the will 'has liberty radically and primarily' (*Quodlibet* IV, q. 21 (p. 257a)). His idea is that the intellect can present different desirable actions to the will – the intellect can be, in Giles's word, 'bifurcated' – and the will simply be free to choose between the two actions. This gives the will a role in what Aquinas calls the 'specification' of an action. But the will's control is not complete: according to Giles, activation – doing something, acting rather than not acting: exercise, as Aquinas labels it – is caused by the intellect (*Quodlibet* III, q. 15). Notice, incidentally, that all of this is compatible with the *propositio magistralis*. Giles uses his account of the bifurcation of the intellect to explain the possibility of *akrasia* – hence all cases of *akrasia* involve intellectual error, as the *propositio magistralis* might lead us to expect. (Though in any case note that the *propositio magistralis* in fact makes no statement about *akrasia*, and focuses on the rather worse case of malice.)

Giles is also notable for his contributions to medieval political philosophy. His early *De regimine principium* is a handbook for kings that, in the course of its argumentation, defends the superiority of monarchy over other forms of government. And his *De ecclesiastica potestate* – scathingly attacked by Ockham later on – argues that the Pope has supreme power over both spiritual and temporal orders: there is no legitimate temporal power unless it be delegated from the Pope, and no legitimate property rights without Papal consent.

Godfrey of Fontaines

Godfrey's views on the common nature are like Aquinas's, and like his closely related to Avicenna's: he talks of the nature's two-fold existence (real, in particulars, and conceptual, in the mind) and three-fold consideration (as real, as conceptual, and in itself). And, even more explicitly than Aquinas, he maintains that the nature in itself lacks any kind of *esse* (*Quodlibet* VI, q. 6). His opponent is Henry. According to Godfrey, Henry posits *esse essentiae* to account for God's knowledge of non-existent possibles: essences must have sufficient extramental being to count as objects of knowledge, even if the essences are not instantiated (*Quodlibet* II, q. 2). For reasons that I have already made plain, I think this is a misreading of Henry. But setting that aside, Godfrey responds to the theory as he presents it by noting that it entails some kind of composition of essence (*esse essentiae*) and existence (*esse exsistentiae*) in an existent individual (*Quodllibet* II, q. 2). Against Aquinas, Godfrey maintains that even Aquinas's more ontologically minimalist reading of Avicenna on common natures does not require (as Aquinas seems to maintain) some kind of distinction between essence and existence. And, of course, rejecting any such distinction pushes Godfrey in a far more Aristotelian direction even than Aquinas (recall that Aristotle restricts the potency/actuality binary to subject or substrate, on the one hand, and form, on the other: for Aquinas, the picture is more complex, since form and essence themselves are in potency to existence; I return to the question of matter in Godfrey in a moment).

But on the interpretation of Avicenna on common natures, Godfrey insists that 'things exist merely singularly [...]; they do not exist commonly or according to their commonality' (*Quodlibet* II, q. 2). We can *think* about things as common, but there are no such things in reality. In line with this, Godfrey denies that there is any distinction between an individual or its nature or essence, and goes as far as to claim that (e.g.) Socrates is just rationality + animality. Still, we can think about, and talk about, kinds of things: but Godfrey claims that, in so doing, we are thinking or talking merely about individuals, under a certain description: indeterminately, rather than determinately, as he puts it (following Aquinas's language in *De ente*).

Even given this, however, Godfrey believes that he needs an account of individuation. After all, if Socrates is just rationality + animality, and Plato likewise, it seems that Socrates and Plato will be identical – will have all the same properties. Godfrey ends up defending quite a curious view. In a way not unrelated to Giles's views, he makes a distinction between what he thinks of as the *explanation* for individuation and the necessary condition or conditions for individuation. Briefly, (substantial) form is the explanation for the individuation of substances of the same kind, and extension the relevant necessary condition for individuation (of different items of the same kind) – and I consider these two claims in turn. As Godfrey sees it, what *explains* the fact that things of the same kind are distinct from each other is that they are 'indivisible into many things of the same kind' (*Quodlibet* VII, q. 5 (p. 323)). Something is indivisible in this sense if it is impossible for there to be instances of it. For example, there can be instances of human nature; one of them is Socrates. But there cannot be instances of Socrates. So, Godfrey claims, the fact that a thing cannot be instantiated explains the fact that it is distinct from all other things of the same kind. The connection between indivisibility in this sense and individuation – the distinction of things of the same kind from each other – is that indivisibility is the mark of *unity*; and what explains something's being one will likewise explain its distinction from other things. Now, according to Godfrey indivisibility is explained by (substantial) *form*, and the reason for this, it seems, is that 'form is that through which an individual is that which it is, and subsists in a nature': a thing 'subsists in being through its form' (*Quodlibet* VII, q. 5 (p. 323)). Lying behind this is a commonplace Aristotelian assumption: a form, F-ness, is that in virtue of which such-and-such is F; but for *x* to be a property-bearer – for *x* to be F – presupposes that *x* is, or that *x* exists. And Godfrey appeals to the case of angels to buttress his case: we know that substantial form is a suitable candidate for the explanation for indivisibility, and thus individuation, since it is such an explanation in the angelic case.

   It might be thought that this would allow Godfrey to posit the existence of more than one angel of the same species, as *per* the 1277 requirements – since angels are subsistent forms, and forms according to Godfrey are particular of themselves. But not a bit of it: Godfrey claims to be agnostic on the question of how this kind of angelic plurality might be maintained: as he rather laconically puts it, the issue is 'difficult to understand' (*Quodlibet* VI, a. 16 (p. 259)). His reason is that he supposes inherence in different chunks of matter to be a necessary condition for distinction between different substances of the same kind. Godfrey talks about the extension of matter as a 'dispositional principle' of individuation: extension allows for *division* – for *cutting up* – and thus for the possibility of the manifold reception of different forms (of the same kind). (So while the basic division between explanations for and necessary conditions of individuation is related to Giles's approach, the details are quite different.)

   Why should Godfrey make inherence in discrete chunks of matter a necessary condition for individuation? After all, if forms are of themselves indivisible, it might look as though the requirement for matter is in fact superfluous. But Godfrey argues – following an interpretation of certain claims in Averroes (see Averroes, *In metaphysicam* IV (VIII, fo. 67rb)) – that number 'results from quantitative division', and thus that countability within a kind requires the inherence of substantial forms in separate chunks of matter. I think the idea is that indivisibility accounts for distinction, but it can only do so in appropriate circumstances. An angel is just a form, and while this form is indivisible in the required sense, there could not be another form with the same structure unless there were some further way of, as it were, allowing the two forms to be 'apart' from each other – and this is the role that extended matter plays in material entities. But Godfrey's claim that only particular natures really exist makes him reluctant to posit as the explanation for this something intrinsic to the particular over and above the nature (the only available feature would be an accident, and Godfrey argues that accidents are posterior to substances, and thus cannot individuate them). By arguing that the substance is intrinsically individuated (in virtue of its indivisibility, secured by its form), but that it presupposes a discrete chunk of matter for its indivisibility to render it discrete from other particulars, Godfrey sees his way between individuation by accidents, on the one hand, and a kind realism that would allow for really existent common natures or universals, on the other. (For the whole discussion of individuation, see *Quodlibet* VII, q. 5.)

I mentioned above Godfrey's Aristotelian identification of matter and form as the potential and the actual, respectively. In making this identification, Godfrey accepts the view that matter is pure potency, much as Aquinas did in the previous generation. He takes this view to follow from the unicity of substantial form thesis: if there is one essential actuality (one substantial form) in a substance, then matter must lack actuality. Of course, Godfrey maintains, matter is not absolutely nothing: it is not non-being. But it is pure potency, lacking any kind of actuality. (One reason why the opponents of the pure-potency thesis are such is that they believe the notion of pure potency, distinct from non-being, is simply unintelligible, since there is nothing that pure potency actually is, and in that case it is surely nothing.) This view is entirely in line with Godfrey's rather rigid Aristotelianism. (For the best discussion of the issue, see *Quodlibet* X, q. 9.)

Godfrey clearly rejects any view according to which we might think of a nature – common or particular – as a constituent of a thing. In line with this, he rejects any such view of existence too. We can think of individuals as existing (or not), and kinds as instantiated (or not), but none of this requires any kind of extramental distinction between essence and existence. Godfrey's basic line is very simple, and eminently reasonable: contingency does not require anything more than a conceptual distinction between essence and existence, and the fact that we can consider an essence in abstraction from existence does not mean that an existent individual includes some feature over and above the individualized essence. He deals with his opponent's inference from the identity of essence and existence to necessary existence by, in effect, arguing that existence is no more than the 'positing' of a thing: if we think of something in abstraction from existence, we are rejecting 'both its *esse exsistentiae* and […] its *esse essentiae*' (*Quodlibet* III, q. 1 (p. 171)). Note the assumption: there is no *esse essentiae* apart from actual existence: something that Giles, but not Henry, would accept.

Godfrey, as we might anticipate given his general intellectual orientation, reacts strongly against the voluntarist tendencies I have just highlighted in Henry and Giles. Henry is his particular opponent. He believes Henry's position to violate a basic principle of Aristotelian philosophy: the impossibility of self-motion. Henry's account of freedom – as including what we would call liberty of indifference – requires that the will can cause its own choice. Given that this is impossible, Godfrey argues that mere non-coercion is necessary and sufficient for freedom: for liberty of spontaneity, as we would put it. The will of necessity follows the moving command of the intellect (*Quodlibet* VIII, q. 16). Godfrey expresses all of this in terms of the object. The activities of intellect and will are both determined by their respective objects: the intellect is moved by its initial cognition of principles to the cognition of conclusions, and the will is moved by the goal – i.e. the goal and whichever of two contraries 'is more ordered to the goal'. The intrinsic indifference of the will to different volitions, and to willing or not, entails that the will 'needs to be put in act by something determinate' – i.e. the object (*Quodlibet* VI, q. 7 (p. 158)). Godfrey here takes a more extremely deterministic line than Aquinas, explicitly maintaining that reasoning is automatic: the outcome of rational deliberation, he maintains, is determined by the object, and the way in which the object impacts on the cognizer depends (merely) on the 'natural disposition and […] habits' of the cognizer (*Quodlibet* X, q. 13 (p. 372)).

Further reading

On the early Thomists and the *Correctorium* literature, the most extensive source is still Frederick J. Roensch, *The Early Thomistic School* (Dubuque, IA: Priory Press, 1964). For Henry of Ghent, the recent *A Companion to Henry of Ghent*, ed. Gordon Wilson (Leiden: Brill, 2011) replaces all other sources. There is no single volume on Olivi; the best collection is *Pierre de Jean Olivi (1248–1298)*, ed. Alain Boureau and Sylvain Piron (Paris: Vrin, 1999). There is nothing similar in English. There is no general monograph on Giles of Rome, either; perhaps the best overall summary of his thought is Giorgio Pini, 'Giles of Rome', in *Theological Quolibeta in the Middle Ages: The Thirteenth Century*, ed. Christopher Schabel, 2 vols (Leiden: Brill, 2006), I, pp. 233–86. Godfrey is well served in John F. Wippel, *The Metaphysical Thought of Godfrey of Fontaines: A Study in Late Thirteenth-Century Philosophy* (Washington, DC: Catholic University of America Press, 1981).

Notes

1   In what follows, I rely in part on the account in Pasnau, 1997a.
2   Here I summarize the account of Giles I offered in my *The Metaphysics of the Incarnation: Thomas Aquinas to Duns Scotus* (Oxford: Oxford University Press, 2002).

CHAPTER 6

Duns Scotus (c. 1266–1308)

Russell L. Friedman has recently argued that the Trinitarian theology of the first decade or so of the fourteenth century was marked by what we might think of as the search for explanations:

> What is involved in coming up with an explanation for a certain state of affairs? It seems clear that we need to analyse the state of affairs itself. And as part of this analysis, we have to figure out what comes first and what comes second, and how various things are related to one another such that precisely this state of affairs obtains. In other words, as soon as we start explaining something, we proceed to break it up into parts, and give those parts some kind of order and mutual relationships. Succinctly put: in order to explain something we need to draw distinctions. (Friedman, 2010, p. 99)

We have seen this tendency towards explanatory accounts in the thinkers we examined in the last chapter, but if any features mark the thought of Duns Scotus as distinctive, they are, first, a focus on identifying the grounds and explanations that are fit for purpose, as it were; and, secondly, since the grounds all turn out, as we shall see, to be *entities*, an attempt to work out the kinds of relations (sameness, constitution, and so on) that might exist between the entities themselves and the items for which they perform some kind of explanatory role. In the process, as we shall see, Duns Scotus – who is the lead in all of these matters – is able to formulate for the first time a notion that seems to us obvious and central to philosophy, but which to the ancients and early medievals seems to have played very little role: the notion of absolute identity. (This sounds like an outlandish claim; here I can only sketch the notion as Scotus defended it.)

There is little doubt in my mind that Scotus was the most philosophically talented of all the medieval theologians. His intellectual achievements clearly made a profound impression on his successors – even those who disagreed with him. Having lectured on the *Sentences* in Oxford, his Franciscan superiors, recognizing his great talent, moved him to Paris, where he lectured again – a unique educational pattern – so that he could become a Regent Master in what was then the pre-eminent of the two universities. According to Ockham, he 'surpasses all others in the subtlety of his judgment' (Ockham, *Ordinatio* d. 3, q. 6, n. 6 (trans. Spade, p. 153)). Peter Auriol (*c.* 1280–1322) reacts to Scotus's view on the common nature with both intellectual and aesthetic wonder: 'this opinion is subtle, and quite beautiful' (Auriol, *Reportatio in libros sententiarum* II, d. 9, a. 1, a. 2 (107b)). The most striking of all is the description from Adam Wodeham, reflecting the memories of the Franciscan house at Oxford in the 1320s: Scotus was 'a man […] lively and rational' (*homo* […] *vivax et rationalis*) (*Lectura secunda*, d. 10, q. unica, § 5 (III, 153)). He does not, to be sure, have the range of Aquinas, and certainly not the systematicity. But he is a more original and creative philosopher, and the sheer power of the arguments he comes up with in defence of his (usually novel) positions is astonishing. What is most notable about his contribution is its global reach: he aims at theories of maximal generality, which for him means including both God and creatures under the scope of the relevant theories. Someone who thinks this aim is mistaken from the very beginning will have little sympathy with Scotus's thought; but such a person will perhaps have little sympathy with philosophy generally in any case.

Scotus is, as I just suggested, not as systematic as Aquinas. This, I think, is in part a function of his early death: elements of his thought are fully worked out and integrated into a systematic whole – most notably, his metaphysics. Parts are very much work in progress, and in these areas it is hard to form one coherent systematically developed theory – most notably, his philosophy of mind and theory of cognition, but also (probably) his ethics. But his thought moves in such powerfully anti-Aristotelian directions, highly original, that it is tempting to suppose that he could not have achieved his goals without rejecting far more of Aristotle than he actually did. Had he done so, he would perhaps have ended up looking more like a rather later thinker on whom he was immensely influential, albeit indirectly: namely, Leibniz.

The easiest way into Scotus's forbiddingly complex thought is to consider his treatment of Avicenna's discussion of common natures – wisely highlighted by Etienne Gilson back in 1927[1] as the starting point for Scotus's metaphysics. Defending the reality of the common nature, Scotus appeals to the thought that similarity between two particulars of the same kind cannot be basic: it requires real, extramental grounding, and thus real, extramental, commonness, between two similar things:

> The same, the similar, and the equal are all based on the notion of one, so that, even though a similarity has for its foundation a thing in the genus of quality, nevertheless such a relation is not real unless it has a real foundation and a real proximate basis for the founding. Therefore, the unity required in the foundation of the relation of similarity is a real one. (*Ordinatio* II, d. 3, p. 1, q. 1, n. 18 (trans. Spade, p. 61))

The 'foundation' here is the common nature. Since this nature is supposed to perform some kind of explanatory function, Scotus reasons that it must be some kind of *entity* – it must be real: 'In the thing [viz. in extramental reality] the nature according to [its primary] entity has true real being outside the soul' (*Ordinatio* II, d. 3, p. 1, q. 1, n. 34 (trans. Spade, pp. 64–5)). And this entity is Avicenna's nature as such:

> 'Horseness is only horseness.' […] The what-the-thing-is is the *per se* object of the intellect and is *per se*, as such, considered by the metaphysician and expressed by the definition. (*Ordinatio* II, d. 3, p. 1, q. 1, nn. 31–2 (trans. Spade, p. 63, slightly altered))

The reason that the nature has some kind of entity is that it is supposed to be subject to the accidental modification of existing as this or that particular, and it is not possible for the subject of a real modification not itself to be real:

> Although it [the nature] is never without some one of these features [viz. being in extramental particulars or being thought of], yet it is not any of them of itself, but is naturally prior to all of them. (*Ordinatio* II, d. 2, p. 1, q. 1, n. 32 (trans. Spade, p. 63))

Given the medieval assumption that anything that has some kind of reality has some kind of unity, Scotus argues that the common nature, since it has some kind of entity, must also have some kind of unity: 'According to that [primary] entity, it has a unity [viz. less-than-numerical-unity] in proportion to it' (*Ordinatio* II, d. 3, p. 1, q. 1, n. 34 (trans. Spade, pp. 64–5)). If the common nature had numerical unity, then, Scotus reasons, it would be a determinate particular. If a nature does not include 'determinate singularity' in its *ratio*, then it cannot be numerically one:

> Whatever from its own notion (*ratione*) is in something *per se* is in it in every instance; therefore, if the nature of the stone were of itself a 'this' then whatever the nature of stone were in, that nature would be 'this stone'. The consequent is nonsense. (*Ordinatio* II, d. 3, p. 1, q. 1, n. 3 (trans. Spade, p. 38))

Since (e.g.) *being human* does not include *being Socrates*, then *being human* must lack real numerical unity. The notion of non-numerical unity is supposed to allow the 'same' nature to be in different particulars. This unity is what Scotus calls a 'proper passion' of the nature (*Ordinatio* II, d. 3, p. 1, q. 1, n. 34); but since the nature as it actually exists is always instantiated, the non-numerical unity is a feature of the nature merely as 'potential' (*Ordinatio* II, d. 3, p. 1, qq. 5–6, n. 173).

So, what is it for the nature to exist as a particular? Scotus accounts for this by introducing a further component into his ontology: a haecceity or thisness, an individuating feature. He argues for the haecceity by excluding other candidates for being individuators (e.g. matter, actual existence) by showing that these things too are common, and thus themselves require individuation (see *Ordinatio* II, d. 3, p. 1, qq. 3, 4, and 5–6). They thus cannot explain particularity. (On this view, of course, there is no reason to deny a multiplicity of immaterial substances in one species – so Scotus has identified a philosophical argument in support of the 1277 condemnation.) The haecceity somehow combines with the nature to form an individual substance. The haecceity is what Scotus calls 'primarily diverse' from anything to which it is not joined: its diversity is not explained by anything other than itself. It is a bare particular whose particularity is a primitive feature of itself. In virtue of its possession of a haecceity, a complete particular is *per se* diverse from anything else. The nature gains its particularity in virtue of its union with the haecceity:

> Whatever is in this stone is numerically one, either primarily or *per se* or denominatively. Primarily, say, as that through which such a unity belongs to this composite. *Per se*, the stone itself, of which what is primarily one with this unity is a *per se* part. Only denominatively, what is potential and is perfected by the actual and is so to speak denominatively related to its actuality. (*Ordinatio* II, d. 3, p. 1, qq. 5–6, n. 175 (trans. Spade, p. 103))

This gives us an abstract particularized nature ('denominatively' or extrinsically one) and an abstract haecceity (primarily one) as the 'components', as it were, of a concrete substance (the item that is *per se* one: that includes its individuator). On this picture, the haecceity is extrinsic to the particularized nature, but not to the whole substance that includes both. The item that is denominatively one, the particularized nature, turns out to be extremely important in this picture. Scotus sometimes labels such entities 'distinctive (*propria*) individuals' (*Ordinatio* I, d. 8, p. 1, a. 3, n. 148). Distinctive individuals are abstract particulars – items that Scotus sometimes labels not (concrete) things (*res*) or forms (*formae*), but (abstract) thing-nesses (*realitates*) or formalities (form-nesses, *formalitates*) – and to see why they are needed we need to look a little more closely at Scotus's account of sameness and distinction. Basically, a substance and its nature are supposed to be in some sense the same: and to be the same, they must, according to Scotus, be inseparable. And if the substance and the common nature were inseparable, then the substance would not be accidental to the common nature. Equally, if they were separable, the substance would not be one simple concrete object.

Why associate sameness and inseparability? (Why could not the common nature be an essential constituent of the substance without the substance's being necessary to the common nature?) Because, I think, Scotus holds that all changes are grounded in the production or destruction of something concrete, and if the common nature were (in some sense) a constituent of a substance, and could persist in the absence of the substance, then the destruction of the substance would be grounded in the destruction of something abstract – namely, the haecceity, the other constituent of the substance.

Scotus makes these points about change when discussing his
theory of relations. According to Henry of Ghent, a relation is
an (abstract) *mode* of its ground: Socrates's similarity to Plato, for
example, is a mode of Socrates's whiteness (see Henry, *Summa
quaestionum* LV, q. 6). Scotus objects: in that case, if Socrates remains
white but ceases to be similar to Plato, there is in Socrates nothing
more than a modal change, a change in *abstract* constituents; and
there are no such changes (see e.g. *Lectura* II, d. 1, q. 5, n. 214).
The particular argument here may not have much to commend it,
since it seems to result in a curious view of relations as analogous to
one-place predicates or monadic properties. But the point is clear
enough: changes in the abstract features of a thing are parasitic on
changes in its concrete constituents. Scotus's world, in fact, is a kind
of building-block world, in which changes in the things composed
from these concrete parts result from the production or destruction
of the concrete building blocks themselves.

The contrast with Aquinas's Aristotelianism is vivid. For example,
Aquinas agrees that concrete things are the building blocks of the
world. But the concrete things that Aquinas has in mind are complete
substances. Their accidents, and their substance-parts (prime matter
and substantial form) are not themselves concrete things. For Scotus,
contrariwise, prime matter, substantial form, and accidents, are
paradigm cases of concrete things – they are the building blocks from
which material substances are constituted. Thus Scotus rejects any
kind of prime matter identified as the purely potential. He believes
that the notion of pure potency is indistinguishable from nothingness,
and holds that, in order for it to be the substrate persisting through
substantial change, matter must include some positive actuality of its
own (*Lectura* II, d. 12, q. un., n. 37): there is something that matter is
'all the time' (contrast Aquinas's view, outlined in Chapter 4). And, as
Scotus's discussion of individuation makes clear, a chunk of matter is
a concrete particular with its own haecceity (see *Ordinatio* II, d. 3, p.
1, qq. 5–6, nn. 187–8, and n. 201). The same discussion makes it clear
too that Scotus thinks of substantial forms as concrete particulars,
including their own haecceities. Unsurprisingly, Scotus says the same
thing about accidents too, though for a different reason, of oddly
Aristotelian inspiration: he argues that the different Aristotelian
categories need to be kept apart from each other, as it were: if an item
in one category were individuated by an item in another category,
the individuated item would belong to both categories, in the sense

that it would include an accident-part and a substance-part, and the whole basic categorial taxonomy would break down (see *Ordinatio* II, d. 3, p. 1, q. 4, n. 91). This hypostatization of accidents has a delightful theological consequence: explaining transubstantiation is, for Scotus, child's play (see *Ordinatio* IV, d. 12, p. 1, q. 1, nn. 17–43)).

One of the appeals of Aquinas's view is that it has no trouble explaining the unity of a composite substance. For Scotus, the situation is far more problematic. In virtue of which of their features do prime matter and substantial form constitute a substance that is one thing? And is a material substance anything other than an aggregate of concrete particulars? And, if so, what might distinguish a substance from a mere aggregate (of prime matter and substantial form)? On the first of these questions, Scotus is agnostic: they do so just because each is the kind of thing that it is. Scotus appeals to notions of potency and actuality here: prime matter is the right kind of potency, and substantial form the right kind of actuality, to compose a substance (*Lectura* II, d. 12, q. un., n. 50). But the notion of potency here is nothing much like Aquinas's Aristotelian one, because it amounts merely to the claim that matter, as a concrete particular, is (sequentially) receptive of certain kinds of form – substance-constituting forms. And the notion of actuality is just the notion of being a concrete structure (of matter). For Aquinas, there is a lot more theory involved: actualizing matter's passive potency, whatever it is, certainly does not involve the production of anything new other than merely the actual substance itself.

On the second question, Scotus has a very distinct proposal. Aggregates are identical with (the sum of) their parts; substances are *constituted* by their parts, and count as things over and above (the sum of) their parts: a substance 'is a third thing other than its causes [viz. matter and substantial form]' (*Ordinatio* III, d. 2, q. 2, n. 84 (Vatican edn, IX, 153)). Scotus gives as his example a substance's distinctive individual, the 'form of a whole':

The form of a whole [...] is form [...] with respect to whole composite: not indeed an informing form, but a form by which the composite is a being quidditatively, and in this way the whole being formally is the form of a whole (just as something white is said to be white by whiteness): not indeed that the form of a whole is as it were a cause of its [viz. of the whole substance], causing as it were a whole along with matter and the partial form, but is the whole considered precisely, according to the way in which Avicenna speaks in *Metaphysics* 5: 'Horseness is just horseness'. (*Ordinatio* III, d. 2, q. 2, nn. 82–3 (Vatican edn, IX, 153))

The components here are distinctive individuals (of prime matter and substantial form). But presumably the same relation obtains at the concrete level too: the concrete substance is something over and above the concrete particular matter, form, and relation that constitute it.

On the third question, Scotus is likewise very clear. If a whole substance were simply identical with the aggregate of its parts,

> there would be no being in which proper passion and proper operation would be, or any proper accident, because these inhere in the species, and not in matter or form, or in both together, other than as they are one in some *per se* whole. [...] Neither does a proper passion or a proper operation or any other non-relational accident follow the whole precisely as relational. (Scotus, *Ordinatio* III, d. 2, q. 2, nn. 77 and 79 (Vatican edn, IX, 150–1))

A substance is something over and above the aggregate of its parts, and in virtue of this fact there are properties that inhere in the whole that cannot inhere in either of the parts alone, or in any mere aggregate of the parts.

Clearly, this allows Scotus a way of accounting for the unity of a substance with more than one substantial form – the very worry that Aquinas appealed to in rejecting the plurality thesis. And Scotus does indeed accept the plurality thesis, at least in the case of animate substances. His reasoning is simple: the identity of a dead body with its living ancestor (*Ordinatio* IV, d. 11, p. 1, a. 1, q. 2, nn. 189–206). Unity is explained by the ordering of the parts in terms of potency/actuality relationships (the matter is potential to the bodily form; the body potential to the animating form) (*Ordinatio* IV, d. 11, p. 1, a. 2, q. 1, nn. 252–3). Scotus even accepts that the radically different structures of the different organs suggests that they too have different forms: and unity is again explained by the ordering of the parts within the whole (*Ordinatio* IV, d. 11, p. 1, a. 2, q. 1, n. 254). Again, Scotus finds philosophical underpinnings for one of the key components on the late thirteenth-century condemnations.

In fact, the metaphysical picture is even more complex than this, since the concrete building blocks, and the things that they compose, include abstract particular constituents too – for example, haecceities and distinctive individuals, as we have already seen. Scotus introduced his famous 'formal' distinction to give an account of the distinction of such abstract particular constituents within one concrete thing. (The formal distinction is a clear descendent of Henry's intentional distinction; and other late thirteenth-century thinkers posited similar kinds of distinction too.) At one point, Scotus gives an exhaustive list of the different kinds of unity that he acknowledges:

> Just as we can find many degrees of unity –
>
> firstly, the minimal degree is unity of aggregation; in the second degree is unity of order; in the third is accidental unity, which adds to order the informing, albeit accidental, of one by the other of those things that are thus one; in the fourth is the *per se* unity of something composed of essential principles one of which is *per se* act and the other *per se* potency; in the fifth is the unity of simplicity which is truly sameness (*identitas*) (for whatever is there is really the same as each thing [there], and is not merely one with it by the unity of union, as in the other modes)
>
> – so, further, not every sameness is formal. I call that sameness formal when, [in the sixth degree], that which is said to be thus the same includes, *per se* in the first mode, that with which it is the same in its formal quidditative notion. (*Ordinatio* I, d. 2, p. 2, qq. 1–4, n. 403 (Vatican edn, II, 356–7))

The idea is that the first four types of unity involve really distinct components united to each other by means of certain real relations. I have examined these kinds of unity already. The fifth type of unity is of abstract particulars really the same (i.e. inseparable), but, as Scotus would put it, formally distinct, or non-adequately the same. Real sameness is sameness *simpliciter*, according to Scotus. Qualified sameness – aka formal or adequate sameness – is (roughly) our Leibnizian kind of identity. More accurately, *adequate* sameness is satisfied by two things if, first, they either are or belong to one and the same substance or accident (as Scotus puts it, they are the same in 'predication and [...] convertibility'); and, second, they are the same in kind (as Scotus puts it, they are the same in 'excellence and perfection' – recall that no kind is exactly as perfect as any other, according to the medievals) (*Reportatio* I, d. 33, q. 2, n. 62, 65 (trans. Wolter and Bychkov, II, p. 330)). Unsurprisingly, Scotus is explicitly committed to the indiscernibility of identicals: 'if contradictories are said of things, then [...] they seem to be not the same' (*Ordinatio* II, d. 1, qq. 4–5, n. 201 (Vatican edn, VII, 102)) – the contrapositive of Leibniz's identity principle (namely, if two things are the same, then everything true of one is true of the other). The principle was enthusiastically embraced by Ockham – see e.g. Ockham, *Ordinatio*, d. 2, q. 6, n. 27. In fact, the principle is a commonplace in the Middle Ages, but as far as I can tell Scotus was the first thinker to distinguish clearly between absolute identity and relative identity, or some kind of sameness that falls short of identity (both of which latter seem to be adopted in earlier thinkers without any attempt to clarify the nature of absolute identity).

Formal sameness obtains both in cases of adequate sameness and in cases in which the definition of one abstract particular is included in the definition of the other (in which case, the first is formally the same as the second, but not *vice versa* – see *Reportatio* I, d. 33, q. 2, n. 66). Adequate sameness is indeed Leibnizian identity; formal sameness is not really a kind of sameness at all, since it fails to be symmetrical. It is, rather, a principle of unity: saying that a part is formally the same as its whole while the whole is formally distinct from any proper part is a way of prioritizing the whole: a whole includes its part, even though the part does not include (exhaust) the whole.

Scotus puts all of this material to much wider use than merely the discussion of individuation. He holds that some distinctive individuals are identical with more than one abstract particular, or somehow include such particulars (see e.g. *Reportatio* II, d. 16, q. un., n. 18, discussing the relation between the (particularized) essence of the soul and some of its properties; and, importantly, *Ordinatio* I, d. 8, p. 1, q. 4, n. 219 on the distinction between *animality* and *rationality* in a human being: really the same, but united in virtue of their union with the whole distinctive individual or concrete substance of which they are abstract constituents). Claiming that these abstract particulars are really the same as each other is a way of asserting that they are united together to constitute a concrete object without this union requiring any real relation between them.

The underlying intuition in all this, I think, is that wholly unstructured or non-compositional concrete objects – monads, as it were – would be indistinguishable from each other. That they are composed of formalities – of abstract particulars – is what it is for them to be structured and thus distinguishable. With the Aristotelian, then, Scotus maintains that their abstract features distinguish kinds of concrete object. But he differs from the Aristotelian both in the analysis of which concrete objects there are (not just substances, but prime matter, and substantial and accidental forms), and in how the abstract features relate to their concrete wholes (not by inherence, but by real sameness).

Scotus holds, furthermore, that the same analysis obtains in the divine case also – indeed, it is in his discussion of the divine nature that Scotus makes the point about things and their abstract constituents most clearly. For example, Scotus holds that there are formal distinctions between the different divine attributes, since he does not see how it could ever be true to claim that (e.g.) wisdom is *identical* with goodness, and thus that divine wisdom is identical with divine goodness. What it is to be good, and what it is to be wise, are distinct; and what it is for God to be good is likewise distinct from what it is for God to be wise (*Ordinatio* I, d. 8, p. 1, q. 4, nn. 192–3). Again, the alternative would have God to be merely an unstructured monad; and how, Scotus wonders, could such a monad ever ground distinct predications about itself? The same obtains in the case of the Trinity, too: there is a formal distinction between the divine essence and the personal properties, with essence and property coalescing, as it were, to form a person (*Ordinatio* I, d. 2, p. 2, qq. 1–4, nn. 389–90). This, incidentally, allows Scotus to solve Trinitarian puzzles about identity: the Father is the same as the divine essence, and the Son likewise; but neither is identical with the divine essence, and thus neither is identical with the other. And – crucially – the transitivity of both sameness and identity is preserved.

This gives Scotus a metaphysics of maximal generality, including both the created and the uncreated realm in the same formal and conceptual scheme. This generality has a semantic consequence: that we can talk of God and creatures using our words in just the same standard senses in both cases. We can talk of God and creatures *univocally.* (We do not have to, of course; some religious language is analogical or even metaphorical.) For Scotus, this fact is required to underwrite the whole project of theology as a deductive science. The senses of words are *concepts*, and Scotus's claim is that God and creatures fall under the extensions of (some of) the same concepts. That there are in general univocal concepts is, according to Scotus, required for our ability to contradict each other, and for our ability to reason syllogistically:

> I designate that concept univocal which possesses sufficient unity in itself, so that to affirm and deny it of one and the same thing would be a contradiction. It also has sufficient unity to serve as the middle term of a syllogism, so that wherever two extremes are united by a middle term that is one in this way, we may conclude to the union of the two extremes among themselves without the fallacy of equivocation. (*Ordinatio* I, d. 3, p. 1, qq. 1–2, n. 26 (trans. Wolter, *Philosophical Writings*, p. 20, slightly altered))

The idea is that, for any concept φ, if we have grounds for thinking that '*x* realizes φ' and 'it is not the case that *x* realizes φ' are contradictories, then φ is univocal; and for any concept ψ, if we have grounds for thinking that ψ is the sense of a syllogistic middle term, then ψ is univocal. So Scotus rejects Aquinas's claim that analogy is sufficient for syllogistic reasoning – for avoiding the fallacy of equivocation. And I think his rejection is fully intelligible: if our terms do not mean precisely the same thing in our syllogistic reasoning, we will have no way of discerning whether our inferences are valid.

Scotus's argument in favour of univocity is simple enough, and well-known:

> Every intellect that is certain about one concept, but dubious about others has, in addition to the concepts about which it is in doubt, a concept of which it is certain. [...] Now, in this life already, a human being can be certain that God is a being and still be in doubt whether he is a finite or an infinite being, a created or an uncreated being. [...] For every philosopher was certain that what he postulated as a first principle was a being (for example, one was certain that fire was a being, and

another that water was a being). Yet he was certain whether it was first or not first. He could not be certain that it was the first being, for then he would have been certain about something false, and what is false is not strictly knowable. Neither was he certain that it was not first; for then he would not have claimed the opposite. (Scotus, *Ordinatio* I, d. 3, p. 1, qq. 1–2, nn. 27 and 29 (trans. Wolter, *Philosophical Writings*, p. 20, slightly altered))

The idea is that thinkers can genuinely contradict each other when claiming respectively (e.g.) that God is an infinite being, and that God is a finite being. In order for them to contradict each other, however, two conditions need to be satisfied: first, that they are genuinely talking about the same object, and secondly that they are ascribing contradictory properties to that object. To satisfy at least the second criterion, it is clear that (e.g.) *being* needs to be univocal.

How does Scotus relate this to the practice of theology? Here is what he says about a part of the 'identification' stage (as opposed to the 'establishment' stage) of the cosmological argument:

Every metaphysical inquiry about God proceeds in this fashion: the formal notion of something is considered; the imperfection associated with this notion in creatures is removed, and then, retaining this same formal notion, we ascribe to it the ultimate degree of perfection and then attribute it to God. Take, for example, the formal notion of wisdom or intellect or will. Such a notion is considered first of all simply in itself and absolutely. Because this notion includes formally no imperfection or limitation, the imperfections associated with it in creatures are removed. Retaining this same notion of wisdom and will, we attribute these to God, but in a most perfect degree. Consequently, every inquiry regarding God is based upon the supposition that the intellect has the same univocal concept which it obtained from creatures. (*Ordinatio* I, d. 3, p. 1, qq. 1–2, n. 39 (trans. Wolter, *Philosophical Writings*, p. 25, slightly altered))

Elsewhere, Scotus makes the same point in connection to revealed theology:

> Unless being implies one simple concept, theology will simply perish. For theologians prove that the divine Word proceeds and is begotten by way of intellect, and the Holy Spirit proceeds by way of will. But if intellect and will were found in us and in God equivocally, there would be no evidence at all that, since a word is begotten in us in such and such a fashion, it is so in God – and likewise with regard to love in us – because then intellect and will in these two cases would be of a wholly different kind. (*Lectura* I, d. 3, p. 1, qq. 1–2, n. 113)

If our words do not have univocal meanings in these various contexts, we will be unable to draw valid inferences about God and his nature – or at least, incapable of distinguishing when we have done so from when we have not.

Scotus does not mean that there is a common nature, *wisdom* (for example), instantiated in God and creatures. He is merely talking about the meanings of words, and claiming that there is a *concept*, wisdom, under whose extension both God and creatures fall. Of course, God and creatures can realize this concept in wholly different ways, as the first passage makes clear (God is infinitely wise, creatures finitely wise). But there is no reason to suppose that the structure of reality is closely mapped by the semantic and syntactic structures of our utterances, or the noetic structure of our concepts.

In fact, while it is clear that formalities in Scotus's metaphysics are *explainers* – they ground the truth of particular predications – we go wrong to infer from this that Scotus believes that there must be distinct formalities for *every* predication that we can truly assert. For example, there is no formality *being*. *Being* is just a concept, and predications of the form '*x* is a being' are grounded in *other* features of *x*; it is in virtue of these other features that *x* falls under the extension of the concept *being*. It is in virtue, for example, of being a human, a rational animal, that Socrates is a being. The task of the metaphysician, as Scotus sees it, is to discern the correct structure of reality, which includes discerning cases in which we need formalities, and cases in which we do not. We do this, oddly enough, by parsimony – discerning the minimal number and kind of formalities required to ground our true predications.

The concept of being is, itself, central to the work of the metaphysician. First of all, Scotus holds that this concept is the subject of metaphysics. The concept is univocal to God and creatures; to this extent, making being the subject of metaphysics makes metaphysics the science of both God and creatures – thus, in a way, resolving the Aristotelian *aporia* about the subject of metaphysics that I introduced in Chapter 3 (*Quaestiones in libros metaphysicorum* VI, q. 4, nn. 10 and 12). Secondly, Scotus holds that *being* is the primary object of the intellect (that feature in virtue of which things can be known), and thus that all beings are what he calls the *per se* object of the intellect – things that can be known (*Ordinatio* I, d. 3, p. 1, q. 3, n. 137).[2] Further, the concept of being is univocal to both actual and possible objects, so Scotus's view is that the proper object of the human intellect includes all actual and possible entities (*Quodlibet*, q. 3, n. 2). This univocity claim probably underpins Scotus's move towards theoretical generality that I mentioned above.

All of this metaphysical and related material seems clearly and systematically worked out, and perhaps forms the kernel of Scotus's thinking. But Scotus died young, and in the midst of complex on-going revisions to his various works, none of which works he successfully completed in final draft. One nice example of the resulting mess comes from his theory of cognition: his defence of the existence of intelligible species, against Henry of Ghent's denial of such items. Scotus objects: intelligible species, prior to cognitive acts, are required to explain the content of such acts (*Ordinatio* I, d. 3, p. 3, q. 1, nn. 352–8). But this claim is inconsistent with Scotus's considered (internalist) view on the content of cognitive acts, which is that content is explained simply by the real structure of such acts themselves, irrespective of their relations either to species or to objects (*Quodlibet*, q. 13, n. 13). And, in any case, the species that Henry rejects, species as defended by Aquinas, enter into a very particular kind of relationship with the corresponding cognitive acts: the acts are simply actualizations of mental content existing habitually in the mind as intelligible species – and this Aristotelian account of actuality, central to Aquinas's formulation of and defence of the theory of intelligible species, is unintelligible in the context of Scotus's reifying ontology. For Scotus, intelligible species and cognitive acts are both real qualities: one of them disposes the mind to produce the other in appropriate circumstances (see *Quodlibet*, q. 13, n. 32 for species, and, q. 13, n. 25 for acts). Scotus, it seems, did not have the chance to think the question through sufficiently thoroughly. If he had, he might well have found himself agreeing with Henry at least to the extent that someone with a notion of cognitive habits, posterior to mental acts – such as Henry has – has no need of intelligible species, however understood.

If Scotus's theory of cognition is work in progress, his theory of action is far more clearly worked out. Basically he follows the Augustinian trajectory, building on the accounts of Henry and Olivi in defending the will's radical freedom. To a greater extent than either of these thinkers, however, he attempts to give an account of the grounding of this freedom. He uses Olivi's introspective argument in favour of the existence of the liberty of indifference, claiming that 'the person who wills experiences that he could have nilled or not willed what he did' (*Quaestiones in libros metaphysicorum* IX, q. 15, n. 30 (trans. Wolter, *Will and Morality*, p. 153); 'nilling' is willing the opposite of something; 'not willing' includes refraining from willing). The grounding of the will's freedom – of its being a power such that it can 'perform either this act or its opposite, or can either act or not act at all' (*Quaestiones in libros metaphysicorum* IX, q. 15, n. 22 (trans. Wolter, *Will and Morality*, p. 151)) – is simply the will's nature: 'one can give no other reason why it elicits its action in this way except that it is this sort of cause' (*Quaestiones in libros metaphysicorum* IX, q. 15, n. 24 (trans. Wolter, *Will and Morality*, p. 151)). Equally, any given free action is such that its explanation is simply the will itself: 'Why does the will will this [action]? There is no other cause to be found except that the will is the will' (*Quaestiones in libros metaphysicorum* IX, q. 15, n. 29 (trans. Wolter, *Will and Morality*, p. 153)). This might make it look as though any given free action is underdetermined, and thus random. But Scotus disagrees. Nothing external to the will actualizes it; but it is a self-actualizer, and can simply sufficiently cause its own contingent activity:

> What reduces such a potency to act, if it is of itself undetermined towards acting or not acting? I reply that [...] there is an indeterminacy [...] of a superabundant sufficiency, based on unlimited actuality. [...] And something indeterminate in this [...] sense [...] can determine itself. [...] The indetermination ascribed to the will [...] is the indeterminacy of surpassing perfection and power, not restricted to some specific act. (*Quaestiones in libros metaphysicorum* IX, q. 15, nn. 31–4 (trans. Wolter, *Will and Morality*, pp. 153–5))

(The earlier Scotus supposed that the intellect was a partial cause of the will's activity; the later Scotus understandably rejects this view, and supposes that the intellect's activity is simply a necessary condition for the will's total self-motion.)[3] Scotus knows well enough that his view represents a radical departure from Aristotle, though he cannot quite bring himself to claim more than that Aristotle 'apparently says nothing' about the will in the sense in which Scotus takes it (*Quaestiones in libros metaphysicorum* IX, q. 15, n. 36 (trans. Wolter, *Will and Morality*, p. 155)).

Scotus says quite a lot about the scope of human freedom, too, wondering about the kinds of context in which we are capable of free action. He seems to think that it is intelligible to talk about freedom only in cases of explicitly *ethical* decision making. He supposes that we are motivated to act for our own advantage – and he uses Anselm's language of the affection for the advantageous to talk about this: the affection for the advantageous 'inclines the will in the highest degree to advantage'. The affection for justice, on the contrary, 'regulates it so that [...] it does not have to follow its inclination' (*Ordinatio* II, d. 6, q. 2, n. 50). The will is *motivated* by its advantage; but it can act justly, and thus against its natural motivation. (Note the difference from Anselm: for Anselm the will has two motivations – the affections for the advantageous and for justice – for Scotus, only the first of these affections is a motivation or inclination.) And it is in its capacity for acting justly that Scotus locates the will's freedom – the feature that distinguishes it from other appetites. Peter King has shown that the crucial issue for Scotus is *motivation*: we might act justly, and have reasons for acting justly, even in the absence of any internal motivation so to do.[4]

What of the *propositio magistralis* and *akrasia*? We can, of course, be motivated to act badly even when we know what we should do, and we might in this case freely act badly. Indeed, Scotus maintains that the embodied will is naturally inclined to follow passion – the pleasurable – and can do so even in cases in which we know what we should do (*Ordinatio* II, d. 43, q. un., n. 5). Scotus's externalism about reasons for acting morally make *akrasia* a readily intelligible phenomenon.

Underlying Scotus's theory of the will are some radical insights on the nature of contingency and possibility. Scotus believes that his account of the will requires alternative possibilities synchronically: if there is to be alternative possible actions, then the following must be true: *x* does A, and possibly, *x* does not do A (*Lectura* I, d. 39, qq. 1–5, n. 52). More generally, 'I call something contingent [...] whose opposite can be actual at the very moment when it occurs' (*Ordinatio* I, d. 2, p. 1, qq. 1–2, n. 86). This implies unrealized possibilities, and regimenting such possibilities in terms of sets of alternative states of affairs. Scotus never quite makes this latter move, though he invents the term 'logically possible', and uses it in much like our modern sense (non-contradiction) (*Ordinatio* I, d. 2, p. 2, qq. 1–4, n. 262). Again, the emphasis on divine freedom stressed in 1277 pays a remarkable philosophical dividend in the hands of Scotus.

Scotus's proof for God's existence likewise makes extensive use of certain rather unusual modal notions: in particular, the belief that 'Nothing can not-be unless something positively or privatively incompossible with it can be' (*De primo principio*, q. 3, n. 6 (trans. Wolter, p. 53)): in effect, that, at the level of concrete substances, it is non-existence, not existence, that requires explanation. Putting it crudely, if there is nothing about the causal constitution of the actual world that prevents something from existing, then that thing exists. If there is nothing incompatible with the existence of a first being, then that being exists. Scotus's argument attempts to show that the existence of such a being cannot be incompatible with the causal features of the actual world. Having shown that, he argues straightforwardly that such a being exists:

> Something simply first, able to produce an effect, is actually existent, and some actually existing nature is thus able to produce an effect. It is proved: anything with whose nature is it incompatible to have the possibility of existence from another (*cuius rationi repugnat posse esse ab alio*), has the possibility of existence from itself, if it can be. But it is incompatible with the nature of anything simply first, able to produce an effect, that it have the possibility of its existence from another [...]; and it can exist. [...] Therefore anything simply first, able to produce an effect, has the possibility of existence from itself. But what does not exist of itself does not have the possibility of existence from itself, for then non-being would produce something in being, which is impossible; and furthermore the thing would then cause itself, and thus would not be entirely uncausable. (*De primo principio*, q. 3, n. 5 (trans. Wolter, pp. 51–3))

In brief: if it is possible that there is something simply first, such a thing has the possibility of its existence from itself. But it is possible that there is something simply first. Therefore anything simply first has the possibility of existence from itself. But anything that has the possibility of existence from itself exists if no feature of the universe prevents it. There is no such feature; therefore something simply first is actually existent. (Note the inspiration not only of Anselm but also of Richard of St Victor (in the claim that something simply first 'cannot have the possibility of its existence from another').)

The emphasis on the contingency of divine willing has a powerful effect on Scotus's ethics and metaethics, too. To start with, it affects the account of natural law. Scotus does have a theory of natural law, and, like Aquinas, he holds that natural law has first principles, and precepts entailed by those principles. Also like Aquinas he holds that this entailment is grounded in a teleological claim about the ultimate good of human nature as fulfilled in the beatific vision. But, unlike Aquinas, Scotus does not believe that the precepts of the second table of the Decalogue have any intrinsic connection with human teleology. And unlike Aquinas, he does not believe that the first principle of natural law is that good should be done. Rather, it is this: 'God […] must be loved alone as God' (*Ordinatio* III, d. 37, q. un., n. 20 (trans. Wolter, *Will and Morality*, p. 277, slightly altered)), which Scotus describes as a law 'with which God's will would rightly agree' (*Ordinatio* IV, d. 46, q. 1, n. 3 (trans. Wolter, *Will and Morality*, p. 241)). As far as I can see, the reason for this shift from Aquinas's view is simply that the norms of natural law are supposed to be exceptionless and universally binding. And the only norm that can bind *God* is this one, or norms entailed by it.

No other norms are like this. The precepts of the second table are neither principles of natural law nor entailed by such principles.

In the things that are prescribed [in the second table of the Decalogue] there is no necessary goodness relative to the ultimate goal; neither in the things prohibited is there any malice that would necessarily turn someone away from the ultimate goal. For even if this good was not prescribed, the ultimate goal could be reached and loved; and if that evil was not prohibited, the acquisition of the final goal would be consistent with it. (*Ordinatio* III, d. 37, q. un., nn. 17–18 (text in Wolter, *Will and Morality*, p. 277))

So what makes the claims about moral duties outlined in the second table true? It is simply God's (contingent) attitude to those claims – i.e., his approval. These attitudes are determined not by further reasons but rather by God's perception of the ways in which, first of all, the precepts of the second table are harmonious with the first (*Ordinatio* III, d. 37, q. un., nn. 25–6) and, secondly, the precepts are harmonious with the natures of things (*Ordinatio* IV, d. 46, q. 1, n. 8). Moral harmony is not the only kind of 'harmony' that can be intellectually perceived. Logical or metaphysical compatibility can be too:

> The sense powers, which are less cognitive than the intellect, immediately perceive inappropriateness (*disconvenientiam*) in their object: this is clear in the case of hearing relative to an inappropriate object. Therefore if infinite were incompatible with being, the intellect would immediately perceive this inappropriateness and incompatibility, and then it could not have infinite being as its object. (*Reportatio* I, d. 2, p. 1, qq. 1–3, n. 72 (trans. Wolter and Bychkov, I, p. 137))

This view of the second table of the Decalogue makes the moral relation with both the first table and the natures of things far looser than Aquinas does, since 'harmony' and 'appropriateness' are far looser relationships than entailment. And Scotus makes use of this looseness to give an account of the contingency of the second table: in all such cases, God could have commanded other than he did. Scotus makes the point most clearly in the context of his discussion of the harmony of the two tables:

> The single justice [in God], which inclines him deter-ministically merely to his first act [i.e. self-love], modifies his secondary acts, although none of them necessarily, such that it could not modify them in the opposite direction. Neither does justice precede the [divine] will, by inclining it naturally to some secondary act. Rather, the will determines itself to any secondary object, and from this the act is modified by that first justice, because it is harmonious with the will to which it

is conformed, as if the first justice were the rectitude inclining [the will]. (*Ordinatio* IV, d. 46, q. 1, n. 8 (text in Wolter, *Will and Morality*, p. 249))

The claim that justice does not 'precede' the will is simply a way of expressing the fact that God is not bound by the relevant moral norms; neither is he bound to prefer any given norm over its opposite. There are many possible harmonious scenarios, incompatible with each other and governed by different and conflicting moral norms. I assume that God has options in cases that each alternative choice can be perceived to be aesthetically pleasing; in other cases, he has no choice. Nothing about the choice requires that the two or more alternatives are equally pleasing (though of course they could be), and Scotus presumably could allow too that God might choose the less pleasing. What Scotus is explicit about is that there is no secondary precept that is such that it is *always* more pleasing than its opposite, or than its dispensation.

All this ties in with Scotus's re-reading of Anselm's two affections, just noted. Acting justly is acting in accordance with the divine will (*Lectura* II, d. 6, q. 2, n. 36). Given that the affection for justice is not a motivation but a way of moderating our natural motivations, we act in accordance with justice, if we do, not as a result of any internal motivation, but simply because it is right – I drew attention to this externalism above, when discussing *akrasia*. God, for Scotus, is unlike us in this respect: he is (internally) *motivated* to act in accordance with justice, and is in this sense a moral agent:

> Since justice, properly speaking, is rectitude of a habituated will, and consequently inclines as it were naturally to another, or to oneself as to another, as it were, and [since] the divine will has no rectitude inclining it determinately to anything other than to its goodness as other, as it were […] it follows that it has no justice other than for paying to his goodness what suits (*condecet*) it. (*Ordinatio* IV, d. 46, q. 1, n. 7 (text in Wolter, *Will and Morality*, p. 247))

(See too the previous quotation: 'justice […] *inclines* [God] to his first act'.) Contrast Aquinas, who never talks of God's inclinations in this context: Aquinas's God acts justly simply because he should – rather like (good) human beings, in Scotus's account.

Much of Scotus's philosophy is strikingly modern – not only its pervasively argumentative and (in every sense) analytic character, but its stress on absolute identity and its invention of haecceity, logical possibility, and contra-causal freedom, to take just four obvious examples. Scotus is, too, as far as I know, the first person to defend something like a modern account of democracy. The question Scotus attempts to answer is the justification for ownership – specifically, since ownership is a post-lapsarian right, what law brought about the division of property after the Fall of humanity. He argues that this was brought about not by divine or natural law, but by positive law. And this in turn prompts him to reflect on the legitimacy of positive law. The legitimacy of positive law derives from the legitimacy of the legislator. And this, Scotus claims, 'can be just by common consent and election on the part of the community' (*Ordinatio* IV, d. 15, q. 2, n. 95 (trans. Wolter, *Will and Morality*, p. 315)), since 'one person can justly submit himself to another' (*Ordinatio* IV, d. 15, q. 2, n. 97 (trans. Wolter, *Will and Morality*, p. 317)). Perhaps not a resounding defence of democracy, but a step on a road along which Ockham, clearly influenced by Scotus, will travel further.

Further reading

As for Aquinas, the literature on Scotus is huge. A good introductory collection of essays is Thomas Williams (ed.), *The Cambridge Companion to Duns Scotus* (Cambridge: Cambridge University Press, 2003). On universals, the magisterial source is Martin M. Tweedale, *Scotus versus Ockham: A Medieval Dispute over Universals*, 2 vols (Lampeter: Edwin Mellen, 1999).

Notes

1 Etienne Gilson, 'Avicenne et le point de depart de Duns Scot', *Archives d'Histoire doctrinale et litteraire du Moyen Age*, 2 (1927), pp. 90–148.
2 More precisely, Scotus holds that (1) all those substances and properties that count as beings, (2) all those substances and properties that fail to be beings but are necessarily united to things that are beings, and (3) all those properties that fail to be beings but that are entailed by the property of being, fall under the proper object of the human intellect. The second of these is supposed to include specific differences (see *Ordinatio* I, d. 3, p. 1, q. 3, nn. 132–3), and the third the transcendentals convertible with being (one, good, true) (see *Ordinatio* I, d. 3, p. 1, q. 3, nn. 134–5).

3   See Stephen D. Dumont, 'Did Duns Scotus Change His Mind on the Will?', in Jan A. Aertsen and others (eds), *Nach der Verurteilung von 1277: Philosophie und Theologie an der Universität von Paris im letzten Viertel des 13. Jahrhunderts* (Berlin: De Gruyter, 2001), pp. 719–94.

4   See his 'Scotus's Rejection of Anselm: The Two Wills Theory', in Ludger Honnefelder and others (eds), *Johannes Duns Scotus 1308–2008: Investigations into his Philosophy*, Archa Verbi, Subsidia, 5 (Münster: Aschendorff; St Bonaventure, NY: Franciscan Institute Publications, 2010), pp. 359–78, on which I rely for this account.

Part IV

SIMPLIFICATION

CHAPTER 7

William of Ockham
(c. 1287–1347)

Scotus and Ockham have been the victims, in recent years, of some curious historiographies, largely driven by modern theological concerns. Scotus has been held responsible for all of the supposed woes of modernity, and Ockham, too, in his small way, for somehow impoverishing both philosophy and theology, destroying some supposed synthesis of the two achieved in the thirteenth century. The eminent historian Etienne Gilson, for example, asserts that Ockham's 'radical empiricism' reduces 'the understanding of faith to a bare minimum'; that 'an Ockhamist intellect is as badly equipped as possible for metaphysical cognition'; and that the result of Ockhamism is that 'the positive collaboration of faith and reason which obtained in the golden age of scholasticism' was replaced by 'a new and much looser regime in which the absolute and self-sufficient certitude of faith was backed by mere philosophical probabilities' (Gilson, 1955, p. 489). All of these claims are, in their most obvious sense, false. In what follows, I hope to provide a rather more nuanced account of Ockham's thought and its place in medieval philosophy. Ockham's rather stormy life – parts of which I discuss later – probably did nothing much to help his reputation.

Ockham is perhaps best known today for two things: his razor, and his nominalism. He was certainly the most talented Oxford philosopher in the array of thinkers inspired by Scotus. The razor was nothing much original – the notion that simpler solutions are methodologically and heuristically preferable to complex ones is plainly expressed in Aristotle, and the principle explicitly is appealed to by Scotus on various occasions (see e.g. Scotus, *Quaestiones super libros metaphysicorum Aristotelis* I, q. 4, n. 41). But there is something quite distinctive about the razor in its context. Scotus posited a large number of entities suitable (as he thought) to do certain kinds of explanatory work. Ockham and some of his contemporaries found the resulting ontology so baroque, so bizarre, that they believed that they had to trim it of formalities and such-like – more an axe than a razor, perhaps. But they did so at huge price. They had no idea how one might go about grounding or explaining the way the world is, the features and properties that things have, and so simply abandoned the task altogether. I think that no one made an intelligent suggestion on this question until the very different kinds of explanation arose with the birth of modern science, a couple of hundred years later. And having said this, it is important immediately to register a significant *caveat* in thinking of the fourteenth century as an era of ontological parsimony: many thinkers over the next couple of hundred years remained thoroughly under the influence of Scotus, and he immediately attracted a large and very significant group of followers. His huge importance and vast influence continued well into the seventeenth century, at which time there were still more 'Scotists' than adherents of any other kind of scholastic philosophy. So while there was a move to simplification and the abandonment of explanation, this movement was far from being the most prevalent in the centuries following the death of Scotus.

Nominalism is a more complex case than the razor. We have already encountered some eleventh and twelfth-century nominalists. (I follow general practice in using the term 'nominalist' to include reference to views, such as Ockham's, more properly labelled 'conceptualist': in the eighteenth century, for example, Bishop Berkeley, in a correction to the rough draft of his Introduction to *The Principles of Human Knowledge*, described Locke's brand of conceptualism as conforming to 'the opinion of that sort of Schoolmen called Nominals' (Berkeley, *Works*, III, 366, n. 10). So there is fine precedent for my usage.) Ockham is explicit that a universal properly so called is a mental concept that is 'naturally predicable of many things', and distinguishes this from words, which are likewise predicable of many, but merely 'by convention' (*Summa logicae* I, c. 14 (trans. Boehner, p. 34)). To demonstrate this, Ockham thinks it sufficient to show that nothing extramental could be universal. A basic assumption in the argument is that 'every substance is numerically one and singular'. Note that this already begs the question against Scotus, since it is precisely this claim that Scotus denies, at least if the domain of substance includes secondary substance. But (as we shall see) some realists – particularly Walter

Burley (1274/5–1344/5) – defend the existence of universals that
have numerical unity. So, given the assumption that every substance
is numerically one and singular, Ockham reasons that there can
be no extramental universals, for the simple reason that universals
cannot be numerically one. As Ockham notes, if a universal were
numerically one, then

> it would follow that Socrates is a universal, since there is no
> stronger reason for one singular substance to be a universal
> than for another. (*Summa logicae* I, c. 15 (trans. Boehner, p.
> 35))

The idea is that universals are supposed to be shared – they are the
'overlap' of different primary substances. But this kind of overlapping
requires that we can distinguish complete things from their overlaps.
And we can do this only if we have some independent way of
carving the world up into natural kinds. If we do have such a way, of
course, there may be a very strong reason for assigning one singular
substance to the category of universal (i.e. one that is the overlap
between two primary substances) and another to the category of the
non-universal (i.e. a primary substance).

Also, no substance could be annihilated without the annihilation
of all other substances of the same kind, since annihilation is total
destruction, and on Burley's view the universal constituent remains
for as long as there are instances of the relevant kind (*Ordinatio*, d.
2, q. 4, nn. 67–8 (trans. Spade, p. 124)). Equally, on the rejected view,
contradictories could be true of one and the same thing, since the
universal substance could be, for example, both happy and miserable:
happy in Christ, and miserable in Judas, to use Ockham's example
(*Summa logicae* I, c. 15 (trans. Boehner, p. 36)).

Clearly, these arguments are not effective against Scotus. But
Ockham has some different strategies for dealing with Scotus's
view. Ockham attacks the view by looking at the coherence (or
otherwise) of the various distinctions that are explicitly or implicitly
presupposed to it. His basic argument focuses on the formal
distinction, which Scotus explicitly appeals to in this context. The
attack seems a little flat-footed, simply asserting that there can be no
extramental distinction other than between distinct *things* (by which
I take it he means complete substances/complete accidents: whole,
independent, things):

> Among creatures it is impossible for some things to differ
> formally unless they are distinguished really. [...] If a nature
> and the contracting difference are not the same in all respects,
> therefore something can be truly affirmed of the one and
> denied of the other. But among creatures the same thing
> cannot be truly affirmed and truly denied of the same thing.
> Therefore, they are not one thing. (*Ordinatio*, d. 2, q. 6, nn. 25
> and 27 (trans. Spade, p. 156))

Scotus would see the question begged in the very first sentence.

Other arguments attack a distinction that Scotus seems to rely
on rather more implicitly: the distinction between the common
nature and any given distinctive individual. Ockham reasons that
'opposites cannot belong to the same thing': in this case, being
'common and proper' (i.e. including both a common nature and an
individuating difference, as Scotus maintains) (*Summa logicae* I, c. 16
(trans. Boehner, p. 38); see *Ordinatio*, d. 2, q. 6, n. 39). Scotus's answer
to this objection – Ockham's problem, as it has come to be known –
is that the real being of the common nature is potential being, and
its unity thus the unity of something real but potential. It is not clear
to me how intelligible this response is. But for some reason Ockham
in any case ignores it.

Finally, Ockham worries about the identity of the distinctive
individual itself. He focuses two distinctive individuals, Plato's and
Socrates's, in abstraction from any other entity (e.g. the contracting
differences), and wonders about their distinction from each other:

> If they are not really the same [as Scotus would maintain],
> then they are really distinguished. Therefore they are really
> distinguished by their own formal notions. But these do not
> include the contracting differences, by hypothesis. And so
> the point is established: they are distinguished by themselves.
> (*Ordinatio*, d. 2, q. 6, n. 74 (Spade, p. 166))

Part of the appeal of this argument is that these distinctive individuals
can be labelled (Ockham calls Plato's *a* and Socrates's *b*), and this
suggests that they can be identified in abstraction from anything else.
But Scotus would doubtless respond that, in this case, we have two
individuals whose identity is parasitic on the identity of something
extrinsic to them, and that Ockham has again begged the question.

So the conclusion is that anything that exists is *ipso facto* individual, and universals are just concepts. Ockham accounts for the fact of natural kinds by appealing to *resemblance* between various particulars. On this view, resemblance is grounded, ontologically, merely by the non-relational properties of things, without appeal to any really *shared* feature – and it was precisely the supposedly unsatisfactory nature of this claim that led Scotus to posit common natures in the first place. Thus Ockham:

> From the very fact that Socrates and Plato differ by themselves only numerically, and Socrates is most similar in substance to Plato, even disregarding everything else, it follows that the intellect can abstract something common to Socrates and Plato that will not be common to Socrates and to a whiteness. One does not have to look for any other cause of this than because Socrates is Socrates and Plato is Plato and each is a man (*Ordinatio*, d. 2, q. 6, n. 160 (trans. Spade, p. 181))[1]

Of course, it is a very real question whether or not Ockham is right about this.

Resemblance is the epistemic ground for our forming universal concepts of natural kinds. But how, as a matter of fact, do we come by such concepts, representing groups of individuals in natural kinds? What cognitive mechanism is operative in the process? Ockham develops the account of intuition and abstraction found in Scotus, insisting (in a way that Scotus merely hinted at) that all intellectual abstraction presupposes direct intuitive cognition of a particular, really present to the cognizer. Ockham holds that such cognition is necessary (and, indeed, sufficient) to allow us to form *judgments* about contingent states of affairs: specifically, the intuitive cognition of (say) Socrates and whiteness causes us to form the judgment that Socrates is white (*Ordinatio*, prol., q. 1 (trans. Boehner, p. 20)). An obvious objection is that sense cognition (non-conceptual cognition) might be sufficient to ground the judgment. But Ockham disagrees, on the grounds of philosophical generality: it is clear that in some cases intellectual cognition is sufficient to ground the relevant judgments – particularly, judgments about our only introspectively intuited mental states; so it should be sufficient in every case (*Ordinatio*, prol., q. 1 (trans. Boehner, pp. 19–21)).

Ockham says next to nothing about the process of abstraction, or about how we come to form general concepts. And what he does say seems remarkably unsatisfactory:

> Given this [intellectual] cognition of that man, [the intellect] comes to have a cognition that is general and common to every man. (*Reportatio* II, qq. 12–13 (*Opera theologica* V, 304, in Adams, 1987), I, p. 526))

The idea seems to be that intuitive cognition of a particular human being automatically gives rise to a concept that equally represents all human beings (*Ordinatio*, prol., q. 1 (Boehner, p. 29)). Marilyn McCord Adams makes a very sensible observation:

> This claim is not very plausible. For it seems that we have intuitive cognitions of many things, a concept of whose most [...] specific species we should find difficult to abstract. We would not experience this difficulty, if the intuitive cognition, together with the intellect, were a total cause of the abstract general concept. (Adams, 1987, II, p. 527)

And the position seems open to a further worry: how can we distinguish between those cognitions that represent just one instance of a kind and those that represent many instances of a kind? Ockham here appeals to his causal theory of mental content:

> We have a cognition proper to one singular thing, not on account of a greater likeness to one than to another, but because this intuitive cognition is naturally caused only by the one and not by the other, and cannot be caused by the other. [...] It is always of the nature of such a cognition (*visio*) to be caused by one object and not by another; and if it is naturally caused, it can be caused only by the one object and not by the other. Therefore the reason why intuitive cognition, rather than [...] abstractive cognition, is said to be proper to the singular thing, is not similarity, but only causality; no other reason can be assigned. (*Quodlibet* VI, q. 6 (trans. Boehner, p. 30))

Intuitive cognitions are caused directly by their objects, and this causal relationship is what explains the fact that the cognition represents just one particular – indeed, just the one that caused it (see *Reportatio* II, dd. 12–13 (*Opera theologica* V, 295–6)).

One very distinctive feature of Ockham's theory is the rejection of intelligible species – indeed, for different reasons, of all kinds of species. In the case of intellectual cognition, Ockham holds that acts cause habits or dispositions, but that (unlike intelligible species, on standard accounts) these habits are posterior to, not prior to, the relevant acts (see *Reportatio* II, dd. 12–13 (*Opera theologica* V, 253)). There is not much at stake here, I think, since everyone allowed for dispositional cognitions caused by acts, and (as I argued in discussing Scotus above) the reasons for positing intelligible species were superseded by the structures of later thirteenth-century cognitive theory, even though the term continued in use. Much more important is Ockham's denial of the *species in medio*. Such species are causal intermediaries between the object and the cognizer. Without such causal intermediaries, Ockham posits action at a distance, which he argues to be possible on empirical grounds (the sun's rays; magnets) (see *Reportatio* III, q. 2 (*Opera theologica* VI, 48)). Given this possibility, parsimony thus allows us to dispense with such species.

At the ellipsis in the passage from *Quodlibet* VI, just quoted, Ockham concedes something that is on the face of it surprising: 'If you say that [an intuitive cognition] may be caused by God alone, I admit that this is true'. This concession seems to undermine the externalist, causal account of mental content. And this is Ockham's notorious claim that it is possible to have intuitive cognition of non-existents, a position that Ockham arrives at on entirely theological grounds (any non-relational thing that can be caused by a secondary cause can be caused by the primary cause – i.e. God) (*Quodlibet* VI, q. 6 (trans. Boehner, pp. 25–6)). It must be admitted that Ockham's position is a little slippery here. Clearly, God could cause a belief that the object exists even when it does not; but this, Ockham maintains, would be a case of abstractive cognition, not intuitive, since the content of intuitive cognition is determined precisely by the way the world is at the time of cognition. (It is this claim that led earlier commentators to identify some form of scepticism in Ockham. But in fact I think any medieval theologian could have made such a claim: it has nothing to do with epistemology, and a lot to do with theological claims about the nature of divine goodness. Anyone could maintain, for example, deception by an evil spirit, as in a case considered by Descartes.) But – and this is the slippery bit – if any *knowledge* is caused, Ockham maintains, it will be a cognition that the object does not exist. Ockham reasons that intuitive cognitions standardly give rise to both positive and negative judgments, and hence sees no reason why this intuitive cognition would not simply give rise to a negative judgment (*Quodlibet* VI, q. 6, ad 1). This is in a way fair enough: we cannot have knowledge of what is not the case, and the content of intuitive cognition is determined by the way the world is at the time of cognition. But the mechanism is left unclear: what it would be to cause an intuitive cognition of an object such that the cognition gives rise to the judgment that the object does not exist? (Adam Wodeham, incidentally, found the view deeply puzzling, and proposed (much more plausibly, I think), that the negative judgments to which intuitive cognition can give rise are explained *inferentially*, from positive intuitions and judgments: see Wodeham, *Lectura secunda*, prol., q. 2, § 2. This seems right: we cannot 'see' negations.)

Ockham's view on the nature of concepts underwent a shift during his career. In his earlier work, he held that concepts are (mental) *objects* of thought – things he labels '*ficta*' (*Ordinatio*, d. 2, q. 8 (trans. Boehner, pp. 41–3)). Later, an application of the razor helped Ockham realize that he has no need for *ficta*: concepts are just the *thoughts* themselves (the acts of cognition): such acts are themselves simply natural signs for collections of particulars (*In perihermeneias* (trans. Boehner, pp. 43–5)).

In fact, Ockham has quite a lot to say on concepts and the nature of thought. One of the ways in which Ockham's thought overlaps considerably with certain modern developments in philosophy of language and philosophy of mind is his belief that conceptual thought is fundamentally *linguistic* in nature, and that this characteristic is best understood in terms of some kind of mental language. (There are antecedents to this view in Scotus; but Scotus does not develop them in any systematic or extended way.) One motivation that Ockham has for positing mental language is to provide suitable objects for assent. He holds that the objects of assent (be it belief or judgment) must be the kinds of thing that can have truth-values, and thus be linguistic complexes. But written or spoken discourse will not do, since these kinds of linguistic complexes are merely conventional. Hence, the objects of assent must be either the complex (mental) objects of acts of apprehension (on the *ficta* view of concepts), or simply these acts themselves (on the act view of concepts). For example, on the earlier view the object of the judgment that Socrates is white is not Socrates or any extramental state of affairs but rather the mental sentence SOCRATES IS WHITE; and on the later view the judgment lacks any object at all, and is simply identical with the asserted mental sentence (see *Ordinatio*, prol., q. 1 (*Opera theologica* I, 16–17) for the *fictum* view, and *Quodlibet* III, q. 8 for the act view).

As we shall see in the next chapter, a number of philosophers in the early fourteenth century adopt nominalist views on universals. Part of Ockham's unique genius lay in his grasping that this metaphysical shift requires – for consistency's sake – a parallel shift in logic and semantics. After all, common terms cannot signify common natures, since there are no such things. Ockham argues that what he labels 'absolute' terms – basically, *substance*-sortals – signify particulars: all particulars of a given kind. Absolute terms are contrasted with connotative terms: terms that signify particular substances in a certain respect (paradigmatically, in relation to their accidental forms). Connotative terms do not have real definitions – they do not pick out the essence of anything. They merely have nominal definitions, and such definitions simply pick out the primary and secondary significates of the term. Nominal definitions, like real definitions, are not metaphysically neutral, however: the correct nominal definition of a connotative term will bring out precisely the metaphysical structure of the realities it signifies (e.g. 'wise' means 'a substance endowed with wisdom': it signifies a substance or substances and connotes the quality *wisdom*) (*Summa logicae* I, c. 10). Abstract substance terms signify in just the same way as concrete terms: they signify what they standardly refer to (i.e. particular substances) (*Summa logicae* I, cc. 5–6). It also follows reasonably obviously that the subject and predicate in a true sentence (e.g. 'Socrates is wise') refer to the same thing, and the truth conditions for an assertoric proposition consist simply in this identity of reference (the so-called 'two-name' theory of predication) (*Summa logicae* II, c. 2). The instructive contrasting case is Scotus, who uses abstract nouns to refer to all sorts of *abstracta* (common natures, distinctive individuals) the existence of which Ockham simply denies.

Ockham uses some of this machinery to analyse his predecessors' talk of common natures. Central to nominalist semantics is the notion of 'supposition': part of which is more or less our notion of reference, what it is in the world that a word in a particular syntactic context points to. If the word has *personal* supposition, it refers to real particular things of a given kind – i.e. it refers to what it primarily signifies, since (common) nouns primarily signify collections of particulars. If it has simple supposition, it stands for a (universal) concept. And if it has material supposition, it stands for a word – it is a case, as we would say, in which a word is *mentioned*. Ockham uses this to analyse Avicenna's claims about horseness, much beloved of the realists. In 'horseness is a universal', 'horseness' has simple supposition; in 'horseness is a singular' it has personal supposition (*Ordinatio*, d. 2, q, 6, n. 190 (trans. Spade, p. 187, slightly altered)). Ockham also uses it to expose an equivocation in Scotus's main argument in favour of the non-numerical unity of the common nature. According to Scotus, as we saw in the previous chapter, 'if the nature of stone is this stone, then whatever the nature of stone is in is this stone'. Ockham disambiguates: if 'nature of stone' has personal supposition, then the antecedent is true but the inference invalid (since there are many stones and many stone natures, and 'nature of stone' can refer to any of them). If it has simple supposition, then the antecedent is false, since a concept is never identical with something extramental (*Ordinatio*, d. 2, q. 6, n. 115). This looks fatal for Scotus's argument – though not necessarily, of course, for his conclusion. At a stroke a vast amount of metaphysics is simply excised by a simple semantic distinction, and if Ockham were to be believed it would be hard to see what all the fuss was about.

Ockham's ontological reductionism goes further than this rejection of *abstracta* of the Scotist variety: he claims that the only concrete objects that exist are substances and qualities. The remaining categories admit of merely linguistic analysis. Ockham arrives at this conclusion on a case-by-case basis, applying the razor as much as possible. A substance's extension is nothing over and above a substance – it is just the distance between the parts of the substance (*Quodlibet* IV, q. 25). And Ockham argues that relations are nothing over and above related substances by showing that Scotus's reifying position entails various absurd conclusions: relation words are connotative, signifying absolute substances and connoting their existing in a certain way with respect to other substances. As he sees it, relational predications are made true simply by substances and their non-relational properties, and Scotus's argument – that a view such as this entails that something real (x's being really related to y) presupposes something mind-dependent (the relational predication) – is clearly mistaken (*Ordinatio*, d. 30, q. 1 (*Opera theologica* III, 309–10, and p. 316 responding to Scotus's evidently specious argument at Scotus, *Ordinatio* II, d. 1, qq. 4–5, n. 223)) – a good use of the razor, it seems to me.

The category of quality is different from this. Ockham argues that changes other than in the category of quality can be explained either by the production or destruction of substances, or by changes in position. But qualitative changes are not like this, and this seems to suggest that (at least some) qualities must count as things distinct from substances (*Quodlibet* VII, q. 2). Ockham accepts that matter and form are concrete entities, but he rejects Scotus's claim that material substances are constituted from matter and substantial form or forms. He claims instead that such substances are *identical* with their matter and substantial form(s), provided these various parts are spatially coincident (*Ordinatio*, d. 30, q. 1). Ockham objects to Scotus's view for a couple of reasons. First, it offers no plausible causal explanation for the 'emergence' of the constituted substance from the union of its parts (*Quaestiones variae*, q. 6, a. 2 (*Opera theologica* VIII, 216)); secondly if the constituted substance is composite, then it is nothing other than the composite that is *identical* with all its parts (*Summulae physicorum* I, c. 19 (*Opera philosophica* VI, 206)). I do not think that Scotus should be at all worried by the second of these, which just amounts to an assertion that substances are identical with the collection of their substance parts. Against Scotus's reasoning in defence of his view, Ockham asserts that simple accidents inhere in a substance's simple parts, and complex accidents in the complex whole (*Quaestiones variae*, q. 6, a. 2 (*Opera theologica* VIII, 216–17)). The case of sensation is rather tricky. We might think that Scotus is right to think that it inheres immediately in the whole, in which case Ockham should say that, since it inheres in both matter and form, it is itself in some way complex, with both material and formal (intentional or immaterial) elements. In fact, in the passage just cited Ockham rather implausibly claims that it is simple and inheres merely in the form – a claim which seems to downplay the inextricably psycho-physical character of sensation in Aristotelian psychology.

Ockham's views on universals, as he himself notes, make it hard for him to make rational sense of the doctrine of the Trinity. Of course, this is perhaps a Herculean task in any case; but Ockham's predecessors believed themselves to have succeeded in just the ways that Ockham believed himself to have failed. His approach involves embracing some version of the formal distinction – and a very odd version, as we shall see. Basically, the divine essence and a divine person are really one thing, but non-identical (since they are subject to different predicates) (see *Ordinatio*, d. 2, q. 11). This of course is flatly contradictory of Ockham's usual denial of the coherence of the formal distinction. And it has disastrous consequences in logic: syllogistic form is not universal (since it fails in cases such as the following: 'The numerically one essence is the Son; the Father is not the Son; therefore the Father is not the essence' (*Ordinatio*, d. 2, q. 6, n. 32 (trans. Spade, p. 157)). Neither is the principle of non-contradiction universal in scope, since it fails in the divine case (since contradictories can be true of one and the same thing: 'Paternity is incommunicable [...] paternity is that thing which is communicable' (*Ordinatio*, d. 2, q. 11 (*Opera theologica* II, 374)). This is unlike Scotus's view, since it simply defines, or at least describes, the formal distinction in terms of its entailing the falsity of these logical principles, without invoking Scotist formalities at all. This – unlike Scotus's view – seems to me simply unintelligible.

There is an alternative route open to Ockham here – he could simply claim that the distinctions between the persons are primitive. After all, the formal distinction is required only if we assert that the personal properties somehow explain the distinctions between the divine persons. But it would be possible for us to make no such assertion at all – we could omit all talk of personal properties – and in this case we would not need the formal distinction. Ockham is unwilling to make just this kind of appeal to mystery, though some of his immediate successors did (see Friedman's (2010) discussion of Walter Chatton (*c.* 1285/90–1343/4) and Gregory of Rimini (*c.* 1300–58), ch. 4). But in some ways Ockham's position is even more mysterious than theirs, since it requires denying that the principle of non-contradiction and syllogistic logic hold globally – they do not hold in the case of God.

These Ockhamist beliefs about the Trinity perhaps lend some credence to Gilson's kind of scepticism about the theological adaptability of Ockham's philosophy – though we should keep in mind that it is the rejection of the formal distinction, not nominalism about universals, that fundamentally causes Ockham's difficulty here. Another area in which Ockham has in modern times come under assault from the point of view of the Catholic faith is his argument – or supposed lack thereof – for God's existence. It is clear enough that Ockham denies the cogency of any proof from the fact that things in the universe are caused: he does not believe that, even in the case of essentially-ordered causes, there is any reason to posit a first cause. In an infinite sequence of essentially-ordered causes, each member is sufficiently explained by its relation to the member immediately prior in the sequence, and in this sense the whole sequence is sufficiently explained (*Quaestiones in libros Physicorum Aristotelis*, q. 135 (trans. Boehner, p. 120)). But Ockham does believe that it is possible to demonstrate the existence of a first *conserving* cause: conservation relationships are of necessity simultaneous, and if there were no first conserver, then there would be infinitely many ordered conserving relationships: and according to Aristotle an actual infinite is impossible (*Quaestiones in libros Physicorum Aristotelis*, q. 136 (trans. Boehner, pp. 122–3)). And Ockham is happy with something like Scotus's argument from eminence too: there must be a being 'than which nothing is more noble and more perfect', otherwise there would be infinitely many beings of ever increasing perfection (*Quodlibet* I, q. 1 (trans. Boehner, p. 126)). But Ockham does not believe that we could show that there is just one such being – it does not follow from the claim that there is a being than which none is more eminent that there is just one such being; and nothing about the impossibility of an actual infinite could ground the conclusion that there is a such a being (*Quodlibet* I, q. 1 (trans. Boehner, p. 126)). If this is theological scepticism, it is scepticism of a rather restrained kind.

One aspect of Ockham's theology of God has been of some influence recently: Ockham has made a small name for himself in modern philosophy of religion for his views on the correct way to solve the dilemma posed by God's knowledge of future contingents – his endorsement of what Alvin Plantinga has labelled 'Ockham's way out'. As we shall see in the next chapter, Peter Auriol held, and held that Aristotle held, that contingent propositions about the future do not obey bivalence – roughly, the principle that a proposition is either true or false. Ockham – for reasons that we do not need to pause on now – holds that God's existence is everlasting, not timeless, and thus that, if God is to know future contingents, propositions about them must be either true or false. His solution is ingenious, though not uncontroversial. Ockham asserts that there are true propositions about future contingents – indeed, it is possible to formulate a true proposition about *any* future contingent, and God knows all of these (*Predestination, God's Foreknowledge and Future Contingents*, Assumption 6). He holds, however, that the truth of these propositions, prior to the occurrence of the contingent event itself, does not subject that event to any kind of inevitability or necessity: it is and remains *contingent*. The crucial move is to identify such propositions as

> about the present as regards their wording only and more evidently about the future, since their truth depends on the truth of propositions about the future. Where such [propositions] are concerned, the rule that every true proposition about the present has [corresponding to it] a necessary one about the past is not true. (*Predestination, God's Foreknowledge and Future Contingents*, Assumption 3 (trans. Adams and Kretzmann, pp. 46–7))

Propositions are, if true, always true, and hence true in the past. On the face of it, the past truth of such propositions makes them (now) necessary. If it was true yesterday that Socrates is just today, then it is now necessary that Socrates is just, since the past cannot be changed. Ockham claims, however, that this rule does not obtain for all propositions – there is a group of propositions, those about future contingents, for which the rule does not hold. As Ockham puts it, such propositions are 'about the future', and thus (now) as contingent as the future. The truth value of the proposition is, in effect, caused by the future event, and some such events are (now) contingent. As Ockham notes, the view is puzzling, since it requires that God have access to the future – to what *is not* yet – without determining it. But in other ways it is not as puzzling as it might seem: on the face of it, the truth, even the fixed truth, of a proposition about the future does not require that the future itself is fixed: the truth of the proposition is indeed determined by the future contingent event; and were things to be such that they turn out differently, the proposition would have been false.

One of the features of Ockham's philosophy that has most exercised his modern detractors is his apparent acceptance of a divine-command metaethic: the view that (with one notable exception) an act is morally right if, and only if, it is commanded by God; and (with one exception) morally wrong if, and only if, it is prohibited by God. Ockham's position is worked out with some care. At its core is the claim that the duty to perform such-and-such an act follows automatically from the act's rightness: 'Everything right is to be done and everything that is wrong is to be avoided' (*Quodlibet* II, q. 14 (trans. Freddoso and Kelley, II, p. 149)). God's command, in other words, does not explain the duty to perform such-and-such an act; that duty follows automatically from the act's rightness.[2] But the scope of God's possible commands is very wide: God can command anything other than hatred of himself. The reason for this last restriction is simply that loving God is the one necessarily good act – the only act that cannot be altered by circumstances (*Quodlibet* III, q. 16).

In fact, this last point is slightly ticklish. What would happen if God were to command us to refrain from loving him for a period of time – perhaps (to use Ockham's examples) for study or some other good work? Ockham clearly accepts that this is a possibility – unlike the possibility of God's issuing a command that God should be hated.[3] An objection to Ockham's view which he himself raises is this: surely in such a case the act of loving God would indeed be altered by its circumstances, and become bad. Ockham's reply is that such an act would, since committed against a divine command, fail to be a genuine act of love for God (*Quodlibet* III, q. 14).

I have already drawn attention to the possibility that the early fourteenth century represents a period of momentous change in political philosophy. The nature of this change is much debated, and I do not want to enter into the details of the debate here, since it would take us on a long detour into the secondary literature. The question that commentators have focused on is this: can we trace the origin of the notion of (subjective) *rights* to the early fourteenth century? In Ockham, the issues are woven into the discussion of Franciscan poverty. It seems to me clear enough that something akin to the notion of subjective rights can be found in Ockham's claim that prelapsarian Adam and Eve had a right – a *power*, as Ockham puts it – to the simple use of the earth's resources, without *ownership* of these resources.[4] But it is clear enough too (as Tuck, 1979, points out) that this notion has its origins in Roman civil law, and, though put to particular theological work, is not really novel. In some ways, it seems that the more innovative claims in Ockham concern what happens *after* the Fall.

In the case of postlapsarian humanity, Ockham treats property-ownership and what he terms 'temporal jurisdiction' in precisely parallel ways: both were introduced as the result of the Fall, to protect human beings from each other – from 'the immoderate appetite of the wicked':

> Aristotle considered that the crowd is bad and given to evil, and therefore common things are by most people less loved, and consequently less cared for, than things which are their own; among such people, therefore, the appropriation of things is better than community. (*Short Discourse* III, c. 7 (trans. Kilcullen, p. 90))

Ownership and temporal jurisdication things are *powers*, and after the Fall, God gave both powers to all human beings:

> Power, therefore, to appropriate temporal things to a person or persons or to a collectivity was given to the human race by God. And for a like reason God gave, without human ministry or cooperation, power to establish rulers with temporal jurisdiction, because temporal jurdisdiction is one of the things necessary and useful for living well. (*Short Discourse* III, c. 7 (trans. Kilcullen, p. 90))

(Note, then, that these things, while not quite *natural* subjective rights, since they are the result of divine positive law, are still highly akin to such rights: they are powers, presumably inalienable by anything other than divine decree, to do things required for survival in the postlapsarian world. And I will quote in a moment a passage that makes at least the second of these look like a natural right too.) The view targets papalist writers such as Giles of Rome (and, of course, the political claims of Pope John XXII, the great scourge of the Franciscans, responsible for canonizing Thomas Aquinas): temporal power of all kinds derives directly from God, to the people, without any papal or ecclesiastical intermediary.

Ockham goes into some detail on the manner in which human beings exercise political power (one of the rights given by divine law in the light of the Fall) – how they 'establish rulers with temporal jurisdiction'. Ockham holds that temporal jurisdiction is bestowed on rulers by God. But not directly; rather, God gives to the people the power to establish such rulers, and in exercising this power the people act as God's agent in God's conferring political power. Ockham likens the role of the people to that of the minister in baptism: the activity of the minister is a necessary condition for the conferral of grace. (He makes the mechanism very clear in another example: the election of the Pope: *Short Discourse* IV, c. 5 (trans. Kilcullen, p. 113).)

So one way of establishing temporal rulers is by the consent of the people – presumably in some form of democratic process, analogous to the election of a pope. And while it is not the only way of establishing temporal power (Ockham mentions just war and direct divine decree too), it is clearly the primary way, and is the first that he mentions when discussing the way in which the Roman Empire was established:

[The Roman Empire] could have become a true empire [...] without any violence, through the free and willing consent of peoples voluntarily subjecting themselves to the Romans. For from God and nature all mortals born free and not subject to anyone else by human law have the power voluntarily to set a ruler over themselves. (*Short Discourse* IV, c. 10 (trans. Kilcullen, p. 124))

This power, again, looks very much like a subjective right, and here it is not only from God but also even 'from nature'.

Ockham worries a bit about the metaphysics here, in a way that might seem odd from the perspective of modern political theory. Just as in the sacramental and papal cases, he believes that the relevant power is exercised just once; after baptism, or the election of a pope, the power or jurisdiction conferred on the recipient 'depended regularly on no one but God alone' (*Short Discourse* IV, c. 6 (trans. Kilcullen, p. 114)) – the continuing consent of the people, in other words, has no rule in the continuing legitimacy of the ruler; though (Ockham seems to imply) their explicit *dissent* might render the rule illegitimate (*Short Discourse* IV, c. 6).

The background to all this is the rather fraught and vitriolic debate surrounding Franciscan poverty, which came to a catastrophic head in the 1320s. The point about the distinction between use and ownership is that it provided a way for the Franciscans to live in the world without violating the vow of absolute poverty that the rule held them to. By appealing to the prelapsarian condition, Ockham tries to find a concrete case in which the distinction between use and ownership does not look simply specious, since, after all, a right to use might on the face of it look just like ownership. Ockham disagrees, and holds that among the 'perfect' there is no sense in, and need for, ownership:

> But it is otherwise in a multitude of the perfect, or of those who are striving for perfection with their whole strength, because the perfect love and care for common things (*communia*) more than for their own (*propria*); whence we read that some Romans, unbelievers even, cared much more for common things than for their own. (*Short Discourse* III, c. 7 (trans. Kilcullen, p. 90))

Of course, in some ways this looks like vain utopianism. But intended or not Ockham's identification of the Franciscans with prelapsarian humanity – in contrast, presumably, with the rest of the Church – must have been rather provoking to his opponents. Still, maintaining that property ownership requires a decree of positive law (by a legitimate law-maker: in this case, God) provides a way for Ockham to distinguish it from mere use.

This rather voluntarist or positivist theory of government and political power – this defence, in short, of (postlapsarian) *democracy* – contrasts powerfully with Aquinas's more absolutist vision. Aristotle held that government is somehow *natural*: any appropriately sized body of people would naturally form a political society (see *Politics* I, cc. 1 and 2). Aquinas explores this question theologically when discussing the presence (or otherwise) of political power in the Garden of Eden. As Aquinas sees it, political society would arise naturally and necessarily even in the absence of human sin and the need for mutual protection from the sinful depredations of others. Human beings are naturally social, and this requires 'one person to preside [...] to direct to the common good'; and they differ in knowledge and ability, such that 'it would be inappropriate for the person [with a higher degree of knowledge and justice] not to use this for the utility of the others' (Aquinas, *Summa theologiae* I, q. 96, a. 4 c)). Aquinas explicitly appeals to the opening of Aristotle's *Politics* here, and there is no doubt that his position represents a way of presenting a fundamentally Aristotelian position within a

Christian context. There is no need here for a specifically voluntary or contractual agreement to set up a political society: it emerges naturally from human nature, just as Aristotle held.

The contrast with Ockham could hardly be more striking; neither could the shift from Aristotelian to more modern, voluntarist notions of the state. In particular, the notion that human beings voluntarily agree with each other to submit to political power in order to protect themselves from each other (from 'the immoderate appetite of the wicked') cannot help but bring to mind a similar, if more dismal, thought in Hobbes:

> The finall Cause, End, or Designe of men, (who naturally love Liberty, and Dominion over others,) in the introduction of that restraint upon themselves, (in which wee see them live in Commonwealths,) is the foresight of their own preservation, and of a more contented life thereby; that is to say, of getting themselves out from that miserable condition of Warre, which is necessarily consequent [...] to the naturall Passions of men. (Hobbes, *Leviathan*, pt. II, c. 17)

Hobbes claims that there is a natural law to the effect that human beings ought to introduce such restraints on themselves:

> [The second law of nature is] that a man be willing, when others are so too, as farre-forth, as for Peace, and defence of himselfe he shall think it necessary, to lay down his right to all things; and be contented with so much liberty against other men, as he would allow other men against himselfe. (Hobbes, *Leviathan*, pt. I, c. 14)

This is close to, but not quite, Ockham's view; Ockham argues not that there is a *duty* to behave in this way, but merely a *right* (*ceteris paribus*). Still, for what it is worth, Ockham's view looks to me to belong more to the modern voluntarist-positivist family pioneered by Hobbes than to the naturalistic position defended in the Aristotelian-Thomist tradition; and claiming that we have a right to political self-determination seems to look forwards to much later developments, towards democracy, in political theory. And in making these moves, Ockham develops in a rather systematic way some of the insights of Scotus's that I described in the previous chapter.

Ockham is not alone in making these kinds of defence of democracy. I mentioned Scotus above, but worthy too of brief notice is Marsilius of Padua (1275/80–1342/3), arts master and eventually Rector of the University of Paris (1312–13). Both he and Ockham ended their days at Munich, excommunicated by a pope whose jurisdiction they did not acknowledge (since, they maintained, John XXII had fallen into error over the scope of his power, and a heretical pope is no pope at all). Ockham had been summoned to Avignon in 1324 to answer certain worries about his orthodoxy, probably the result of the personal animosity of the Dominican John Lutterell, Chancellor of the University of Oxford from 1317 to 1322. While in Avignon Ockham fell in with the spiritual Franciscans, including the Franciscan Minister General Michael of Cesena, also in Avignon, in his case to answer papal worries about the Franciscan teaching and practice of poverty. The whole group fled to the Emperor, Ludwig of Bavaria, in 1328. Marsilius, in the meantime, had been with Ludwig since 1326, helping the Emperor in his power struggle against the Pope.

Marsilius's concerns were more political than Ockham's, and his cast of mind less speculative and metaphysical. His basic line, like Ockham's, is the independence of civil jurisdiction from ecclesiastical. But his approach is recognizably more modern: the efficient cause of (positive) law, and thus of the legislative power, is the whole people 'or the weightier part thereof' (*Defensor pacis* I, c. 12), and likewise the efficient cause of government (i.e. the executive power) (*Defensor pacis* I, c. 15). The reason given in both chapters is that human beings come together into political society solely for the purpose of living well (*Defensor pacis* I, c. 4 – the Aristotelian assumption), and thus must themselves have power over the things that are necessary for them to achieve this goal. Ockham's presuppositions are utterly different from this: he follows Augustine in making civil society a consequence of the Fall, whereas for Marsilius, contrariwise, democracy is natural, and he repeatedly discusses the opening two chapters of Aristotle's *Politics* – where civil society (though not, of course, democracy as such) is presented as a natural consequence of human nature (Aristotle, *Politics* I, cc. 1–2, discussed in detail in *Defensor pacis* I, cc. 3–4). Ockham's theory is more like Scotus's than Marsilius's is; but Marsilius's conceptual arguments in favour of democracy clearly owe more to Scotus's inchoate conceptual arguments than Ockham's rather historical ones do.

Further reading

The best book on Ockham is Marilyn McCord Adams, *William Ockham*, 2 vols (Notre Dame, IN: University of Notre Dame Press, 1987). Also useful is Paul Vincent Spade (ed.), *The Cambridge Companion to Ockham* (Cambridge: Cambridge University Press, 1999). For Ockham's theory of mind and mental language, see Claude Panaccio, *Ockham on Concepts* (Aldershot: Ashgate, 2004).

Notes

1   Ockham's thinking here is perhaps influenced by the Oxonian Henry of Harclay (*c.* 1270–1317), who made just the same claim a couple of years earlier: 'Something common can still be abstracted from what are ultimately distinct in reality, which are not one in any thing, for things like this can be similar or agreeing. Therefore, one common concept can correspond to each on the part of the intellect' (*Quaestiones ordinariae*, q. 14, n. 92 (trans. Henninger, I, p. 157)). Or perhaps, as I suggest in Chapter 7, he derived this view from the Parisian Auriol. Nominalism was in the air in both great university cities.

2   This principle cannot be quite right, since it seems to extend the web of duty too far, not allowing space for supererogation. I am not sure what Ockham says about this, and in any case do not know of a discussion of supererogation in his works.

3   In his early *Reportatio*, Ockham affirms that God could command or cause hatred of himself. But since God is not obliged by any precept not to command or cause such an act, God would, in causing such an act, not be doing anything wrong (*Reportatio* II, q. 19). This does not look quite right: it is (according to Ockham) not by a positive precept but by a necessarily true principle of natural law that we are obliged not to hate God. I take it that Ockham, in later rejecting this view, comes to be more consistent on the issue.

4   This is the argument that Richard Tuck makes in his ground-breaking study, *Natural Rights Theories: Their Origin and Development* (Cambridge: Cambridge University Press, 1979).

CHAPTER 8

From 1310 to 1350

Durand of St Pourçain (and Hervaeus Natalis)

While Scotus was ploughing his own highly original furrow, the Dominicans were, in the meantime, pursuing their own lines of research too, and (as it turns out) restricting their intellectual vitality in ways that seem with hindsight to be mere folly. One of the more interesting thinkers working in Paris in the years immediately after Scotus is the Dominican Durand of St Pourçain. We have three versions of Durand's *Sentence* commentary: an early working draft (now conveniently known as 'A'), composed in advance of the lectures themselves, probably in 1307–8. This work was circulated (Durand claims against his will), and provoked something of a small storm in Dominican circles. Durand's commentary diverged from Aquinas on many points, and he was constrained to compose a second version (version 'B'), more in line with the Thomist party line, which doubtless formed the basis of his lectures at Paris, delivered 1310–12. Durand became Master of Theology in 1312, but spent his time from 1313 in Avignon and elsewhere performing various ecclesiastical duties for the Pope – apparently with a high degree of diplomatic competence. His troubles with the Dominican order persisted: 93 theses were condemned by the order in 1314, and in 1317 no fewer than 235 theses, considered contrary to the teaching of Aquinas, were censured. But in this year Durand was consecrated a bishop, and thus effectively placed outside Dominican jurisdiction. He was involved on the Pope's side in the controversies on Franciscan poverty, and was part of the Avignon commission in 1326 investigating the doctrinal orthodoxy of Ockham – and which led ultimately to Ockham's flight to Munich. But between 1318 and 1325 Durand found time to produce a third version of his *Sentence* commentary (version 'C'), published in 1327. A is relatively autonomous from its Dominican authorities; B rather conformist; and C a revision of A in a truly independent way.

Of course, the Parisian Dominicans found themselves in an awkward position, since the order in effect required them to defend theses that had been condemned by the Bishop of Paris some years earlier. As we have seen, one of the key issues concerned individuation: could there be more than one angel in one species? Aristotelians of all stripes were challenged, of course. Durand's near contemporary, the Dominican Hervaeus Natalis, in his *Sentence* commentary (dating from 1302–3), having defended a complex and original version of the Thomist position, proposes two possible ways of reading the condemnation in a way compatible with Thomism. First, the condemnation could be read as rejecting the view merely that it is a lack of divine power that grounds the impossibility of more than one angel in a kind; or, 'perhaps better', secondly, the condemnation could be read as rejecting the view that angelic immateriality is the explanation for the impossibility. And he comments on the second that

> if [the Bishop] understood [the article] in this way, he indeed understood it well. But if he understood it differently, then whatever was contrary to his intention would have to be inferred from what he did not say (*habeatur per non dicto*). (Hervaeus, *In quatuor libros sententiarum commentaria* II, d. 3, q. 2, a. 2 ad 3 (p. 211a))

Both readings seem rather forced. The condemned proposition (as I noted in Chapter 5 above) is that God cannot make more than one angel in a species, and that the reason for this is that angels lack matter. I take it that a natural reading of this would make the target of the condemnation the conclusion (viz. that God cannot make more than one angel in a species), rather than merely the reason for this restriction – albeit that proponents of this restriction hold as a matter of fact that angelic immateriality is the reason for this. But Hervaeus capitalizes on the possible ambiguity. He believes, of course, that there cannot be more than one angel in a species, and so needs to find a reading of the article that will allow his view while yet condemning some other, closely related, view. The first interpretation, admittedly, seems flatly contradictory to the sense of the article, since what is condemned is not the view that it is God's lack of power that causes the restriction, but rather angelic immateriality. The second gloss is, as Hervaeus himself claims, indeed better, and, as we have seen, the same move was made by Giles of Rome.

So what reason does Hervaeus propose for the impossibility of multiple instantiations of one angelic kind? He suggests that what allows forms to be multiply instantiated is their including a certain 'latitude' (*latitudo*), and that this latitude is something 'other than the absolute notion of the form'. This latitude 'implies potentiality and imperfection', such that something including such potentiality can be a part of something else (e.g. as an individual can be part of a species, or as a human soul can be part of a human person). So Hervaeus concludes that angels lack such latitude:

> An angel neither is a part of a whole, nor is naturally able to be such; [...] therefore [...] among angels one cannot differ from another other than specifically; on account of which there cannot be many in one species. (Hervaeus, *In quatuor libros sententiarum commentaria* II, d. 3, q. 2, a. 2 c (p. 210b))

Not a particularly fine piece of philosophizing, and clearly some kind of descendent of Giles's view (that angelic forms lack the restriction in degree that would allow them to admit of multiple instantiations); but the point of the rather tortuous argumentation, I take it, is to distinguish the case of an angel from that of a human soul, since the medievals generally admit, against the Averroists, that there can be more than one human soul. And Hervaeus is safe from 1277, as he interprets it. It is, after all, not the non-inclusion of matter that prevents there being more than one angel of a given kind, but the lack of the imperfection of 'latitude'.

Durand has no such difficulties, at least in versions A and C of his commentary. (Version B is different: clearly, Durand cannot provide a discussion of the issue that would satisfy his Dominican colleagues, so he simply omits it.) He is not concerned to defend (in any way, even one as forced as Hervaeus's) the position of Aquinas, and he has no problem with positing a plurality of angels in one species.

On the question of universals, he is someone who, I think, aims to be a nominalist. Unlike Aquinas (and Scotus, for that matter), he claims not merely that universals are mental entities, but also that common natures are: 'the common nature, in many individuals, is one thing merely in reason, and many in reality'; and, more significantly, Durand draws from this claim the conclusions that there is no need to seek for a principle of individuation, and that the common nature and the individual differ 'as concept and existent thing' (*Scriptum super quatuor libros sententiarum* II, d. 3, q. 2 (§ 14, versions A and C)). The difference from Aquinas on this latter point is that the common nature, for Aquinas, is not a concept, but something that can receive the accidental modifications of being a real thing, in the individuals, or of being a concept, in the mind. Durand identifies the common nature as the concept, and he has an account of individuation in general that avoids reference to any intrinsic principle. According to Durand, there can be many instances of a kind if and only if there is a cause or causes that can produce such instances: and doing so simply requires the possibility of a 'repeatable action' (*Scriptum super quatuor libros sententiarum* II, d. 3, q. 3, § A15; § C14).

Over the two versions, the nominalist position remains the same; but the influence of Hervaeus diminishes. To start with, version A accepts Hervaeus's view that the latitude of a form explains its repeatability (*Scriptum super quatuor libros sententiarum* II, d. 3, q. 3, § A7; § A15), but Durand rejects the view that angelic forms lack such latitude (*Scriptum super quatuor libros sententiarum* II, d. 3, q. 3, § A14). In any case, as it turns out, Durand, in this early version, does not understand the latitude of a form in just the way that Hervaeus does. According to Hervaeus, the latitude is explained by something extrinsic to the form, whereas Durand (perhaps rather more like Giles) believes that latitude is an *intrinsic* feature of the form: it is simply the 'nature of the form, to which it is not repugnant to be found in many' (*Scriptum super quatuor libros sententiarum* II, d. 3, q. 3, § A13). Be that as it may, Durand comes to abandon any kind of endorsement of latitude as an explanation for repeatability. Among other things, he criticizes, in his later account, Hervaeus's argument in favour of his view that there cannot be more than one angel in a species, rightly claiming that it simply begs the question (since there is no reason to associate the impossibility of being a part with the question of individuation) (*Scriptum super quatuor libros sententiarum* II, d. 3, q. 3, § C9). Rather, Durand claims, simply being an existent entity – simply being an instantiation of a form – explains individuation (*Scriptum super quatuor libros sententiarum* II, d. 3, q. 3, § C8). And existence is explained simply in terms of efficient causation: having a causal origin of the right type explains existence, and the existence of more than one thing of the same kind is explained by there being more than one possible causal origin of the right type (*Scriptum super quatuor libros sententiarum* II, d. 3, q. 3, § C14). The contours of the position remain much the same between the two versions; but the explanatory role of formal latitude disappears. Durand is silent about his reasons for the shift, but I assume that he came to see that the theory did not work in the context of a view that allows for multiplicity within an angelic species, and was thus superfluous to requirements.

Peter Auriol

Doubtless the most important thinker between Scotus and Ockham is the Franciscan Peter Auriol. Like Durand, he embraces a nominalist view on the question of universals. But he distinguishes carefully between different kinds of realist views, and clearly allows himself to be influenced by, and target, Scotus, in a way that is not evident in the work of Hervaeus and Durand. The relevant part of Auriol's *Sentence* commentary dates from 1316 to 1318, and includes critiques of views similar to those of Durand. It also provides arguments strikingly similar to those formulated in 1317–19 by Ockham, lecturing in the *Sentences* in England during those years – and it is possible that Auriol's treatment of these problems was influential on Ockham's. And Auriol's nominalism, like Ockham's, is more carefully thought through than that of Durand.

In particular, Auriol distinguishes the view of Scotus – which he interprets as positing 'a reality [...] to which neither universality nor particularity is repugnant, [...] not the same as that to which universality is repugnant' (*Reportatio in libros sententiarum* II, d. 9, q. 2, a. 2 (II, 107a)) – from that of Plato, according to which 'there is a reality in which Socrates and Plato coincide, and other realities through which they differ', and notes that, in his opinion, 'many today really fall into [this view]' (*Reportatio in libros sententiarum* II, d. 9, q. 2, a. 1 (II, 103b)). As I show below, the position is Burley's. And Auriol rejects both of these views.

Auriol rejects Burley's view by arguing – as Ockham will do a year or two later – that something can be annihilated only if all of its components are annihilated. So if Burley's view is true, something can be annihilated only if its nature is annihilated; and its nature can be annihilated only if all instances of its kind are annihilated. But God can clearly annihilate any single thing he chooses. So Burley's opinion is false (*Reportatio in libros sententiarum* II, d. 9, q. 2, a. 1). On the way through his discussion, Auriol makes it clear that Burley's view is in effect committed to the claim that a universal has 'numerical unity' (*Reportatio in libros sententiarum* II, d. 9, q. 2, a. 1 (II, 106a)). Against Scotus's view, Auriol's main argument is that Scotus is committed absurdly to the real existence or entity of something that lacks numerical unity – as Auriol puts it, is 'indifferent' to this or that unity. His first argument is one Ockham uses too. Socrates includes 'an indifferent thing and a non-indifferent thing', the common nature and the distinctive individual: 'therefore there are two humanities in Socrates, one proper to him, one indifferent' (*Reportatio in libros sententiarum* II, d. 9, q. 2, a. 2 (II, 107b)). And this is absurd.

Given that realism is false, Auriol opts for a very clearly articulated nominalism, one that he explicitly makes compatible with epistemological realism about natural kinds:

> To the third question [viz. whether specific unity is merely a unity in resemblance, and in quality]: I reply and say 'yes'. (*Reportatio in libros sententiarum* II, d. 9, q. 2, a. 3 (II, 108b))

And he goes on to describe the process according to which we form common concepts:

> This is the sequence: a particular thing is naturally disposed to form similar impressions, of the same kind, in the intellect; therefore [particular things] cause a species of the same kind in the intellect. From species of the same kind in the intellect there follows one act of the same kind – and I do not now care whether the species is that act or not. Therefore individuals that can share one species share one act. And from one act there follows one [objective] concept in the intellect. [...] But an objective concept is nothing other than the thing appearing as an object (*res apparens obiective*) through an act of the intellect, which is called a concept. (*Reportatio in libros sententiarum* II, d. 9, q. 2, a. 4 (II, 109a))

Clearly, Ockham adopts something like this externalist view too. (I return to Auriol's distinctive theory of concepts as items with *esse apparens* below.)

For something to be an individual is for it to be indivisible – such that it cannot be instantiated, we might say (*Reportatio in libros sententiarum* II, d. 9, q. 3, a. 2). And according to Auriol nothing real can be instantiated. So no explanation for indivisibility is required, other than the real things themselves. Auriol's strategy is rather unexpected: he follows Scotus in showing that anything that might be added to the individual to explain its indivisibility will itself be common (*Reportatio in libros sententiarum* II, d. 9, q. 3, a. 2). Still, Auriol acknowledges that the question of indivisibility is different from the question of the distinction between particulars in the same species – since, after all, two particulars with all the same properties ought to be identical. So, he claims, what prevents there being two particulars with all the same properties is (in the case of material substances) the fact that they are different chunks of matter; and (in the case of immaterial substances such as angels) that they are receptive of different properties (*Reportatio in libros sententiarum* II, d. 9, q. 3, a. 4). The theory leaves many questions unsolved; but it is plain that Auriol is right in supposing that there might be two different accounts needed for the distinct questions of indivisibility and distinction within a kind.

Auriol does not explicitly consider in this context the formal distinction that is at the heart of Scotus's theory. But he does so elsewhere, in a more theological context. As we saw, Scotus posits formal non-identity between the divine attributes, and between the divine essence and personal properties in the Trinity. Auriol rejects the distinction in both cases. In the first – that of the divine attributes – he believes that it posits too much. If there is any way in which the attributes are not the same, or non-identical, they are distinct (*Scriptum super primum sententiarum*, d. 8, q. 3, a. 5 (Buytaert, §§ 149–57)), and if they are distinct but somehow united they must enter into composition (*Scriptum super primum sententiarum*, d. 8, q. 3, a. 5 (Buytaert, §§ 158–63)) – a conclusion which both Auriol and Scotus would deny. Furthermore, if the non-identity of the attributes is not real distinction – if it is *secundum quid* non-identity – then the attributes themselves cannot be fully-fledged beings, but merely beings *secundum quid* (*Scriptum super primum sententiarum*, d. 8, q. 3, a. 5 (Buytaert, §§ 142–48)). Again, Scotus denies this, since he thinks the attributes are fully real; and Auriol denies it, since he thinks that each attribute simply *is* the divine essence (under a certain description). Thus, Auriol holds the divine attributes are simply concepts: these concepts signify *being* directly (*in recto*) 'indeterminately' (i.e. not any given kind of being); but they connote (*in obliquo*) determinate *rationes* – determinate descriptions, we might say. These concepts have extensions, and asserting that God has such-and-such an attribute is a way of asserting that he falls under the extension of such-and-such a concept. For example, when we claim that God is just, 'just' signifies a being, indeterminately, and connotes the fact that this being is such that it gives to everyone what is her due. Or consider the case of God's immensity:

> The immense is that which can reach every place, and immensity that by which he can do this. It is certain that the whole concept of being is included principally here and in *recto*, even though a certain something (*certum quid*) is included also, in *obliquo*. (*Scriptum super primum sententiarum*, d. 8, q. 3, a. 5 (Buytaert, § 62))

This is clearly a way of trying to preserve divine simplicity: the only thing, concrete or abstract, is the divine essence. Auriol has a similar instinct about the divine essence and personal properties in the Trinity, too, though he develops what he wants to say in a rather different direction. In a way, just as Auriol thinks that Scotus posits too much *distinction* in the case of the divine attributes, he thinks that Scotus posits too little *reality* in the case of the essence and properties. The divine attributes signify the same thing *in recto*, but not *in obliquo*. The essence and any personal property signify the same thing *in obliquo*, but not *in recto*: there is some sense in which they signify (different) concrete objects. Essence and property are fully real, and it is this that Auriol thinks that Scotus has got wrong. Auriol argues that the concepts that we can form of the essence and of the property are determinate (not applicable to any other object) and non-overlapping (*Scriptum super primum sententiarum*, d. 33, a. 2 (p. 736b)): they are distinct *in recto* (*Scriptum super primum sententiarum*, d. 33, a. 2 (p. 737b)). And what grounds the applicability of these concepts to God is the fact that the essence and the property is each a thing, 'grounding the same unity and indivision in reality' (*Scriptum super primum sententiarum*, d. 1, q. 1, a. 4 (Buytaert, p. 370, § 111));

contrast the case of the divine attributes, which are merely concepts, not things). So here we have fully real concrete things, really the same as each other. Auriol sometimes speaks of them as 'constituents' of a person, in something like the way bricks and mortar constitute a house (*Scriptum super primum sententiarum*, d. 26, a. 3 (p. 587b).[1] So Auriol is fully serious about the claims to their concrete reality. But, unlike the bricks and mortar of a house, they are 'indistinct' (*Scriptum super primum sententiarum*, d. 33, a. 2 (p.737b)). I take it that we might best think of something like the statue case beloved of modern metaphysicians: the bronze lump and the statue are concrete objects, grounding different concepts, but in some crucial sense indistinct: fully overlapping. Or, to borrow another modern example, we might think of a wooden pillar, at once a statue and a wall support. But instead of thinking of the wood constituting the statue and the support beam, we might think of the constitution relation running the other way round: the statue and the beam constitute the wooden object. (Odd, I know, but it might be something along the lines of what Auriol is thinking: two concrete constituents, fully overlapping.) At any rate, the essence and property are inseparable, and thus signify each other *in obliquo*:

> The divine properties are the essence through every kind of indistinction, both real and rational, even though they can be distinguished conceptually, in relation to their being conceived in *recto*. So two concepts can be formed, of the property and of the essence, of which each of necessity includes the property and the essence. But one includes the property in *recto*, and the indistinct essence in *obliquo*, and the other one *vice versa* [i.e. the essence in *recto* and the property in *obliquo*]. (*Scriptum super primum sententiarum*, d. 33, a. 2 (p. 741a))

Auriol develops an original account of the distinction between intuitive and abstractive cognition, in which one of his most celebrated notions plays a central role: the notion of *esse apparens* – the *appearance* of something, or something's being *apparent*. Abstractive cognition is, as Auriol puts it, fundamentally an exercise in imagination, or some intellectual cognate of imagination (*Scriptum super primum sententiarum*, prooemium, q. 2, a. 3 (trans. Pasnau, p. 207, § 111)), quite different from the phenomenally rich occurrence of real *experiences*. Experience is the mark of intuitive cognition: intuitive cognition is (to cite Auriol's four conditions for intuitive cognition) 'direct'; it is such that the object is or seems to be 'present'; it is such that the object is or seems to be 'actual'; and such that the object is or seems to be 'existent' (*Scriptum super primum sententiarum*, prooemium, q. 2, a. 3 (trans. Pasnau, p. 206, §§ 105–9)). And the *content* of such experience, be it sensory or intellectual, is *esse apparens* – as Auriol puts it, the acts of sensation and intellection 'place' the object in *esse apparenti* or in *esse intentionali* (*Scriptum super primum sententiarum*, d. 3, q. 4, a. 1 (Buytaert, p. 696, § 31)). Abstractive cognition is quite different: species *lack esse apparens* – they are simply real qualities inherent in the various media of cognition (Tachau quotes relevant passages from unpublished sources in *Vision and Certitude*, pp. 98–9). Auriol argues the necessity for such *esse apparens* by considering cases of sensory illusion: after-images, dreams, hallucinations (*Scriptum super primum sententiarum*, prooemium, q. 2, a. 3, nn. 81–6 (trans. Pasnau, pp. 200–1, §§ 82–6)), optical illusions, and the well-known example of the appearance of motion in stationary trees when viewed from a moving boat (the key passage is *Scriptum super primum sententiarum*, d. 3, q. 4, a. 1 (Buytaert, p. 696, § 31)). In all these cases we have actual experiences, with sensory or conceptual content, but no corresponding object – hence the experiences' having *esse apparens*. An obvious corollary of this is that intuitive cognition need not be veridical. In fact, Auriol does not posit a mechanism to allow us to discern between real and veridical intuitions. To this extent, his theory has understandably been seen to usher in some kind of scepticism. Auriol takes precisely the opposite view: he argues that someone *denying esse apparens* would have no way of distinguishing the true from the seemingly true (*Scriptum super primum sententiarum*, d. 3, q. 4, a. 1 (Buytaert, p. 697, § 31)). But without a way of distinguishing between the two cases (illusion and veridical cognition), be it phenomenally or through judgment, Auriol looks vulnerable.

In his lifetime and after, Auriol was most well-known for, and most criticized for, his views on future contingents. In effect, Auriol endorses the view that the medievals ascribed to Aristotle in his discussion of the sea battle in *De interpretatione*, c. 9: there are no future contingent facts, and thus propositions about future contingents lack a determinate truth value. This view is committed to the falsity of bivalence – the principle that every proposition is either true or false: there is no third truth value; and neither can propositions lack truth values altogether (on bivalence, they cannot be both true and false either, but we do not need to worry about that here). Future contingent propositions do not satisfy this principle:

> No singular proposition can be formulated about a future contingent about which it can be conceded that it is true and its opposite false. Each is neither true nor false. (*Scriptum super primum sententiarum*, d. 38, a. 3 (http://www.peterauriol.net/ auriol-pdf/SCR-38.pdf, p. 14))

Auriol's reason is that if a future proposition is true, it is always true; and if it is always true it is true now, and was true in the past; and if so, it is inevitable. And if it is inevitable, it is not contingent (*Scriptum super primum sententiarum*, d. 38, a. 3 (http://www.peterauriol.net/ auriol-pdf/SCR-38.pdf, p. 14)).[2] Auriol notes that this teaching – that some propositions are neither true nor false – does not violate the principle of non-contradiction, since, as he puts it, this principle claims no more than that 'if one [proposition, p,] is true, then the other [proposition, not-p,] is false' (p and not-p cannot be true together); but it says nothing about the case in which p is neither true nor false, which is what Auriol supposes for future contingent propositions (*Scriptum super primum sententiarum*, d. 38, a. 3 (http:// www.peterauriol.net/auriol-pdf/SCR-38.pdf, p. 17)). (Note that Auriol says nothing here about the principle of the excluded middle, the principle that p and not-p cannot be false together, though Auriol's denial of bivalence is as far as I can see consistent with accepting this principle too.)

Auriol's view represents quite a challenge: we have already seen the lengths to which Ockham went to refute it. The only obvious strategy I can think of is to maintain that future contingents have a truth value that cannot (yet) be known. And, in the absence of some other way for God to know the future, that would represent an assault on divine knowledge that the medievals would not be happy to make. Auriol's view itself resurfaced at the University of Louvain in the fifteenth century. Peter of Rivo (*c.* 1420–1500) adopted something like Auriol's rejection of bivalence, and was condemned in 1473 by Sixtus IV. And there, I suppose, we find the rather unsatisfactory end of the story.

Ockham's Oxonian contemporaries, followers, and opponents

Ockham and Auriol were not alone in their nominalism: as we have seen, various late thirteenth and early fourteenth-century thinkers held this kind of view. In Oxford – which in the years after Scotus tended to surpass Paris in both the quality and the originality of its philosophical contributions – several of Ockham's contemporaries accepted somewhat more realist views – even if we set on one side avowedly Scotist thinkers. Walter Chatton, for example, defends Scotus's views on the question against Ockham's attacks. Chatton's arguments against Ockham are not all that strong – they nit-pick on certain technicalities that, I think, Ockham could, if so minded, simply deny (see Chatton, *Lectura super sententias* I, d. 2, q. 5 (I, 359–61)). More interesting is the case of Walter Burley, whom I mentioned above. Burley's view is that a universal

> has being merely in its singulars, and that a universal is according to its whole self in each of its singulars. (*Tractatus de universalibus* (p. 20, ll. 16–17))

His most substantive reason in favour of his view is that similarity cannot be basic:

> If there were no intellect, still two stones would be more alike than a stone and a donkey. But all likeness is in something that is one. […] Therefore there is some extramental thing in which two stones are alike, and a stone and a donkey are not. (*Tractatus de universalibus* (p. 26, ll. 24–8))

And he offers replies, too, to some of Ockham's criticisms. He does not seem moved by the worry that we would have no way of distinguishing concrete particulars from abstract universals. But he devotes some time to the worry that contradictory properties would belong to one and the same thing (i.e. the universal) – for example, being in motion and being at rest. The reply distinguishes between two ways of being numerically one: generally, whatever can be counted; and strictly, what is 'distinguished from the one in species and the one in genus is numerically one' (*Tractatus de universalibus* (p. 32, ll. 19–23)). The point is that we can count specific natures, but they are still such that they can have subjective parts. Burley draws two consequences. The first is that contradictory properties can belong to something that is numerically one in the first sense, since these properties are merely accidentally properties of the nature:

> just as it is not inappropriate that contraries are in what is specifically the same, so it is not inappropriate that contraries are (at least accidentally) in what is numerically the same understood generally. (*Tractatus de universalibus* (p. 34, ll. 12–13))

The second is that the nature in the particular is neither numerically the same nor numerically distinct from the particular (we can count particulars, and we can count natures, but we cannot count particulars and natures *together*) (*Tractatus de universalibus* (p. 34, ll. 25–8)). Burley uses this strategy to deal with a version of the famous third man argument, and offers a rather nice, original, reply. An objector worries that we can count a universal man in addition to any given particular man (*Tractatus de universalibus* (p. 30, ll. 23–30)). But Burley's rules about counting, just given, render this objection wrong-headed, and he says as much in reply (*Tractatus de universalibus* (p. 38, l. 24–p. 40, l. 4)). Clearly, Burley wants to make a radical distinction between two kinds of numerical singularity, and denies that we can count such singulars together. It is not clear exactly what the distinction is, but it is evidently some kind of concrete/abstract distinction. For example, at one point, replying to a version of Ockham's contradiction argument, Burley denies that universals are *parts* of particulars. I assume he means *concrete* parts, in some sense, since his examples of parts are matter and form, which Burley takes to be concrete items ('Socrates, who is a particular effect, is composed only of particular causes, namely, matter and form') (*Tractatus de universalibus* (p. 40, ll. 10–11)).

As I noted above, one of Ockham's motivations for developing a theory of mental language was to provide objects for propositional attitudes such as knowing and believing. Reflection on this amongst some of Ockham's immediate successors led to one of the most powerful alternatives to standard Aristotelian metaphysical views: namely, the Aristotelian view that all that there is is either substance, accident, or (perhaps) accidental whole. (Scotus and his followers perhaps give us one kind of alternative, non-Aristotelian, universe, since substances and accidents are according to them composed of

formalities, abstract particulars; here we will see another, perhaps
even more radical.) The background is Ockham's view on the objects
of belief, which came under immediate attack from one of his most
able contemporaries, Walter Chatton. Ockham's view requires
that the object of belief simply is the complex apprehension itself,
a mental state: and in this case, Chatton worries, Ockham's view
requires that, whenever we believe such-and-such, we are *aware* of
our apprehending such-and-such – and, he asserts, it is not the case
that we are always aware of the apprehension as such. He concludes
that the object of belief must simply be the external object itself,
the item signified by the terms – the mental acts – in the mental
sentence that is the act of apprehension (*Collatio et prologus*, q. 1, a. 1
(p. 21, ll. 106–111)). More specifically, my belief that (e.g.) Chatton
is intelligent has simply Chatton himself as its object. And Chatton
is, according to the theory, signified by any of the terms of the mental
sentence (*Collatio et prologus*, q. 1, a. 1 (pp. 24–5 (ll. 213–20)).

Chatton's argument relies on the claim that we can have mental
acts – in this case, our act of apprehension – of which we are unaware.
On the face of it, this raises a problem for the internal coherence of
Chatton's view, since he elsewhere seems to insist that there are *no*
such acts: all mental acts are conscious, or such that we are non-
reflexively aware of them: they automatically contain or bring along
with themselves awareness of themselves (see *Collatio et prologus*, q.
5, a. 2 (pp. 121–3)). Chatton considers precisely this objection to his
alternative to Ockham's view, and puts it with devastating clarity:

> Here it could be said that the major premise [viz. that we
> can assent to a complex without apprehending it] includes a
> contradiction, and therefore should be denied: for the complex
> proposition is the apprehension of itself, since a proposition's
> being apprehended is simply for it to be in the mind, since a
> reflex act is not distinguished in this case from a direct act.
> (*Collatio et prologus*, q. 1, a. 1 (p. 22, ll. 127–31))

Chatton tries a couple of replies to this, neither of which is to my
mind particularly convincing. First of all, he claims that component
parts of a mental sentence are temporally successive (just like
written or spoken words), and thus that they *cannot* be apprehended
altogether (*Collatio et prologus*, q. 1, a. 1 (p. 22, ll. 133–52)). Secondly,
he argues (more cautiously) that the fact that we are automatically

aware of the all of the parts of the mental sentence does not in any case entail that we are automatically aware of the whole complex (*Collatio et prologus*, q. 1, a. 1 (p. 23, ll. 172–9)). The first of these seems particularly odd. It seems to be false (and in any case not required by Chatton's anti-Ockham argument) that we cannot be aware of a whole complex apprehension; and it seems curious to suppose that the items composing a mental sentence are ordered temporally (though it may be that Chatton derives this assumption from Scotus, who seems to presuppose it in his discussion of the words of consecration in the Eucharist: see *Ordinatio* IV, d. 8, q. 2, n. 105). And, on the second argument, it is not clear what it would be to be aware of the whole complex if it is not to be aware of all of its parts.

The theory is in any case rather puzzling for another reason: it makes the object of assent a simple item (a substance); and it is not clear (to me at least) how one might assent to a substance. It was not clear, either, to Adam Wodeham, a successor of both Ockham's and Chatton's – one of the most intelligent and interesting of all medieval philosophers. Wodeham agrees with Chatton's criticism of Ockham, and argues further that an act of assent *cannot* simply have something mental as its object. As he sees Ockham's view, it involves the following process:

> First, the [extramental] thing is apprehended by a simple act of understanding. Secondly, an evident [...] composition is formed [i.e. the mental sentence apprehending the object]. Thirdly, that composition or complex is apprehended by a simple act of apprehension. Fourthly, one assents to the complex, in such a way that, although the assent is a kind of apprehension, [...] still, it is not an apprehension that things are as the proposition signifies. (For that, the evident proposition suffices.) Instead the assent concerns only the complex itself. By this, one apprehends its correspondence to what is apprehended through it. (*Lectura secunda*, prol., q. 1, § 4 (trans. Pasnau, p. 329))

Thus presented, Ockham's view is open to an obvious objection: our only access to 'what is apprehended through' the mental complex is the mental complex itself: and simply reflecting on this complex gives no ground for judging that it corresponds to reality, and thus for assenting to it. The mental complex itself, apprehending reality, brings its assent along with itself, as it were: it 'necessitat[es] the assent' (*Lectura secunda*, prol., q. 1, § 7 (trans. Pasnau, p. 335)). As Wodeham sees it, it is not clear why the assent itself requires more than one mental complex (*Lectura secunda*, prol., q. 1, § 5 (trans. Pasnau, p. 329)).

But, likewise, Wodeham does not see how Chatton's view can account for assent at all (as opposed to just believing *in* an individual): he agrees with Ockham that the objects of assent cannot be simple (this is the gist of the arguments at *Lectura secunda*, prol., q. 1, § 3 (trans. Pasnau, pp. 324–6)). So, Wodeham concludes, the object of assent must be 'the total significate' of the mental complex (*Lectura secunda*, prol., q. 1, § 7 (trans. Pasnau, p. 334)). This move results in perhaps the greatest threat to Aristotelian metaphysics countenanced in the Middle Ages: the objects of assent must be, in some sense, real complexes – they must be (what we would call) *facts*, or (actually obtaining) *states of affairs*:

> The total object of a proposition is its significate. Its significate is either being-so-as-the-proposition-denotes or not-being-so. For example, the object of *God is God* is God-being-God and the significate of *Man is pale* or *Paleness inheres in man* is man-being-pale, or paleness-inhering-in-man. (*Lectura secunda*, prol., q. 1, § 8 (trans. Pasnau, p. 335))

Now, this is a threat, because it seems to introduce a whole new class of entities into the Aristotelian framework: facts, somehow over and above substances, accidents, and accidental wholes. Wodeham is aware of the potentially revolutionary nature of his insights.[3] For example, he wants to resist the claim that the items he is talking about are complex: they are, he maintains, neither simple nor complex, but merely 'something signifiable by a complex' (*Lectura secunda*, prol., q. 1, § 8 (trans. Pasnau, p. 337)) – hence, as the Parisian theologian Gregory of Rimini later labelled it, such an item is a *complexe significabile* (something complexly signifiable: see Gregory, *Lectura super primum et secundum sententiarum*, prol., q. 1 (I, 8)). Equally, Wodeham wants to deny that a fact is either 'something or nothing': it is 'not something but rather man-being-something'; 'not a what (*quid*) but rather being-a-what' (*Lectura secunda*, prol., q. 1, § 8 (trans. Pasnau, p. 337)). The aim, I take it, is (among other things) to try to blunt the anti-Aristotelianism of all this. (Wodeham also uses this move to try to make his view hospitable to the problem of the objects of beliefs about the future and past: past and future objects do not exist; but they do not not-exist, and thus are suitable for being the objects of belief: they are (e.g.) something-going-to-exist (*Lectura secunda*, prol., q. 1, § 10 (trans. Pasnau, p. 340)).)

A little later, in Paris, Gregory, of Rimini, who adopts Wodeham's view here, grasps the bull by the horns, and simply asserts that, although not a thing in the sense of something having an essence, a *complexe significabile* is none the less a thing in the sense of being something that makes a locution true (Gregory, *Lectura super primum et secundum sententiarum*, prol., q. 1 (I, 8–9)); and Gregory appeals to Aristotle here, who uses the word 'thing' to pick out such states of affairs: 'When a thing is or is not, necessarily, a locution is said to be true or false' (*Categories*, c. 12, (14b21–2), quoted at Gregory, *Lectura super primum et secundum sententiarum*, prol., q. 1 (I, 8)). Parisian philosophers by and large rejected Gregory's view. Marsilius of Inghen is typical. Gregory asserts that facts (*complexe significabilia*) exist; Marsilius believes this position to be 'incomprehensible', simply on Aristotelian grounds that there is no existent that is neither substance nor accident (*Quaestiones super quatuor libros sententiarum*, prol., q. 2, a. 3). And, of course, if it is held (as Wodeham and Gregory probably do) that the world includes states of affairs *in addition* to substances and accidents, then clearly the view is susceptible to worries about parsimony: adherents of *complexe significabilia* ought simply to reject Aristotelian metaphysics altogether.

The nexus of Chatton, Wodeham, and Gregory of Rimini was involved in another very significant issue, too: the nature of a continuum. The origin of the debate was Henry of Harclay, who adopted a view that bears some resemblance to that of Grosseteste some 80 years earlier. But Harclay's motivations for his view were very different from Grosseteste's. Grosseteste was interested in physics, and an attempt to explain the nature of light. Harclay comes at the issue from a decidedly *theological* perspective. His view is that a continuum is composed of infinitely many indivisibles, such that each one of these indivisibles touches at least one other, and at most two others. They do this by being in places that are immediately adjacent to each other. Henry accepts the Aristotelian assumption that any continuum is infinitely divisible: it can be divided at any possible point. But, he claims, the omniscient God can see *all* the points at which a continuum can be divided. The argument as usually discussed by thinkers of the fourteenth century is found reported in William of Alnwick:

> God actually sees or knows the first beginning point of a line, and any other point which it is possible to pick out in the same line. Therefore, either [i] God sees that, in between this beginning point of the line and any other point in the same line, a line can intervene, or [ii] not. If not [i.e. (ii)], then he sees point immediate to point, which is what we propose. If so [i.e. (i)], then, since it is possible to assign points in the intermediate line, those points will not be seen by God, which is false. The consequence is clear, for according to what we have posited a line falls between the first point and any other point (of the same line) seen by God, and consequently there is some midpoint between this point and any other point seen by God. Therefore this midpoint is not seen by God. (William of Alnwick, *Determinationes*, q. 2 (quoted in Wodeham, *Tractatus de indivisibilibus*, p. 289, n. 2))

When dealing with the first disjunct, Harclay presupposes two claims: (1) that the two points seen by God are such that God sees no further points between them; and (2) that any line contains points. Thus, Harclay attempts to disprove the first disjunct by showing that accepting it entails – absurdly – that there will be points which God does not see. So the second disjunct – Harclay's view – must be true. There is a quick and dirty answer to this argument: points are not real, and so there is nothing for God to know. This was a standard nominalist view about points (it is nowadays known as 'non-entitism': the denial that points have any entity or reality), and it is clearly related to Aristotle's view that points on a continuum (barring the limits) are merely possible, not actual. Wodeham accepts this quick and dirty response (*Tractatus de indivisibilibus*, p. 105). But he tries to argue, too, that even supposing the reality of points, Harclay's argument is fallacious: it does not follow from the claim that the whole collection of points (other than the end point or limit of the continuum) is immediate to the end point that there is some one point that lacks a point between it and the end point (*Tractatus de indivisibilibus*, p. 106).

228 *The Medieval Christian Philosophers*

Chatton tries something different by way of response: a continuum is composed of finitely many indivisibles. He thus denies even the Aristotelian claim that there are *potentially* infinitely many points in a continuum. For Aristotle, we can divide a continuum at any point, and there is no limit to our doing so. For Chatton, there is such a limit – and his reason for so thinking is that a finite extension must have a finite number of components (see Wodeham, *Tractatus de indivisibilibus*, q. 1, a. 1, n. 18). Of course, Chatton's account raises tremendous mathematical difficulties, since if he is correct Euclidian geometry turns out to be false.

A more sensible solution can be found in Gregory of Rimini. Henry of Harclay held that the Aristotelian claim that every whole is greater than its parts obtains for finite but not infinite numbers, and thus is committed to different kinds of part-whole relations in the case of finite and infinite quantities. Gregory builds on this insight, and attempts to give it some theoretical underpinning. He holds that a continuum is composed of actually infinitely many *extended* parts. The parts are not discrete – in fact, they (obviously) overlap – but they can be counted, and they are infinitely many. Both Aristotelians and indivisibilists such as Harclay maintain that, were a continuum to be composed of an actual infinity of parts, then each such part would be immediately adjacent to at least one and at most two others. Gregory rejects this conditional: each part, he maintains, is immediately adjacent to infinitely many other parts (since each (extended) part contains infinitely many extended parts: infinitely many ever smaller proportional parts (for the whole discussion, see *Lectura super primum et secundum sententiarum* II, d. 2, q. 2, a. 1)). Gregory summarizes his view, and makes its theological context clear, as follows:

And just as every continuum in fact has infinitely many potential parts, and each [part of it], however small, includes infinitely many [parts] (and no part can be understood to be indivisible; nor is there a potential infinity of such [indivisible] parts), so I say that in God's conception, the continuum is totally actually divided into parts, of which each is also totally actually divided, and includes infinitely many actually divided [parts]. (*Lectura super primum et secundum sententiarum* I, dd. 35–6, q. 1, a. 1 ad 7 (III, p. 224, ll. 7–12))

This is Gregory's solution to Henry's worry that, if God cannot know the infinitely many potential points on a line, then divine omniscience is compromised. According to Gregory, God can know all the infinitely many possible ways in which a continuum can be divided up. This knowledge, according to Gregory, does not require that there be infinitely many points on a line. And in working out his account of the infinite, Gregory has a crucial insight that was then lost for many years – arguably until the transfinite mathematics of Cantor. He puzzles about how continua might have different extensions, given that they all contain the same number of parts (i.e. an infinite number). He has two solutions. The first, which applies specifically to extended magnitudes, is that the parts of continua of greater and lesser magnitude can be paired, but such that each part on the greater extension is larger than the corresponding part on the lesser extension (*Lectura super primum et secundum sententiarum* II, d. 2, q. 2, a. 1). The second is more general: part can be paired with part, such that there are no more parts in a greater magnitude than in a lesser one; but the lesser one is contained as a subset of the greater one, 'even though it does not include more unities' than any of its parts (*Lectura super primum et secundum sententiarum* I, dd. 42–4, q. 4, a. 2 ad 2 (III, p. 458, l. 35–p. 459, l. 1)). The first solution is rather elegant as an account of unequal extension given the insight that continua are composed wholly of extended parts. But it is this second solution that anticipates much later developments in the mathematics of the infinite.

Of course, all of these infinitist views remained minority views: Aristotelians of all stripes denied the possibility of an actual infinite; and nominalists (and many others too, including Gregory of Rimini) were by and large non-entitists, and certainly denied that a continuum could be composed of points. A vigorous defender of the standard Aristotelian view is Thomas Bradwardine (*c.* 1300–49). Bradwardine argued, correctly, that Euclidean geometry excludes a view such as Chatton's; and he argued too (not wholly soundly) that Grosseteste's position (that a continuum is composed of infinitely many mediate indivisibles) entails that the same continuum is composed of finitely many immediate indivisibles. But the conclusion is false, so by *modus tollens* a continuum cannot be composed of infinitely many mediate indivisibles, and Grosseteste's view is excluded (see *De continuo*, concl. 120, quoted in Sylla, 1998, p. 72, on whom I rely for this account of Bradwardine).

Bradwardine himself was the first and most important member of a group, clustered around Merton College but including Richard Kilvington (1302/5–61) at Oriel, known as the 'Oxford Calculators'. The assumption of the infinite divisibility of a continuum was central to the vast strides Bradwardine made, in his revolutionary *Tractatus de proportionibus*, in the calculation of velocity and acceleration. It was well known that velocity varies in accordance with variation in the proportion between force and resistance. Bradwardine calculated, simply focusing on the mathematical requirements that any theory of velocity must satisfy, that

> squaring the proportion of force to resistance means doubling the velocity, and raising the proportion to the third, fourth, or fifth power entails a threefold, fourfold, or fivefold increase in velocity. [...] In modern terms: $V = \log\frac{F}{R}$ (where V = velocity, F = motive force, and R resistance). (Maier, 1982, p. 73)

Bradwardine went on to become Archbishop of Canterbury in 1349, though he died of the plague in the same year. One might wish that all holders of that position had been as intelligent.

William Heytesbury (before 1313–72/3) and Richard Swineshead (*fl. c.* 1340–54), perhaps even greater mathematicians than Bradwardine, developed a theorem about uniform acceleration (though not one that they knew how to prove), in effect measuring acceleration in terms of its velocity at the middle instant of the period of acceleration:

> The Merton theorem can be expressed in modern symbols as [...] $S = \frac{1}{2}V_f t$, for acceleration from rest, where S is the distance traversed, V_f is the final velocity, and t is the time of acceleration. (Clagett, 1959, p. 255)

Part of the significance of this lies in the fact that it requires the notion of *instantaneous* velocity – and thus implies an inchoate understanding of infinitesimal analysis. It is also an expression of the law of free fall, something like the law later demonstrated empirically by Galileo.

Meanwhile, in Paris, John Buridan was involved in equally revolutionary reappraisals of the physical and causal processes involved in local motion. Aristotle held that motion requires contact between the mover and the moved body. Unsurprisingly, then, he found the notion of projectile motion rather puzzling. He proposed two possible accounts. According to the first, known as *antiperistasis*, a moving body displaces the air in front of it as it moves; this air moves behind the body and acts as its mover. According to the second, which Aristotle seems to prefer, the air is moved by the original mover, and this motion gives it the power to move the body through the air (see Aristotle, *Phys.* VIII, c. 10 (266b27–267a20)). Both theories seem remarkably implausible, even by the standards of Aristotelian physics. In the sixth century, John Philoponus hypothesized (rather more plausibly) that the *projectile* receives from the mover some kind of impressed force that enables it to move away from the mover (Philoponus, *On Aristotle's Physics*, IV, c. 8 (trans. Huby, p. 43). This theory seems to have been known in the thirteenth century (perhaps through Avicenna; Philoponus's commentary was not available in the medieval west), though was unanimously rejected. In the fourteenth century, however, it was revived in a rather more sophisticated version. The Franciscan Francis of Marchia defends a view much like Philoponus's (see *On the Sentences* IV (trans. Clagett, 1959, pp. 526–7)). But Buridan makes a crucial amendment: he proposes that the relevant force is in fact an intrinsic quality of a body – its *impetus* – susceptible of quantification as a product of the quantity of the body's prime matter and its velocity (although Buridan never suggested exactly how this quantification might be done). Among other things, Buridan used his account to explain the motion of the heavenly bodies, and to explain acceleration in free fall (*Super octo libros physicorum* VIII, q. 12).

Clearly, it is a small step from impetus conceived as a permanent and intrinsic quality to Galileo's theory of inertia, which basically maintains the quantitative analysis of inertia (as a product of weight (according to Galileo; actually mass) and velocity), while abandoning the analysis in terms of Aristotle's category of quality. Of course, it does not make for good history to talk about one theory's *anticipating* another; neither does it do so to consider a thinker's most significant contribution simply in the light of what happened to prove influential. For this reason, commentators have recently been inclined to downplay the significance of these fourteenth-century innovations. But it seems to me that there are clear continuities here, and that they can be properly acknowledged.

Nicholas of Autrecourt

Some support for Gilson's negative assessment of Ockham might perhaps be found in an unexpected place: the University of Paris itself, in the late 1330s and early 1340s. In 1339 the University prohibited the 'dogmatizing' of the teachings of William of Ockham; and in 1340 condemned a set of teachings, and included in the final paragraph of the statute a reiteration of the prohibition connected with Ockham in 1339. Oaths in relation to the 1340 statute were imposed in 1341. But the impression that this prohibition relates to Ockham's teaching is misleading. The first of these statutes does not condemn any teachings; what it does condemn is taking these teachings as in any sense authoritative, or worthy of special attention. And it seems that the second of these statutes was directed specifically at teachings of another thinker altogether – Nicholas of Autrecourt (*c.* 1296–1369) – and that the decree has nothing much to do with the teachings of Ockham. It would, after all, be odd on the face of it for a statute in 1340 to condemn Ockhamist teachings: the Chancellor of the University in 1340 was John Buridan, a philosopher who explicitly assumed Ockham's positions as his philosophical starting point. I return to Autrecourt in just a moment. On the alleged anti-Ockhamism of mid-fourteenth-century Paris, we should keep in mind that the relevant ban appears in any case to have been lifted sometime between 1355 and 1368. In the fifteenth century the picture seems to have been similar. The 1341 oath was imposed again in 1474, and rescinded in 1482; but there is no evidence that there was any sort of school of nominalists or Ockhamists at the University of Paris in the late fifteenth century. Neither should it be thought that official reaction to the denial of extramental universals was always negative. The condemnation of Wyclif and the execution of Hus at the Council of Constance in 1415 – both avowed realists – led in the early fifteenth century to a theological reaction against certain forms of realism, for example, at Paris under John Gerson (1363–1429) (not himself a nominalist) and at Heidelberg.

Autrecourt himself is more anti-Ockhamist than he is any kind of adherent of the teachings of Ockham. His target was a Franciscan, Bernard of Arezzo (d. 1342). Bernard – whose opinions survive merely in Nicholas's letters to him – defended a rather sceptical variant of Ockham's view on the intuitive cognition of non-existents, according to which

> '[1] Clear intuitive cognition is that by which we judge a thing to exist, whether it exists or not. [...] [2] The inference "An object does not exist, therefore it is not seen" is not valid; nor does this hold "This is seen, therefore this exists"; indeed, both are invalid. [...] [3] Intuitive cognition does not necessarily require the existing thing' (*First Letter* (trans. Hyman, Walsh, and Williams, p. 652), quoting Bernard of Arezzo, *In sententias* I, d. 3, q. 4)

The first of these conclusions, in particular, is sceptical in thrust: if God causes an intuitive cognition of a non-existent, that cognition leads to a judgment that the object exists. Setting aside the question of the content of the judgment that follows on the perceptions, Nicholas held a far stronger position, one that allows the possibility of supernatural intervention any causal relation, and thus that automatically undermines *all* natural causal relations, and *a fortiori* any causal link between an object and our cognition of it: a far more radically sceptical conclusion than Bernard's, since as Nicholas understands it our judgments about existence are always necessarily insecure (*First Letter* (trans. Hyman, Walsh, and Williams, pp. 652–3)). Of course, Ockham does not make this kind of move: not only does he not accept that the possibility of supernatural intervention undermines all natural causal relations; he explicitly maintains that God's causing an intuitive cognition of a non-existent would cause a judgment that the object does not exist – as we saw above. Still, Nicholas goes further along the sceptical path: the only things that we can know – of which we can have an evident cognition – are logical tautologies (e.g. the principle of non-contradiction), and our own souls (*Second Letter* (trans. Hyman, Walsh, and Williams, p. 657)). But the rules of logic require that conclusions are synonymous with their premises, and thus that we cannot infer the existence of one thing from that of another (*Second Letter* (trans. Hyman, Walsh, and Williams, p. 655) – e.g. infer the existence of extramental realities from the existence of our own souls. These are genuinely sceptical claims, and explicitly opposed to the views of Ockham defended by Bernard. And Nicholas was condemned for them at Paris in 1346: in 1347 he had his academic degrees voided and was constrained to burn his writings. But he lived out the rest of his days, more than 20 years, happily enough for all we know, and certainly comfortably, as Dean of Metz.

Further reading

With the exception of Buridan, the thinkers I consider in this chapter have not (thus far!) attracted significant systematic work. Buridan is well served, with two excellent monographs: Jack Zupko, *John Buridan: Portrait of a Fourteenth-Century Arts Master* (Notre Dame: University of Notre Dame Press, 2003), and Gyula Klima, *John Buridan*, Great Medieval Thinkers (New York: Oxford University Press, 2009). For Durand's theology, see Isabel Iribarren, *Durandus of Saint Pourçain: A Dominican Theologian in the Shadow of Aquinas* (Oxford: Oxford University Press, 2005). An issue of the journal *Vivarium* was devoted to Auriol (*Vivarium* 38 (2000)). Auriol's philosophy of mind is discussed in Katherine H. Tachau, *Vision and Certitude in the Age of Ockham* (Leiden: Brill, 1988). On Burley, see *A Companion to Walter Burley*, ed. Allesandro Conti (Leiden: Brill, 2013). For questions of the infinite, see Norman Kretzmann (ed.), *Infinity and Continuity in Ancient and Medieval Thought* (Ithaca, NY: Cornell University Press, 1982). For *complexe significabilia*, see Pascale Bermon, *L'assentiment et son objet chez Grégoire de Rimini* (Paris: Vrin, 2007). On mental language and the objects of propositional attitudes, see Elizabeth Karger, 'William of Ockham, Walter Chatton and Adam Wodeham on the Objects of Knowledge and Belief', *Vivarium* 33 (1995), pp. 171–96.

Notes

1   I owe this reference to Russell Friedman, *Intellectual Traditions at the Medieval University: The Use of Philosophical Psychology in Trinitarian Theology among the Franciscans and Dominicans, 1250–1350*, 2 vols (Leiden: Brill, 2013), I, p. 543.
2   Auriol does not think that this claim entails that God does not know the future. Unlike Ockham, he believes that God is timeless, and his cognition of all temporal events, including the future, is by means of (non-propositional) representations in his mind. These representations depend merely on the divine essence, and are 'the cause of the actuality which a future contingent has when it is produced in act'; and the representations cause 'not by efficient causality but by exemplar causality' (*Scriptum super primum sententiarum*, d. 38, a. 1 (http://www.peterauriol.net/auriol-pdf/SCR-38.pdf, p. 8)). Unlike the traditional view deriving from Boethius, Auriol denies that there is any sense in which God is present to, or simultaneous with, created events: as timeless, he is not

present to, or simultaneous with, the events, since these relations require temporality. Rather, God is 'indistant' from the events: 'The opposite of distance is not only simultaneity or durational coexistence, which are contrarily opposed [to distance], but rather indistance, the negation of distance, which are privatively and contradictorily opposed [to distance]. Therefore, a representation that is indistant from the actual existence of a future contingent – given that it is not co-existent or simultaneous, but merely indistant – is such that it cannot fail in representing' (*Scriptum super primum sententiarum*, d. 38, a. 1 (http://www.peterauriol.net/auriol-pdf/SCR-38.pdf, p. 9)). The whole view strikes me as deeply mysterious, and perhaps more so even than Ockham's. Auriol's claims about future propositions means that God must know the future – in fact everything – merely non-propositionally, and that there is no propositional content that cannot be known non-propositionally, else there would indeed be some content that God knows and some that he does not. And this would, I take it, pose a threat to omniscience.

3 The closest analogue, earlier in the medieval tradition, to this kind of move can be found in Abelard. As I showed above, Abelard's views on universals involve denying that a status such as *being a human* is a thing. Abelard makes a similar claim for *x*'s *being a human*: this is what is signified by the proposition '*x* is human' (it is, as Abelard puts it, the *dictum* of the proposition), and is nothing at all ('non est res': *Dialectica*, p. 160). But such *dicta* are required to explain the truth of true conditionals, and are perhaps akin to what we think of as propositions – though, as commentators point out, Abelard sometimes speaks of them as somehow real, akin to states of affairs. On this second reading, Abelard could be taken to anticipate Wodeham's view. For discussion, see Marenbon, *The Philosophy of Peter Abelard*, pp. 202–9. It should be added that some commentators interpret Wodeham not to be positing states of affairs, but rather propositions or sentence-types, and to maintain that these abstract things are the objects of belief (see e.g. Pasnau, *Cambridge Translations*, pp. 318–19). I doubt this is correct – the whole discussion of the entitative status of these items suggests that they have some kind of extramental status, and Wodeham was certainly read in that way by Gregory of Rimini, as we shall see.

Epilogue
Retrospection: John Wyclif (*c.* 1330–84)

Despite the tremendous continuity in philosophical work during the period studied here, it is perhaps worth bearing in mind some of the changes that we find. For example, I have tried to convey the impression here that philosophy became far more subtle and nuanced between the thirteenth century and the fourteenth. Reading Scotus after reading Aquinas reveals the tremendous leap in the complexity and sophistication both of the kinds of question which were being asked and of the answers being given. Not everyone was happy with this increasing refinement, incidentally: Gerson, for example, the Chancellor of the University of Paris, persistently castigated the theologians for neglecting real theology in favour of Oxonian logic-chopping of the Scotist kind. While a very significant thinker, Gerson's interests are more pastoral than philosophical, and I say no more about him. Indeed, there is a clear sense in which much intellectual effort after 1350 shifted from the academic to the pastoral and practical. Part of the reason for this must have been the emergence of significant intellectual heresies that had strong pastoral and practical consequences: Wycliffism and Hussitism. The great schism of 1378–1418 again perhaps added a practical focus to theological discussion.

The devastation of the Black Death (principally during the latter part of 1347, and continuing to 1350) probably made a difference in this respect too, creating a global pastoral problem that became a central concern of the universities. But it had another, more obvious, effect too: a radical reduction in university personnel – there were fewer faculty, and fewer students. In fact, the universities after 1350 were in various ways worse off, intellectually, than those prior to this date. Not only were numbers lower; the 100-years war prevented interchange of students between England and France, and, effectively, between the German parts of the Holy

Roman Empire and France too. The first of a series of universities east of the Rhine – the Charles University, in Prague – was founded in 1347, and was the first university outside of Paris, Oxford, and Cambridge, to include all three graduate schools (that is to say, including theology). One result of all this was a massive decline in *internationalism*: universities became local and insular, with a larger number of them drawing on fewer students. And the result was as one would expect. The white-hot intensity in the intellectual environment that produced thinkers of the calibre of Aquinas, Scotus, and Ockham, was no more. As the European educational system declined in the years after 1350, the intellectual centre of gravity moved away from the universities, and into courts, private societies, private houses, and autodidacts: think of the great intellectual achievements of the seventeenth century, for example, in which the universities were scarcely involved at all. (The Reformation is perhaps an exception, since it at least in part arose in a university context. But it was not fundamentally an intellectual movement at all, but something of a rather different kind.)

From our perspective, another important shift is worth noting, and it brings me to the topic of these concluding comments. Without wishing to stress the trend too strongly, it is clear that there is a further significant difference between philosophy prior to 1350 and philosophy after 1350. After 1350, the efforts of philosophers were by-and-large derivative of the work of the earlier period. At its most extreme, there exist well-known fifteenth-century commentaries on some of the works of Aquinas and Scotus: most famously, John Capreol (1380–1444) on the *Sentence* commentary of Aquinas, written largely with the express aim of defending Aquinas against attack, principally from Scotists. In at least one university, a brief attempt was made to institute a chair specifically for lectures on Scotus and Augustine: in 1479–81, the Louvain theology faculty appointed a professor to give supplementary lectures in Scotus and, on certain days, either Augustine's *De civitate dei* or *De doctrina christiana*, or some other theology book chosen by the students. Equally, for example, the massive treatises of Paul of Venice (1369–1429) basically develop themes from Scotus and Wyclif; the Spanish scholastics enter into an anti-modern tradition of their own that was, for all its originality, explicitly backward-looking (the greatest of them,

Francisco Suarez (1548–1617), begins every discussion with a round-up of the views of thirteenth- and early fourteenth-century thinkers). Similarly, logic became consciously backwards-looking. German universities of the late fifteenth century sometimes organized their Arts faculties into different approaches to the study and theorizing of logic in this way, dividing into the *via moderna* and the *via antiqua*, the former of which was nominalist in orientation, and the latter realist (sometimes split into the *via Alberti*, the *via Thomae*, and the *via Scoti*). After 1350, it is exceptional to find more than a couple of manuscripts for any new work – compared to the far larger numbers of copies of thirteenth- and early fourteenth-century works. (A well-known exception: FitzRalph's (1295/1300–60) *Defensio curatorum*, an anti-mendicant work that appealed both to orthodox churchmen and their Wycliffite and Hussite opponents.) In contrast, the interest in copying the works of the great scholastics prior to 1350 if anything increases during the fifteenth century. Philosophy after 1350 becomes in some way *traditional*: quite the contrast to the originality of the thirteenth century.

So I will not spend much time on this period, though, by way of rounding off the book, I will say a few things about the undeniable philosophical genius of the period after 1350 – John Wyclif (*c.* 1325–84) – since he is the best illustration of the nature of the continuities with the earlier period, as well as the novelties of the later period. In fact, while he was, in his way, startlingly original, it is possible to trace the origins even of his wilder innovative claims to sources in the twelfth and thirteenth centuries. I give three examples, all from Wyclif's metaphysics.

First, Wyclif on universals. Much has been made of Wyclif's realism on the question of universals. Commentators follow Wyclif's own lead on this: in *De universalibus*, for example, Wyclif writes that 'beyond doubt, intellectual and emotional error about universals is the cause of all the sin that reigns in the world', offering in support of this the general political claim that 'universal goods are better than private goods' (*De universalibus*, c. 3 (trans. Kenny, p. 22)) – note the very novel way of grounding a metaphysical conclusion. Wyclif places his theory midway between the nominalism (as he sees it) of Aquinas and Giles of Rome and the more extreme realism of Walter Burley:

Some say that every substance is particular, and is universal only by being apprehended universally; just as an artefact is called human, on the basis of a humanity outside itself, and a thing seen, or understood, or otherwise described on the basis of something outside itself. And this opinion is attributed to St Thomas, Giles and many others.

The second way says that the universal is not any of its particulars since it is contrasted with a particular because it is common, or shared, or predicable, and is prior by nature and imperceptible by the senses and different in many other ways, as is clear in *De Interpretatione*, chapter II. Of actual things, says the Philosopher, some are universal, others particular. And this opinion seems to have been held by Master Walter Burley and many others. [...]

I, for my part, take a middle way, reconciling the extremes; I agree with the first opinion that every universal is particular, and *vice versa*, though the two are formally distinct from each other. (*De universalibus*, c. 4 (trans. Kenny, pp. 27–8))

The view here ascribed to Aquinas and Giles of Rome is that universals are just concepts: these concepts are 'outside' the particulars, in the sense of not being in any way real constituents of the particulars. The view ascribed to Walter Burley makes universals a distinct category of reality, contrasted with particulars. A universal, on this view, is a real constituent of the particulars that exemplify it, such that this relation of exemplification does not involve any way in which the universal 'becomes' any of its particulars. (Notice the backward-looking nature of the discussion: all the way to 100 years earlier and the view of Aquinas.) As we saw above, the view that Wyclif is describing here involves the claim that a universal is itself numerically singular, and thus is a numerically singular constituent of the many numerically distinct particulars that exemplify it. Wyclif's own view involves the claim, not made explicit by him, that universals lack this kind of numerical singularity. A universal is somehow 'divided' into the many particulars that it 'becomes' when instantiated by them:

Every particular of the universal has an essence which is that particular itself, and this essence is a subjective part of the given universal; it follows that every individual receives a

part of the universal, which is its essence, from the universal
from which it takes its origin. And every creature is a being
by sharing in this way. (*De universalibus*, c. 4 (trans. Kenny,
pp. 28–9))

A universal is a real thing that is divided into its particulars in such
a way that it somehow 'becomes' the many particulars that it is.
Nominalism is avoided by the claim that the universal is real: it is the
subject that is modified by division into particulars. In this sense, it 'is
by nature prior to its individual since it can exist without it' (Wyclif,
De universalibus, c. 5 (trans. Kenny, p. 37)) – which is to say that the
universal can exist without this or that particular, though presumably
not without all of them. Wyclif finds this view in Aristotle, Averroes,
and Anselm (*De universalibus*, c. 4), and his position obviously has a
great deal in common with that of Duns Scotus.

Wyclif himself mentions Scotus with approval as 'a loyal
defender of universals' (*De universalibus* c. 7 (trans. Kenny, p. 53)),
and among other things Wyclif draws from Scotus the opinion that
there is a 'formal distinction' between the common nature and the
particular substance that instantiates it. As Wyclif understands it,
a formal distinction between two things obtains when they differ
'even though they are alike within the same single essence or
suppositum' (*De universalibus* c. 4 (trans. Kenny, p. 29)). Things are
formally distinct if they are somehow distinguishable features of
a numerically singular thing. And universal nature and particular
substance are distinguished on the grounds that the universal nature
'can be common to many men, whereas this man cannot' (Wyclif, *De
universalibus* c. 4 (trans. Kenny, p. 30)).

Note that Wyclif holds, in the displayed passage just quoted, that
the particular *is* its essence. He buttresses this view with a theory
of predication that he borrows from Scotus: essential predication,
which is

predication in which the same essence is the subject and
predicate, even though the notion of the predicate differs
from the notion of the subject. (*De universalibus* c. 1 (trans.
Kenny, p. 4))

This allows Wyclif to maintain a relationship of real identity between
an individual such as Socrates and the universal nature – humanity

– that he instantiates. This is the same as Scotus's predication 'by identity', used by Scotus to assert real sameness between formally distinct components neither of which inheres in the other. Now, Wyclif holds that the relationships of formal distinction and real sameness obtain between each of an individual's properties and the individual itself. A formal distinction obtains in the case that

> things differ in accidental form while being alike within the same subject. Thus quantity, quality, relation and the other categories, if they coincide in the same particular subject, are all the same in particular subject, even though in their natures they differ in category. (*De universalibus* c. 4 (trans. Kenny, pp. 29–30))[1]

Wyclif maintains in effect that accidents are somehow modalizations of their substance: they are not things in any way really distinct from it. And he holds that what individuates a substance from any other substance is its unique collection of accidents – an insight that he expressly derives from Anselm. Wyclif claims that there is 'an assemblage (*collatio*) of properties added to the specific nature through which it is distinguished individually from other singulars' (Wyclif, *De incarnacione*, c. 8 (p. 129, l. 31–p. 130, l. 1); Wyclif immediately cites Anselm, *De incarnatione*, c. 7). What is key here is the insight that the kind-nature and accidents combine to compose a numerically singular substance. And the whiteness of (e.g.) Socrates is just Socrates himself.

Now, this immediately makes it clear why Wyclif is forced to reject the doctrine of transubstantiation (*De eucharistia*, c. 2): on the view just outlined, the notion of an accident without a substance is simply contradictory. If Socrates's whiteness is Socrates himself (i.e. Socrates in a certain state or mode of existing), then Socrates's whiteness clearly cannot exist without Socrates. But, again, this view has some precedents. As I just noted, Wyclif wants, in effect, to see accidents as modes: he is implacably opposed to any reification of accidents, perhaps more so than any other medieval thinker. And this is, I suppose, a very plausible reading of Aristotle on the nature of accidents: not beings, but items that belong to a being. All of this, of course, is many miles distant from Scotus's account of the metaphysics of material substance, despite Wyclif's use of the machinery of Scotus's formal distinction.

The denial of transubstantiation can be approached from another angle too, and this is my third case of innovation: Wyclif's view that nothing can be annihilated (hence the bread in the Eucharist can cease to exist only through some natural process). Annihilation is complete destruction. But for something to be completely destroyed, all of its components and properties must be destroyed. And *analogous being* is a feature of any created being; likewise, such a being is the same as its essence (*De universalibus*, c. 13). So, on the first argument Wyclif proposes, the annihilation of a creature would require the annihilation of the whole universe; and on the second it would require at least the destruction of every instance of its kind. The second argument, at least, is the contrapositive of an argument Ockham used against universals: if there were universals, then annihilation would be impossible; given that annihilation is possible, there are no universals. Wyclif accepts the inference, but denies the consequent: there are universals; so annihilation is indeed impossible. Another example of a seemingly innovative claim in Wyclif that turns out to be rather traditional.

Further reading

Wyclif's philosophy is not particularly well served in the literature: perhaps the best places to start are the essays by Anthony Kenny and Norman Kretzmann in Anthony Kenny (ed.), *Wyclif in His Times* (Oxford, Clarendon Press, 1986). There is some useful material in Ian Christopher Levy (ed.), *A Companion to John Wyclif: Late Medieval Theologian* (Leiden and Boston: Brill, 2006).

Note

1   The view seems to bear some resemblance to Auriol's claim that a substance and an accident are two things that have 'the unity of indistinction', a claim that Auriol defends on the grounds that the accident cannot be conceived without the substance: see *Scriptum super primum sententiarum*, d. 1, q. 1, a. 4 (Buytaert, p. 364, § 99).

Glossary

A priori: Known independently of experience

Accident: A non-essential property

Action theory: An account of the processes involved in human activity

Actuality: Form or activity; the actualization of a potency

Agent intellect: The part of the mind responsible for abstracting universal ideas from experience

Akrasia: A defect in character revealed in action that is contrary to an agent's beliefs about what should be done

Analogy: A property of words whose meanings are related but non-identical; a property of such meanings or concepts themselves

Apophaticism: The theory that God cannot be described in human language

Asymmetry, *see* Symmetry

Atomism: The theory that extended items are composed of atoms

Being: The most general concept, predicating possibility or reality of its subject; that which is, in any way whatsoever

Categories: Aristotle's ten categories, an (exhaustive) list of the kinds of predicates there are, or of the kinds of attributes there are: namely, substance, and the nine accidental categories: quantity, quality, relation, action, passion (undergoing), place, time, posture, vesture

Causation, primary: God's being an immediate partial cause of all things

Causes, essentially ordered: Causes ordered such that earlier causes bring about the activity of later ones

Causes, four: Efficient cause, bringing something about; final cause, a thing's goal or purpose; formal cause, form; material cause, matter

Christology: An account of the Christian doctrine of the Incarnation

Common nature: An essence really shared by different particulars

Communicability: Shareability, usually of a universal or common nature

Conceptualism, *see* Nominalism

Concupiscence: Inordinate desire, often sexual

Consequentialism: The theory that the moral worth of an action is determined simply by its consequences

Contingency: Non-necessity; the property of being such that it need not be, or could have been otherwise

Contra-causal freedom, *see* Liberty of indifference

Contrapositive: Of a conditional 'if p, then q', the contrapositive is 'if not-q, then not-p'

Conventionalism: The theory that such-and-such (e.g. language, ethics, scientific law) does not reflect the way the world is, but is merely the result of human choice

Deduction, deductive argument: An argument such that, if the premises are true, the conclusion must likewise be true

Determinism: The theory that all that occurs occurs as a matter of necessity

Disposition: Inclination or tendency to function in a certain way

Distinctions: Among thinkers who distinguish varieties of distinction, a *real* distinction obtains between two separable items; a *formal* or *intentional* distinction obtains between two non-identical but inseparable items

Divine simplicity: The theory that God lacks any kind of complexity, usually even including a lack of properties distinct in any way either from God or from each other

Divisibility: A capacity to be divided, e.g. into quantitative parts or into subjective parts (i.e. the instances of a universal or common nature)

Efficient cause, *see* Cause

Elements: The four elements: fire, air, water, earth

Epistemology: The theory of what constitutes knowledge

Equivocation: A property of words whose meanings are wholly disjoint; a property of such meanings or concepts themselves

Esse: Existence; *esse exsistentiae*, the existence of particular things; *esse essentiae*, the existence of a common nature; *esse rationis*, mental existence

Essence: The necessary or defining properties of a thing (in material substances, essence includes both matter and form)

Extension: The extension of a general term or concept consists of all the items to which the term or concept applies; magnitude

Externalism: In the philosophy of mind, the theory that the content of a concept is fixed by something external to the mind; in the philosophy of action, the theory that the reasons for an action may be independent of any internal motivation for that action

Form, accidental, *see* Accident

Form, substantial: The property or group of properties that determines prime matter (or some lower-order substance) to be a particular kind of thing

Foundation (of property/relation): Feature in virtue of which a property/ relation belongs to a substance

Generation: The production of a substance from a pre-existent substance or matter; in the Trinity, the eternal production of the Son by the Father

Genus: A general class, subdivided into species by specific differences

Haecceity: Non-qualitative property responsible for individuation

Hermeneutics: The theory of the interpretation of texts

Hylomorphism: The theory that material substances are composites of matter and substantial form

Hypostasis: In theological contexts, an ultimate subject of properties; something that cannot be shared; a subsistent

Hypostatization: Treating *prima facie* abstract items as concrete ones

Identity conditions: Criteria to be satisfied for two things to be identical

Identity, Leibnizian: Absolute identity, satisfying Leibniz's Law (the indiscernibility of identicals) that if two items are identical, then whatever is true of one is true of the other

Identity of indiscernibles: The principle that, if whatever is true of one item is true of another, then the two items are identical

Incarnation: The Christian doctrine that a divine person (the second person of the Trinity), while remaining divine, became a human being; a divine person's becoming a human being

Incommunicability, *see* Communicability

Incontinence, *see Akrasia*

Individuation: An account of the distinction of one individual from another; an account of what renders individuals indivisible, such that there cannot be instances of them

Indivisibility, *see* Divisibility

Induction, inductive argument: An argument such that the truth of the premises raises the likelihood of the truth of the conclusion; an argument from specific cases to a general rule

Intellect: Power for conceptual thought

Intellectualism: The theory that the intellect's activity is primary in human action

Intension: The meaning of a term; the content of a concept

Kind, *see* Natural kind

Liberty of indifference: The power to choose between two alternative possibilities

Liberty of spontaneity: The power to act without coercion

Malice: The deliberate choice of the morally bad

Metaethics: The study of the grounds of ethical beliefs

Metaphysics: The study of the nature and extent of being

Modalization: A way in which something exists

Moral psychology: The study of the interrelations between action theory and ethics

Motion: Any kind of accidental change; movement from place to place

Natural kind: A collection of items such that the identity of the collection is not dependent on human choice or convention

Natural law: Universal moral norm, perhaps obtaining independently of any explicit legislation or legislator

Naturalism: The theory that some domain or class of things is as it is independently of God

Nature, *see* Natural kind

Necessitarianism: The theory that the universe cannot be other than it is

Necessity: Of a proposition: such that its opposite is or entails a contradiction; of a property: such that the item that has the property cannot lack it

Nominalism: The denial of common natures or extramental universals

Occurrent belief/cognition: A consciously entertained belief or cognition

Ontology: Metaphysics; the assumptions underlying metaphysics

Personal property: The feature that distinguishes one of the persons of the Trinity from any other such person

Phantasm: An imagined mental representation of an object

Phenomenology: The theory of how things feel, or seem to be, to a conscious subject

Possibility, logical: A proposition is logically possible if it neither is nor entails a contradiction

Possible intellect: The part of the mind responsible for storing conceptual information; according to some also the part of the mind responsible for occurrent cognition

Postlapsarian: After the Fall of Adam

Potency: A capacity to be affected

Power: A capacity to act

Predicables: Different varieties of universals: genus, specific difference, definition/species (constituted of genus and specific difference), *proprium* (necessary but non-defining feature), and accident

Prime matter: The underlying substrate of all substantial change

Privation: The lack of a form

Proper passion: A necessary but non-defining feature of a particular or universal (*see too* Predicables)

Propositional logic: A formal system covering the logical relations between propositions

Proprium, see Predicables

Pure potency: The lack of any property or actuality whatsoever; sometimes taken to be a property of prime matter

Quiddity, *see* Essence

Realism: The theory that common natures exist, or that there exist extramental universals

Rights, subjective: An individual's entitlement to behave in a certain way, or to be treated in a certain way

Science, *scientia*: In Aristotelian philosophy, an axiomatized syllogistic system in which the axioms explain the theorems

Self-motion: Something's changing itself

Semantics: The theory of meaning

Sensible: Can be sensed, or is an object of sense

Sortal: A noun picking out a kind of thing

Species: Kind, defined in terms of genus and specific difference; any kind of cognitive representation

Species, expressed and impressed: An impressed species is a real accident, inherent in a cognitive power, that may be the bearer of semantic content; an expressed species is the semantic content, that may or may not be borne by an impressed species

Specific difference: The feature, proper to a given species, that differentiates different species within a genus

Subsistence: The property of being an independent existent

Substance, primary and secondary: A primary substance is a particular of a given natural kind; a secondary substance is the corresponding universal concept or nature (*see too* Categories)

Substantial change: The natural production and destruction of substances

Substrate: Some item persisting through a change and underlying it

Suppositum, see Hypostasis

Syllogism: A deductive argument comprising three statements (two premises and a conclusion) and three terms, unified through a 'middle term' shared by the two premises

Symmetry: A property of relations such that, if *a* has a relation R to *b*, *b* has the same relation R to *a*

Synchronic: At the same time as

Teleology: The theory that things have natural purposes or goals to which they necessarily tend

Transcendentals: Properties that 'transcend' Aristotle's categories, e.g. by being features of items in all, or more than one, category; or features of God alone

Transitivity: A property of relations such that, if *a* has relation R to *b*, and *b* has relation R to *c*, *a* has relation R to *c*

Transubstantiation: The Christian doctrine that, in the Eucharist, the bread is fully converted into Christ's body, and the wine fully converted into Christ's blood

Trinity: The Christian doctrine that there is one God, and that that God is three persons

Universal: A shared feature, or common concept

Univocity: A property of words whose meanings are identical; a property of such meanings or concepts themselves

Virtue: An (acquired) disposition to act in a morally good way

Virtue ethics: The theory according to which what is morally good is determined by the way in which a virtuous person acts

Voluntarism: The theory that the will has priority over the intellect in human action

Weakness of will, *see Akrasia*

Bibliography

Primary sources and translations[1]

Abelard, Peter, *Philosophische Schriften*, ed. Bernhard Geyer (Münster: Aschendorff, 1919–33) [contains *Logica 'ingredientibus'*]

———, *Commentaria in Epistolam Pauli ad Romanos*, in *Petri Abaelardi opera theologica*, I, ed. E. M. Buytaert, Corpus Christianorum Continuatio Mediaevalis, 11 (Turnhout: Brepols, 1969)

———, *Theologia 'Christiana'*, in *Petri Abaelardi opera theologica*, II, ed. E. M. Buytaert, Corpus Christianorum Continuatio Mediaevalis, 12 (Turnhout: Brepols, 1969)

———, *Dialectica*, ed. Lambert Marie de Rijk, second edition (Assen: van Gorcum, 1970)

———, *The Letters of Abelard and Heloise*, trans. Betty Radice (Harmondsworth: Penguin, 1974)

———, *Theologia 'Scholarium'*, in *Petri Abaelardi opera theologica*, III, ed. E. M. Buytaert and C. J. Mews, Corpus Christianorum Continuatio Mediaevalis, 13 (Turnhout: Brepols, 1977)

Albert the Great, *De bono*, ed. Heinrich Kühle, *Opera Omnia*, XXVIII (Münster: Aschendorff, 1958)

———, *Opera omnia*, ed. A. Borgnet, 38 vols (Paris: Vivès, 1890–99)

———, *Physica*, pars I, ed. P. Hossfeld, *Opera Omnia*, IV/1 (Münster: Aschendorff, 1987)

———, *Super Ethica commentum et quaestiones, libros VI–X*, ed. W. Kübel, *Opera Omnia*, XIV/2 (Münster: Aschendorff, 1987)

———, *Super universalia Porphyrii*, ed. Manuel Santos Noya, *Opera omnia*, I/1A (Münster: Aschendorff, 2004)

Alexander of Aphrodisias, *De anima*, trans. Athansios P. Fotinis (Washington, DC: University Press of America, 1979)

Anselm of Canterbury, *Opera omnia*, ed. F. S. Schmitt, 6 vols (Edinburgh: Nelson, 1946–61)

———, *The Major Works*, ed. Brian Davies and G. R. Evans (Oxford: Oxford University Press, 1998)

Aquinas, Thomas, *In duodecim libros metaphysicorum Aristotelis expositio*, ed, R. M. Spiazzi (Turin: Marietti, 1950)

———, *In libros de generatione et corruptione expositio*, ed. R. M. Spiazzi (Turin: Marietti, 1952)

————, *In octo libros physicorum Aristotelis expositio*, ed. Mariani Maggiòlo (Turin: Marietti, 1954)

————, *Selected Writings*, ed. Ralph McInerny (London: Penguin, 1998) [contains *De aeternitate mundi*]

Augustine, *De diversis quaestionibus*, trans. David L. Mosher, Fathers of the Church, 70 (Washington, DC: Catholic University of America Press, 1982)

Auriol, Peter, *Scriptum super primum librum sententiarum* (Rome, 1596)

————, *Reportatio in libros sententiarum*, 2 vols (Rome, 1605)

————, *Scriptum super primum librum sententiarum* [prologue and distinctions 1–8], ed. E. M. Buytaert, 2 vols (St Bonaventure, NY: Franciscan Institute, 1956)

————, *Scriptum super primum librum sententiarum* [distinction 8], ed. Christopher Shabel, http://www.peterauriol.net/auriol-pdf/SCR-8-3.pdf (accessed online 1 April, 2013)

————, *Scriptum super primum librum sententiarum* [distinction 38], ed. Christopher Schabel, http://www.peterauriol.net/auriol-pdf/SCR-38.pdf (accessed online 1 April, 2013)

Averroes, *Aristotelis opera cum Averrois commentaria*, 11 vols (Venice, 1550)

Avicenna, *The Metaphysics of* The Healing, trans. Michael E. Marmura (Provo, UT: Brigham Young University Press, 2005)

Bacon, Roger, *Opus majus*, ed. John Henry Bridges, 2 vols (Oxford: Clarendon Press, 1893)

————, *Roger Bacon's Philosophy of Nature: A Critical Edition, with English Translation, Introduction, and Notes, of* De multiplicatione specierum *and* De speculis comburentibus, ed. David C. Lindberg (Oxford: Clarendon Press, 1983)

Berkeley, George, *Works*, ed. Alexander Campbell Fraser, 4 vols (Oxford, Clarendon Press, 1901)

Bernard of Clairvaux, *Some Letters of Bernard of Clairvaux*, trans. Samuel J. Eales, ed. Francis Aiden Gasquet (London: John Hodges, 1904)

————, *De consideratione*, trans. John D. Anderson and Elizabeth T. Kennan (Kalamazoo, MI: Cistercian Publications, 1976)

————, *De gratia et libero arbitrio*, trans. Daniel O'Donovan (Kalamazoo, MI: Cistercian Publications, 1988)

Boethius, *Commentariorum in librum Aristotelis Perihermeneias, editio secunda*, ed. C. Meiser (Leipzig: Teubner, 1880)

————, *In Ciceronis Topica*, ed. Eleonore Stump (Ithaca: Cornell University Press, 1987)

————, *The Theological Tractates; The Consolation of Philosophy*, ed. H. F. Stewart and others, Loeb Classical Library (Cambridge, MA: Harvard University Press, 1990)

Bonaventure, *Opera Omnia*, 10 vols (Quaracchi: Collegium S. Bonaventurae, 1882–1902)

————, *The Soul's Journey into God. The Tree of Life. The Life of St Francis*, trans. Ewert Cousins, Classics of Western Spirituality (New York: Paulist Press, 1978)

————, *Disputed Questions on the Mystery of the Trinity*, trans. Zachary Hayes (St Bonaventure, NY: Franciscan Institute, 1979)

————, *Disputed Questions on the Knowledge of Christ*, trans. Zachary Hayes (St Bonaventure, NY: Franciscan Institute, 1992)

————, *On the Reduction of the Arts to Theology*, trans. Zachary Hayes (St Bonaventure, NY: Franciscan Institute, 1996)

Buridan, John, *Super octo libros physicorum* (Paris, 1509)

Burley, Walter, *Tractatus de universalibus*, ed. Hans-Ulrich Wöhler (Stuttgart: Hirzel, 1999)

Cassiordorus, *Institutiones*, ed. R. A. B. Mynors (Oxford: Clarendon Press, 1937)

Chartularium Universitatis Parisiensis, ed. H. Denifle and H. Chatelain, 4 vols (Paris: Delalain, 1889–97)

Chatton, Walter, *Collatio et prologus*, ed. Joseph C. Wey (Toronto: Pontifical Institute of Mediaeval Studies, 1989)

Cicero, *On Duties*, ed. M. T. Griffin and E. M. Atkins, Cambridge Texts in the History of Political Thought (Cambridge: Cambridge University Press, 1991)

Clarembald of Arras, see Häring, Nikolaus M

Conciliorum oecumenicorum decreta, ed. J. Alberigo and others (Bologna: Istituto per le scienze religiose, 1973) [contains Lateran IV and the Council of Vienne]

David of Dinant, *Quaternulorum fragmenta*, ed. M. Kurdziałek (Warsaw, 1963)

De la Mare, William, *Correctorium fratris thomae*, ed. as part of the text in P. Glorieux, *Le Correctorium corruptorii 'Quare'* (Kain: Le Saulchoir, 1927)

Duns Scotus, John, *Opera omnia*, ed. C. Balić and others (Vatican City: Vatican Press, 1950–)

————, *A Treatise on God as First Principle*, ed. Allan B. Wolter, second edition (Chicago, IL: Franciscan Herald Press, 1982)

————, *Duns Scotus on the Will and Morality*, ed. Allan B. Wolter (Washington DC: Catholic University of America Press, 1986)

————, *Philosophical Writings*, trans. Allan B. Wolter (Indianapolis, IN, and Cambridge: Hackett, 1987)

————, *Opera philosophica*, ed. Girard J. Etzkorn and others, 5 vols (St Bonaventure, NY: St Bonaventure University Press, 1996–2005)

————, *Reportatio*, ed. Allan B. Wolter and Oleg V. Bychkov, 2 vols (St Bonaventure, NY: Franciscan Institute, 2004–8)

Durand of St Pourçain, *Scriptum super quatuor libros sententiarum* [...] *Distinctiones 1-5 libri Secundi*, ed. Fiorella Retucci (Leuven: Peeters, 2012)

Fairweather, Eugene R., *A Scholastic Miscellany: Anselm to Ockham*, Library of Christian Classics (London: SCM Press, 1956) [contains Abelard, *Commentary on Romans*]

Francis of Marchia, *Sententia et compilatio super libros physicorum Aristotelis*, ed. N. Mariani (Grottaferrata: Collegii S. Bonaventurae, 1998)

[al-Ghazālī] Algazel, *Metaphysics*, trans. J. T. Muckle (Toronto: St Michael's College, 1934)

Gilbert of Poitiers, *The Commentaries on Boethius*, ed. Nikolaus M. Häring (Toronto: Pontifical Institute of Mediaeval Studies, 1996)

Giles of Rome, *Quodlibeta* (Louvain, 1646)

———, *Theorems on Essence and Existence*, trans. Michael V. Murray (Milwaukee, WI: Marquette University Press, 1952)

Godfrey of Fontaines, *Les quatre premiers Quodlibets*, ed. M. de Wulf and A. Pelzer, Les philosophes Belges, 2 (Louvain: Institut supérieur de philosophie, 1904)

———, *Les Quodlibets cinq, six et sept*, ed. M. de Wulf and J. Hoffmanns, Les philosophes Belges, 3 (Louvain: Institut supérieur de philosophie, 1914)

———, *Les Quodlibets onze-quatorze*, ed. Jean Hoffmans, Les philosophes Belges, 5 (Louvain: Institut supérieur de philosophie, 1932–5)

Gregory of Rimini, *Lectura super primum et secundum sententiarum*, ed. Damasus Trapp, 7 vols (Berlin: De Gruyter, 1979–87)

Grosseteste, Robert, *De luce*, trans. Clare C. Riedl (Milwaukee, WI: Marquette University Press, 1942)

———, *Commentarius in posteriorjm analyticorum libros*, ed. Pietro Rossi (Florence: Olschki, 1981)

Häring, Nikolaus M., *The Life and Works of Clarembald of Arras: A Twelfth-Century Master of the School of Chartres* (Toronto: Pontifical Institute of Mediaeval Studies, 1965) [contains *Tractatus super librum Boetii de trinitate*]

Henry of Ghent, *Quodlibeta* (Paris, 1518)

———, *Summa quaestionum*, 2 vols (Paris, 1520)

———, *Opera omnia*, ed. R. Macken and others (Leuven: Leuven University Press, 1979–)

Henry of Harclay, *Quaestiones ordinariae*, ed. Mark G. Henninger, 2 vols (Oxford: Oxford University Press, 2008)

Hugh of St Victor, *De sacramentis Christianae fidei*, ed. Rainer Berndt (Münster: Aschendorff, 2008)

Hyman, Arthur, James J. Walsh, and Thomas Williams (eds), *Philosophy in the Middle Ages*, third edition (Indianapolis, IN; Cambridge: Hackett, 2010)

John of Salisbury, *Historia pontificalis*, ed. Marjorie Chibnall (Oxford: Clarendon Press, 1986)

Laberge, Damasus, 'Fr. Petri Ioannis Olivi, O.F.M., tria scripta sui ipsius apologetica annorum 1283 et 1285', *Archivum Franciscanum Historicum* 28 (1935), pp. 115–53, 374–407

Littera septem sigillorum, ed. G. Fussenegger, *Archivum Franciscanum Historicum*, 47 (1954), pp. 45–53

Lombard, Peter, *Sentences*, trans. Giulio Silano, 4 vols (Toronto: Pontifical Institute of Mediaeval Studies, 2007–10)

McKeon, Richard, *Selections from Medieval Philosophers*, 2 vols (New York: Scribners, 1929–30) [contains Grosseteste, *De veritate*]

Marsilius of Inghen, *Quaestiones super quatuor libros sententiarum*, ed. Georg Wieland and Manuel Santos Noya (Leiden: Brill, 2000–)

Marsilius of Padua, *Defensor Pacis*, trans. Alan Gewirth (Toronto: University of Toronto Press, 1992)

Moses Maimonides, *The Guide of the Perplexed*, trans. Shlomo Pines, 2 vols (Chicago: University of Chicago Press, 1963)

Natalis, Hervaeus, *In quatuor libros sententiarum commentaria* (Paris, 1647)

Olivi, Peter, *Quaestiones in secundum librum sententiarum*, ed. B. Jansen, 3 vols (Quaracchi: Collegium S. Bonaventurae, 1922–6)

Pasnau, Robert (ed.), *The Cambridge Translations of Medieval Philosophical Texts. Volume 3. Mind and Knowledge* (Cambridge: Cambridge University Press, 2002) [contains Auriol, *Scriptum*, prooemium, q. 2; Adam Wodeham, *Lectura secunda*, d. 1, q. 1]

Pecham, John, *Quodlibeta quatuor*, ed. Girard J. Etzkorn and Ferdinand M. Delorme (Grottaferrata: Collegium S. Bonaventurae, 1989)

Philoponus, John, *On Aristotle, Physics 4.6-9*, trans. Pamela Huby, Ancient Commentators on Aristotle (Bristol: Bristol Classical Press, 2012)

Richard of St Victor, *De Trinitate*, ed. Jean Ribaillier, *Textes Philosophiques du Moyen Age*, 6 (Paris: Vrin, 1958)

———, *Trinity and Creation*, ed. Boyd Taylor Coolman and Dale M. Coulter (New York: New City Press, 2010 [contains *De trinitate*]

Siger of Brabant, *Quaestiones in tertium De anima. De anima intellectiva*, ed. B. C. Bazàn (Louvain: Publications universitaires, 1972)

Spade, Paul Vincent, *Five Texts on the Mediaeval Problem of Universals: Porphyry, Boethius, Abelard, Duns Scotus, Ockham* (Indianapolis, IN; Cambridge: Hackett, 1994) [contains Porphyry, *Isagoge*, Boethius, *Second Commentary on Porphyry's Isagoge*; Abelard, *Glosses on Porphyry*; Scotus, *Ordinatio* II, d. 3, p. 1; Ockham, *Ordinatio*, d. 2, qq. 4–8]

Tugwell, Simon, *Albert and Thomas: Selected Writings*, Classics of Western Spirituality (New York: Paulist Press, 1982) [contains Albert the Great, *Commentary on Dionysius' Mystical Theology*]

William of Auvergne, *De trinitate*, trans. Ronald J. Teske (Milwaukee, WI: Marquette University Press, 1989)

———, *De anima*, trans. Ronald J. Teske (Milwaukee, WI: Marquette University Press, 2000)

William of Ockham, *Opera theologica*, ed. Iuvenalis Lalor and others 10 vols (St Bonaventure, NY: St Bonaventure University Press, 1967–86)

————, *Opera philosophica*, ed. Iuvenalis Lalor and others, 7 vols (St Bonaventure, NY: St Bonaventure University Press, 1974–88)

————, *Predestination, God's Knowledge, and Future Contingents*, ed. Marilyn McCord Adams and Norman Kretzmann, second edition (Indianapolis, IN: Hackett, 1983)

————, *Philosophical Writings*, ed. Philotheus Boehner and Stephen Brown (Indianapolis, IN, and Cambridge: Hackett, 1990)

————, *Quodlibetal Questions*, trans. Alfred J. Freddoso and Francis E. Kelley, 2 vols (Yale, CT: Yale University Press, 1991)

————, *A Short Discourse on the Tyrannical Government over Things Divine and Human*, trans. John Kilcullen (Cambridge: Cambridge University Press, 1992)

Wodeham, Adam, *Tractatus de indivisibilibus*, ed. Rega Wood (Dordrecht: Kluwer, 1988)

————, *Lectura secunda in primum librum Sententiarum*, ed. Rega Wood and Gedeon Gál, 3 vols (St Bonaventure, NY: St Bonaventure University Press, 1990)

Wyclif, John, *De incarnacione*, ed. Edward Harris (London: Trübner, 1886)

————, *De eucharistia*, ed. J. Loserth (London: Trübner, 1892)

————, *Tractatus de universalibus*, trans. Anthony Kenny (Oxford: Clarendon Press, 1985)

Secondary sources

Adams, Marilyn, McCord, *William Ockham*, 2 vols (Notre Dame, IN: University of Notre Dame Press, 1987)

Brower, Jeffrey, E., 'Trinity', in *The Cambridge Companion to Abelard*, ed. Jeffrey E. Brower and Kevin Guilfoy (Cambridge: Cambridge University Press, 2004), pp. 223–57

Clagett, Marshall, *The Science of Mechanics in the Middle Ages* (Madison: University of Wisconsin Press, 1959)

de Rijk, L. M., *Logica modernorum: A Contribution to the History of Early Terminist Logic*, 3 vols (Assen: van Gorcum, 1962–7)

Dronke, Peter (ed.), *A History of Twelfth-Century Western Philosophy* (Cambridge: Cambridge University Press, 1988)

Evans, G. R., *Old Arts. New Theology: The Beginnings of Theology as an Academic Discipline* (Oxford: Clarendon Press, 1980)

Fine, Gail, *On Ideas: Aristotle's Criticism of Plato's Theory of Forms* (Oxford: Clarendon Press, 1993)

Friedman, Russell, L., *Medieval Trinitarian Thought From Aquinas to Ockham* (Cambridge: Cambridge University Press, 2010)

Gilson, Etienne, *History of Christian Philosophy in the Middle Ages* (London: Sheed and Ward, 1955)

Luscombe, David, *The School of Peter Abelard: The Influence of Abelard's Thought in the Early Medieval Period* (Cambridge: Cambridge University Press, 1963)

Maier, Anneliese, *On the Threshold of Exact Science: Selected Writings of Anneliese Maier on Late Medieval Natural Philosophy*, ed. and trans. Steven D. Sargent (Philadelphia: University of Pennsylvania Press, 1982)

Marenbon, John, *From the Circle of Alcuin to the School of Auxerre: Logic, Theology, and Philosophy in the Early Middle Ages* (Cambridge: Cambridge University Press, 1981)

———, 'Abelard's Changing Thoughts on Sameness and Difference in Logic and Theology', *American Catholic Philosophical Quarterly*, 81 (2004), pp. 229–50

Martin, Christopher, *The Philosophy of Thomas Aquinas: Introductory Readings* (London: Routledge, 1988)

Pasnau, Robert, 'Olivi on the Metaphysics of the Soul', *Medieval Philosophy and Theology*, 6 (1997a), pp. 109–32

———, *Theories of Cognition in the Later Middle Ages* (Cambridge: Cambridge University Press, 1997b)

———, 'Science and Certainty', in *id.* (ed.), *The Cambridge History of Medieval Philosophy*, 2 vols (Cambridge, Cambridge University Press, 2010), I, pp. 357–68

Principe, Walter, H., *Alexander of Hales' Theology of the Hypostatic Union* (Toronto: Pontifical Institute of Mediaeval Studies, 1967)

Quinn, Philip, 'Abelard on Atonement: "Nothing Unintelligible, Arbitrary, Illogical, or Immoral about It"', in Eleonore Stump (ed.), *Reasoned Faith: Essays in Philosophical Theology in Honor of Norman Kretzmann* (Ithaca and London: Cornell University Press, 1993), pp. 281–300

Robb, Fiona, 'The Fourth Lateran Council's Definition of Trinitarian Orthodoxy', *Journal of Ecclesiastical History*, 48 (1997)

Sylla, Edith, 'Adam Wodeham's Response to Henry of Harclay', *Medieval Philosophy and Theology*, 7 (1998), pp. 69–87

Tweedale, Martin, M., 'Alexander of Aphrodisias' Views on Universals', *Phronesis* 29 (1984), pp. 279–303

Visser, Sandra and Williams, Thomas, *Anselm*, Great Medieval Thinkers (New York: Oxford University Press, 2009)

Note

1   I include only those works to which I refer, in specific editions, in my text. And I do so minimally: I omit passing references, and references

to material in well-known series (e.g. Patrologia Latina), unless I need a very precise reference that needs details of an edition. I also omit works readily available in multiple English translations (e.g. Plato and Aristotle; Augustine's *Confessions*; Aquinas's *Summa theologiae* and other major works). I cite Latin editions only in the absence of English translations. And I cite English translations only in cases in which I use the translation in the text.

Index